MANAGING the
CHALLENGES
in Human Service
Organizations

MANAGING the
CHALLENGES
in Human Service
Organizations
A CASEBOOK

Published in collaboration with the
Mack Center on Nonprofit Management in the Human Services
University of California, Berkeley, School of Social Welfare

Michael J. Austin
University of California, Berkeley

Ralph Brody
Cleveland State University

Thomas Packard
San Diego State University

Los Angeles • London • New Delhi • Singapore • Washington DC

For information:

 SAGE Publications, Inc.
2455 Teller Road
Thousand Oaks, California 91320
E-mail: order@sagepub.com

SAGE Publications India Pvt. Ltd.
B 1/I 1 Mohan Cooperative
Industrial Area
Mathura Road, New Delhi 110 044
India

SAGE Publications Ltd.
1 Oliver's Yard
55 City Road
London EC1Y 1SP
United Kingdom

SAGE Publications Asia-Pacific
Pte. Ltd.
33 Pekin Street #02-01
Far East Square
Singapore 048763

Printed in the United States of America

Library of Congress Cataloging-in-Publication Data

Austin, Michael J.
Managing the challenges in human service organizations: a casebook/
Michael J. Austin, Ralph Brody, Thomas Packard.
    p. cm.
Includes bibliographical references and index.
ISBN 978-1-4129-4127-3 (pbk.)
    1. Human services—Management. I. Brody, Ralph. II. Packard, Thomas Roy. III. Title.

HV41.A865 2009
361.0068—dc22   2008011029

This book is printed on acid-free paper.

08   09   10   11   12   10   9   8   7   6   5   4   3   2   1

Acquisitions Editor:	Kassie Graves
Editorial Assistant:	Veronica K. Novak
Production Editor:	Kristen Gibson
Typesetter:	C&M Digitals (P) Ltd.
Proofreader:	Kevin Gleason
Indexer:	Monica Smersh
Cover Designer:	Candice Harman
Marketing Manager:	Carmel Schrire

Contents

Preface

Case-based learning is like looking through a one-way mirror to observe the activities on the other side. It provides you with an opportunity to observe the actions of others, in order to speculate on how you might handle the same situations they face. Case-based learning places value on your own prior experiences and how they might inform your views of a case situation. In a similar way, if the case represents a new situation for you, then your learning is enhanced by engaging in a problem-solving process. When cases are assessed in a classroom situation, you also gain the benefit of others who might bring a different perspective based on their own experiences and/or critical thinking skills. In essence, case-based learning is an interesting way to learn about managing the real-life challenges of human service organizations.

This casebook also supplements the various textbooks in human service management by bringing theory to life. It can complement both classroom lectures and field-based internship learning. It provides a tool for those of you who find learning to be more engaging when you are applying practice principles or concepts to real-life situations. Case-based learning builds upon your readiness to learn by providing you with the opportunity to analyze different organizational situations. The cases are designed to give you an opportunity to explore creative alternatives, as well as to engage your initiative in group-based problem solving.

While some of these cases may seem overwhelming to some readers, they all are based on real-life organizational situations. The cases reflect the realities of organizational life, from the specific details of single-issue cases, to the complexities of multi-issue cases in which it is challenging to identify relevant theories or practice principles. These cases also reflect real life with respect to the limited information available in a case. This limitation is similar to the reality of incomplete information in organizational situations that lack a documented history or specific details related to the problem. However, cases are different in that you cannot go back and get more information before planning and acting. In a positive vein, cases are distinct from real life in the sense that case analysis provides a safe place to be creative and take risks with no fear of negative consequences. Finally, while the real world rarely provides practitioners with opportunities to step back and reflect, case-based learning does provide these opportunities for you: to thoughtfully and carefully consider an organizational situation in all its richness, to consciously apply theory or engage in evidence-informed practice, and to assess your own learning about human services management.

Case-based learning also provides you with a way of expanding your base of experience. By reading, discussing, and analyzing the case with a debriefing tool, you are adding to your understanding of the complexities of agency management, as well as testing your analytic and interactional skills by engaging in shared problem solving with peers. The debriefing of a case also creates learning opportunities for you and your peers with regard to refining teamwork skills as you collectively engage in the process of considering and incorporating the views of others. Team facilitation and leadership are often seen by experienced administrators as an essential skill set for effective agency management. In a similar way, you can enhance your advocacy and critical thinking skills as a result of discussing various approaches to case-based problem solving. In essence, case-based learning can enhance some of your core management skills as you work with others to identify alternatives to complex organizational and interpersonal situations.

Case-based learning has value beyond its use as a classroom exercise, especially when instructors select only a few of the cases in this book for use in a course. For example, you could read the entire casebook using a critical self-assessment perspective. In this situation, you could develop a list of issues, skills, and questions that represent the most important learning issues for your current stage of development as a manager. This list could form the basis of: (1) questions you raise in class, (2) questions you explore with your fieldwork instructor, and (3) questions you wish to address through more focused reading related to a term paper. Such a paper might be included in a management course, but it could also be a feature of a human behavior and social environment course in which you could explore theories that might inform the management practices that you found most challenging. This list could also be used to link management issues to the art and science of policy implementation when studying the development and implementation of social policies. For example, what are the management challenges associated with encouraging staff to implement unfunded state-wide child-welfare mandates when additional financial resources are not included in the policy implementation process (often referred to as "doing more with less")?

One of the most challenging aspects of using this casebook can be found in the process of supplementing fieldwork. Given the limited range of experiences that are possible in such an internship, the broad-ranging issues in the casebook can serve as valuable discussion topics within the traditional weekly or biweekly supervisory meetings between you and your field instructor. The cases may represent situations that do not exist in your current fieldwork agency but might appear in other agencies. These discussions can complement the hands-on nature of more narrowly focused fieldwork assignments. In essence, the breadth and depth of case-based learning reflected in this casebook can provide you with fewer surprises as you enter management practice.

The two primary co-editors (Austin and Packard) offer many years of management experience, ranging from executive positions in not-for-profit organizations to program evaluation and organization development in local government and the deanship of a school of social work. We both have teaching experience at the graduate and undergraduate levels. We each keep one of our feet off-campus through active consulting practices that inform our teaching. This helps to keep our teaching real and credible, as we are able to assess the extent to which our teaching does, in fact, adequately address current organizational life and the challenges facing practicing administrators. We both receive student feedback each semester about the relevance of our teaching and about the call for more case examples. As students ask for examples of the application of theories and principles, we continuously learn from them about their perspectives and concerns and how well we are responding. Life-long learning is a central feature of our careers, and case-based teaching is an essential part of our teaching-management practice.

Before exploring the cases themselves, we encourage you to review the first two chapters that are designed to help you maximize your experiences in working with the cases. Chapter 1 reviews some of the uses and benefits of case-based learning and presents several conceptual frameworks for use in analyzing and responding to cases. Chapter 2 describes the process of case assessment and debriefing, and provides several debriefing tools. This chapter also includes a discussion of the casebook's structure and how the cases were organized into different categories that also relate to the features of various textbooks on human service management. This approach should help you and your instructor make the best use of the various cases.

Case-based learning provides an opportunity for students and instructors to learn and grow together. This casebook's development has been a learning opportunity for us, and we are eager to hear from those who use these cases in terms of what worked, what did not work, or what should have been included. The future updating of this case-book will benefit greatly from new cases developed by the students and faculty who use this casebook. We also hope that instructors will share with us their approaches to case-based teaching so that these can be included in future editions.

We encourage you to explore the wide variety of cases for use as classroom discussion springboards, in-class experiential exercises, and/or components of mid-term, final, or end-of-program exams. We hope that the learning experiences will enrich all those who participate and will help prepare the next generation of human services managers to successfully anticipate and address the organizational challenges that they will face in the years to come.

Michael J. Austin, PhD
Thomas Packard, DSW

Acknowledgments

We have many people to thank for their contributions to this casebook. Ralph Brody, prior to his passing, had already acknowledged his deep gratitude for the assistance he received from the following people: Akia Foster-Churn, Alex Sanchez, Alisa Bridges, Ava Lucky, Bill Eyman, Cheryl Lydston, Christopher Trunk, Debra Curlee, Dr. Russ Kaye, Dr. Murali Nair, J. Toth, James Krauskopf, Jane Fumich, Joe Cistone, Joe Gauntner, Karen Ponting, Kimberly Moss, La'Keisha Dorsey, Lisa Thomas, Madhura Shaligram, Martie McParland, Maureen Dee, Meghan Gaines, Michelle Larde, Paul Alandt, Randi Kassan, Ron Hill, Shannon Ingle, Susan Griffin, Susan Schwarzwald, Ted Fabjan, Tiffany Hunt, Tina Burnett, Tom Mendelsohn, Janie Bechtel, Donald Lichi, Eugene Norris, Sherry Gedeon, Chris Buch, Walter Ginn, and Howard Bram. Special thanks to Jessica Forsberg for typing assistance, Phyllis Brody for editing, and Dr. Stuart Mendel and his Nonprofit Management class at the College of Urban Affairs, Cleveland State University.

Tom Packard acknowledges the valuable assistance of Jacquelyn Sorenson, Kay Traube, Dorothy Melia, and David Thomas for sharing their agency experiences and helping in the development of cases. He also has appreciated his Administration students who have enriched his teaching and learning through their participation in stimulating case discussions in classes over the last 20 years.

Mike Austin greatly values the contributions of his management and planning MSW students at the University of California, Berkeley, School of Social Welfare, for assisting with the development and field-testing of many of these cases over the past decade—especially Jennette Claassen and Amy Benton, who helped to organize and assist with the selection of many of the cases, and Sharon Ikami, who helped prepare the manuscript for publication.

We also want to acknowledge the substantial assistance we received from our SAGE editor, Kassie Graves, who brought together the editors when she discovered that we (Mike Austin and Tom Packard) were developing our manuscript at the same time that Ralph

Brody was completing his casebook. We very much appreciate the support and encouragement of Ralph's wife, Phyllis Brody, following Ralph's untimely passing in February 2006. We feel honored that she gave us permission to include his excellent work in order to develop a more comprehensive casebook. We also appreciate the editorial assistance of Kristen Gibson at SAGE.

We are also most grateful to those colleagues who agreed to include their previously published or unpublished cases in this collection. They include William Kahn, Maureen Borland, Janelle Cavanagh, Jonathan Kidde, Wayne Feinstein, Art Blum, Gil Villagran, Dick O'Neil, Sylvia Pizzini, John Oppenheim, and all of the authors whose copyrighted work is also included.

As we put this manuscript together, we learned so much from each other. We both have many years of classroom experience in preparing graduate social work students for careers in the administration of human service organizations. By sharing our different classroom experiences, we were able to construct the conceptual framework for this casebook as well as further refine our approaches to the development of debriefing frameworks used to help students analyze cases and develop practice-oriented strategies for dealing with routine and complex situations. We have reflected on our shared learning in articles being prepared for journal publication, which are identified in the reference section at the end of the casebook.

We want to expand our collaborative process by inviting faculty and students to test these cases in the classroom as well as prepare new cases that we plan to include in future editions of this casebook. We hope you derive as much pleasure out of these cases as we did in developing and compiling them. We welcome your feedback.

Michael J. Austin, PhD
Mack Professor of Nonprofit Management
Director, Mack Center on Nonprofit Management
in the Human Services
School of Social Welfare
University of California, Berkeley
Berkeley, California

Thomas Packard, DSW
Associate Professor
School of Social Work
San Diego State University
San Diego, California

February 2008

1

Introduction

U sing teaching cases in professional education programs has gained increased attention over the past several decades. However, there are very few current casebooks in human service management and leadership (Fauri, Wernet, & Netting, 2004; Mayers, Souffle, & Schoech, 1994). This shortage may be one reason that cases are not a primary focus of teaching in human service management. In a recent assessment of textbooks and casebooks in social work administration, Austin and Kruzich (2004) conclude that new approaches to case study development are needed in this field. This book seeks to address this need by compiling a compendium of management and leadership cases covering a wide range of subjects within a set of conceptual frameworks and debriefing strategies for case analysis.

While the terms *management* and *leadership* can be defined in different ways, our definitions (adapted from Kotter, 1990, by Northouse, 2004) feature management as promoting "order and consistency" related to planning/budgeting, organizing/staffing, and controlling/problem solving. In contrast, leadership focuses on "change and movement" related to establishing direction through vision and strategy; aligning individual and organizational goals; building teams; and motivating, inspiring, and empowering staff (Northouse, 2004, Chap. 9). Both management and leadership are essential to effective organizations. Another approach is to use the term *administration* to capture both aspects of management and leadership (Roberts-DeGennaro & Packard, 2002). In essence, both management and leadership issues should be kept in mind when analyzing the organizational dilemmas in this casebook.

❖ OVERVIEW

This chapter begins with a review of some of the ways in which case-based learning may be used and some of the benefits of case-based learning. Three conceptual frameworks are used to organize the cases that describe and provide opportunities to assess the nature of managerial work. The first framework features the managerial roles perspective developed by Menefee (2000); the second is the classic competing values framework developed by Quinn (1988) and applied by Edwards and Yankey (2006); and the third is the well-established framework of managerial functions associated with organizational processes and systems (Lewis, Packard, & Lewis, 2007). In addition to these three conceptual frameworks, five alternative frameworks for debriefing cases are described in Chapter 2 for students and instructors to analyze and discuss the cases. Chapter 2 concludes with a discussion of ways to use the casebook and a description of the other chapters.

The Uses of Case-Based Learning

Teaching cases are often used to assist students in learning different interventions, to understand multi-problem situations, to illustrate models of practice, and/or to promote new ways of conceptualizing practice (Cossom, 1991). The use of teaching cases helps to create a learner-centered environment in which students become participatory learners through self-directed inquiry (Cossom, 1991). The classroom can become a problem-solving laboratory where students are encouraged to raise thoughtful questions. Case-based teaching helps to generate discussion about the multiple alternatives to diverse situations (Cossom, 1991).

Case-based learning can also help to develop skills related to using data and applying concepts to complex and real-life situations; making decisions in the context of competing alternatives, perceptions, and opinions among colleagues; and exploring different approaches to influencing others. The case-based approach to learning draws upon the existing knowledge and experiences of students while the instructor introduces concepts, theories, and practices within a framework that promotes retention and retrieval.

One of the unique aspects of case-based learning is the opportunity to link real-life managerial dilemmas with the theories and practice principles identified in the literature. Case-based learning also provides a venue for exploring the multiple aspects of practice wisdom—a complex blending of knowledge, skills, and experience that seeks to blend action and reflection. As Birren and Fisher (1990) note, wisdom is tested by circumstances in which we try to decide what is changeable and what is not. Wisdom brings together previously separated processes of logical knowing with uncertainty and reflection. It also relies on interpersonal exchanges in order to develop the ability to balance facts with questions about ambiguous situations while avoiding rigidity in search of the truth.

Cases also provide a unique opportunity for students to critically reflect upon three aspects of practice: (1) the relevance of theory to practice, (2) the role of research that can inform practice, and (3) the use of principles to guide decision-making behaviors. In an analysis of a teaching case, the debriefing frameworks and the questions at the ends of cases are designed to encourage students to acquire a managerial mindset that values and uses research and theory to inform their decisions and future practice.

The Value and Benefits of Case-Based Learning

The multiple benefits of using teaching cases in preparing future human service managers, as well as some of the limitations of case-based learning are described in the following section.

Simulating Administrative Dilemmas

Cases can address the interests of students who want to *experience* different aspects of agency administration, where they can test their understanding and refine their skills in situations that replicate some aspects of actual practice. Many students enter graduate human service administration courses with limited managerial experience (including negative stereotypes of administrators whom they have observed). They are interested in understanding the experience of administration. This is probably one reason why the involvement of practicing administrators as guest speakers on campus is so well received by students. Student interest in management practice is also addressed in their internship experiences, where they work daily with a practicing administrator.

Cases offer multiple dimensions of learning that can capture student interests and go beyond students' own experiences with internships and guest speakers. Cases provide students with opportunities to think like administrators and experience realistic dilemmas. Cases also offer opportunities for an instructor to integrate theory and practice principles into the experiential learning of a case discussion.

Leveling the Learning Field

Students enter graduate human service management programs with different managerial experiences. Case discussions are a way of leveling the learning field. Irrespective of prior work experience, all students can contribute to a case discussion. Equipped with concepts from theory and practice courses, any student can make observations about what is happening in a case, analyze a situation using theory and practice principles, and recommend courses of action based on course readings. Experienced and inexperienced students benefit from class discussions where the critical thinking skills of less experienced students complement the practice wisdom of more experienced students.

Speculating on Challenges

Third, one aspect of teaching management and leadership skills involves orienting students to the challenges of administration by helping them develop mental models linked to the values of client-centered administration (Rapp & Poertner, 2007). Helping students approach the administrative challenges found in teaching cases can be inherently interesting, as opposed to being problematic, overwhelming, or intimidating. Learning in this context can actually enhance students' critical thinking capacities while they take risks within the safe environment of the classroom.

Enhancing Analytic Skills

Fourth, case-based learning can also help students develop a beginning sense of competence and understanding of managerial work while refining their analytic skills. A large part of effective management is the framing of probing questions and weighing alternatives before acting, a process that is not always possible to learn in high-pressure agency internships, but one that is clearly available in case-based learning.

An old axiom related to these pressures suggests that practicing managers make decisions using the targeting process of "ready, fire" without spending time on "aiming," while academics prefer "ready, aim, aim . . ." since they are rarely called upon to "fire" (i.e., analysis paralysis). Case discussions allow time for all phases: assessment, planning, and action. The development of analytical skills is a fundamental component of graduate professional education—a learning opportunity that is not always available through on-the-job experience.

Applying Analytic Frameworks

Fifth, case discussions also offer repeated learning opportunities using different analytical frameworks. Different tools or frameworks are useful when responding to complex practice situations. Practicing administrators develop, often subconsciously, "theories in use" (Argyris & Schon, 1996) that guide their thinking and decision making on a daily basis. Case discussions, informed by relevant theory and facilitated by discussion, help students identify and articulate their mental models. This type of interactive learning enables them to raise questions about their operating assumptions, as well as to identify alternative frameworks to inform their decision making.

Supplement to Fieldwork

Sixth, case-based learning is an important supplement to fieldwork. Consistent with the principles of adult learning, fieldwork is particularly valuable for students who perceive its direct relevance to their goals of becoming effective practitioners. However, the time demands of task accomplishment in fieldwork agencies do not always allow for time to debrief, reflect, assess, and integrate theory and practice. Case-based learning about administrative dilemmas provides more time to reflect and consider a broader array of alternatives than is found in most field experiences. An instructor can introduce cases for any practice situation, whereas internship experiences are sometimes limited, depending on the availability of particular learning experiences. Case discussion also allows for more opportunity to take risks and provides access to experiences not often available in the field (e.g., staff supervision or executive-board relations).

These six benefits of case-based learning need to be balanced with the limitations inherent in an over-reliance on this pedagogic technique for developing managerial competence and confidence. For example, one of the limitations found in teaching only through the case method in MBA programs is that it may overemphasize the skill of speaking "convincingly to 40–90 people" (Mintzberg, 2004, p. 57) while neglecting other skills related to give-and-take dialogue or self-reflection. Another limitation is that students may assume that implementation involves merely "giving orders" (Kelly & Kelly, 1986, p. 32). The major limitation of the case method is that classroom participants can only speculate about how they might act in a given situation. As a result, it is important to place case-based learning within a context of multiple learning opportunities. For example, Mintzberg (2004, p. 267) argues for the blending of several learning experiences; namely, lectures ("for conceptual inputs"), cases ("to widen exposure"), action learning internships ("for new experiences"), and self-reflection to capture the student's own experiences.

❖ CONCEPTUAL FRAMEWORKS

Three conceptual frameworks are used in this casebook to organize the diverse set of cases. As highlighted in Figure 1.1, the frameworks complement each other in the sense that each offers unique strengths and perspectives. The framework of managerial roles describes the different roles that human service managers assume in their daily practice (Menefee, 2000). The competing values framework (Quinn, 1988) captures the tensions created by competing priorities that affect managerial decision making. The management functions framework, grounded in systems theory, focuses on the organizational processes that are needed to achieve organizational effectiveness and excellence (Lewis et al., 2007). The framework elements are aligned in Figure 1.1 to reflect the three major domains, as follows:

- Leadership roles and functions that focus on the external "big picture" perspectives and the internal aspects of human service organizations
- Analytic roles and functions that focus on assessing and managing resources and technical processes
- Interactional roles and functions that emphasize the human dimension of organizational life

These three major domains are vertically aligned to connect the elements of each of the three conceptual frameworks that are horizontally displayed and described in the next section.

❖ MANAGERIAL ROLES

Over the past two decades, Menefee and others (Ezell, Menefee, & Patti, 1989; Menefee, 1997; Menefee, 2000; Menefee & Thompson, 1994) have developed an empirical basis for describing management activity

Figure 1.1   Conceptual Frameworks

	Leadership processes	Analytic processes	Interactional processes
Managerial Roles (Menefee, 2000)	Boundary Spanner	Resource administrator	Communicator
	Innovator	Evaluator	Advocate
	Organizer	Policy practitioner	Supervisor
	Team leader		Facilitator
Competing Values (Quinn, 1988)	Creative/risk-taking (external)	Stability and control (monitoring and coordinating)	Supportive and flexible (facilitating and mentoring)
	Directive and goal-oriented (internal)		
Managerial Functions (Lewis, et al., 2007)	Executive-board relations (governance)	Program planning and design	Human resource management
	Environmental relations and strategy	Program evaluation	Supervisory management
	Organizational design and structure	Information and knowledge management	Organization development
	Leadership, vision, values	Financial management	Change management

in terms of the roles that human service managers perform. Menefee defined a set of roles that capture the nature of managerial work in the human services field (Figure 1.2).

In the area of *leadership*, for example, a manager fulfills several roles. The boundary-spanner role includes managing relationships, including interorganizational relationships and partnerships. In this role, the manager needs to network with and influence stakeholders, including policy makers, funding sources, and other community providers. This role also includes communicating to staff the needs and expectations of external stakeholders, so that the agency can meet these expectations through responsive and effective programs. In order to effectively respond to changing conditions and expectations in the environment, the manager also needs to assume the role of innovator, forecasting trends and developing strategies in order to respond. This role involves designing and implementing new programs, as well as

Figure 1.2   Managerial Roles

Leadership Roles

1. *Boundary-spanner:* Capacity to manage relationships, develop networks, and influence others to foster interorganizational relationships, develop partnerships, and integrate service delivery systems.

2. *Innovator:* Capacity to forecast trends in the external environment and develop alternative and innovative strategies for responding to those forces.

3. *Organizer:* Capacity to arrange and structure the work of an agency to optimize the use of human and material resources (including delegating and staffing) in order to continuously modify internal structures, processes, and conditions to adapt to external, often turbulent, environments.

4. *Team builder/Leader:* Capacity to build coalitions and teams (interagency, intra-agency, interdisciplinary, etc.) by organizing and enlisting groups to ensure service availability and effective agency operations, with special attention to group maintenance and task functions of meeting management.

Interactional Roles

5. *Communicator:* Capacity to exchange written and verbal information, make formal presentations, and keep internal and external stakeholders continuously informed through the extensive use of technology.

6. *Advocate:* Capacity to represent the interests of individuals and groups by lobbying, testifying, and fostering relationships with public officials and community leaders.

7. *Supervisor:* Capacity to direct and guide the delivery of agency services while attending to the socio-emotional needs of staff through the use of coordinating, supporting, and consultant advising activities needed to motivate staff, coordinate workloads, set goals and limits, provide corrective feedback, and monitor work processes and outcomes.

8. *Facilitator:* Capacity to enlist others in accomplishing the vision, mission, and goals of an agency or community coalition by enabling, orienting, training, and empowering others through modeling methods for collaboration and coordination that can change and strengthen organizational culture.

Analytic Roles

9. *Resource administrator:* Capacity to manage efficiently and effectively the human, financial, informational, and physical resources needed by agencies related to fundraising, grant writing, marketing, media relations, and performance management.

10. *Evaluator:* Capacity to conduct needs assessments and program evaluations related to the agency's impact on client populations and community needs based on a strong understanding of research methods, as well as to supervise/contract specialists related to continuous quality improvement and outcome assessment.

11. *Policy practitioner:* Capacity to develop/formulate, interpret, comply with, and influence public policies, and the capacity to understand and articulate to staff the full range of policy implementation issues and challenges.

SOURCE: Menefee (2000).

redesigning organizational structures and processes. In performing the organizer role, managers address not only organizational structure, but also processes such as the human resource management system (from job design, to staff training and evaluation). And finally, the team builder role includes building high-performing teams using group process and meetings-management skills. This role also includes using interagency coalitions to help shape new policies and services.

A key *interactional* role is that of communicator, including the use of oral and written communication, as well as information technology. The major tasks include formal presentations to groups such as agency boards and informal communications with staff to keep them informed about changes and developments inside and outside the agency. As an advocate, the manager represents the interests of stakeholders (e.g., clients or interest groups) in the community and the policy arena, often with a focus on social justice and new service needs. As a supervisor, the manager attends to the socio-emotional needs of staff by coordinating, supporting, motivating, and monitoring. Supervision includes the three distinct elements of the administrative, educational, and supportive supervision functions (Kadushin & Harkness, 2002), as well as fostering a learning culture (Austin & Hopkins, 2004). The role of facilitator involves enlisting others in accomplishing the agency's vision and goals by enabling, orienting, training, and empowering others. This role also includes modeling desired behavior to help shape the organization's culture.

An essential *analytic* role is to serve as a resource administrator, one who manages the agency's human, financial, informational, and physical resources. This includes not only securing resources, but also the effective and efficient ongoing management of these resources—from acquiring new funds, to the oversight of financial management systems. As an evaluator, the manager focuses on agency outcomes and continuous improvement by using needs assessments and program evaluations. Finally, the manager as a policy practitioner helps develop, influence, and implement public policies. This also includes working with staff to ensure that they understand the importance and implications of new policies.

❖ COMPETING VALUES

While the competing values perspective also includes managerial roles, it focuses on the notion that organizational effectiveness is multidimensional and socially constructed, meaning different things to different stakeholders (Herman & Renz, 1999; Quinn, 1988). The competing values framework is built upon two dimensions representing competing organizational values; namely, flexibility versus control and an internal versus an external focus, as noted in Figure 1.3 (Edwards & Yankey, 2006, p. 7).

Figure 1.3 Competing Values Framework

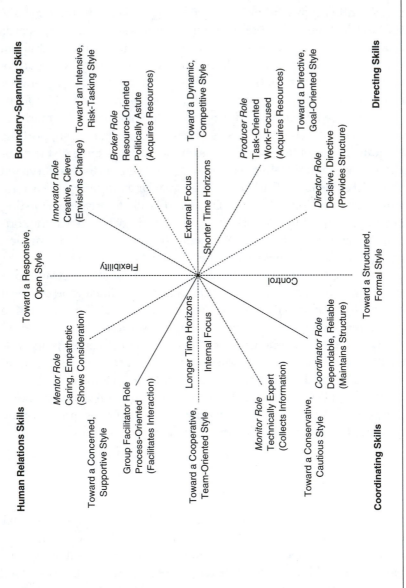

SOURCE: R. E. Quinn, *Beyond Rational Management: Mastering the Paradoxes and Competing Demands of High Performance* (San Francisco: Jossey-Bass, © 1988). Reprinted with permission.

The first dimension of *flexibility and control* is rooted in the findings of Lawrence and Lorsch (1967), who noted that there are countervailing forces toward integration and differentiation in complex organizations. Most human service organizations, except for the smallest, typically have multiple services that serve a range of client populations. In order to effectively and efficiently respond to these populations, organizational units need to differentiate from one another based on both service delivery and management processes. For example, financial management systems need to be implemented in a routine, standard way, while some service delivery processes are by nature nonroutine and require varying types of staff skills. These differentiated functions need to be pulled together through integrating mechanisms that can ensure both coordination and enough control to allow the organization to operate efficiently. *Management functions,* including finances, information systems, and human resources are typically centralized so that they operate in the same way throughout the agency. Service delivery, on the other hand, is typically more decentralized, with different programs requiring different practices and procedures. In fact, both control and flexibility are needed for optimal agency functioning, and part of the administrator's job is to manage this tension.

The second dimension of competing values involves the tension between an *internal* and *external* focus. Internally, the organization needs to be maintained by attending to both the technical aspects of systems, such as financial management, and the social aspects of human resources, such as staff morale and commitment. Administrators need to ensure that proper procedures are being used within the agency, while at the same time monitoring morale and providing socioemotional support to staff. At the other end of the continuum, administrators need to pay attention to the external environment. This includes assessing changes in the environment, strategically positioning the organization, marketing, and ensuring the growth and survival of the organization. As is the case with the dimension of flexibility and control, administrators need to manage both sets of demands: ensuring the effectiveness of the organization's internal functions while constantly monitoring and adapting to external forces.

These two dimensions, when combined, represent four models of organizational effectiveness: (1) the *human relations* model that attends to flexibility and an internal focus, (2) the *open systems* approach that focuses on flexibility and the external environment, (3) the *rational goal* model that uses control to ensure accomplishment of goals expected by external forces, and (4) the *internal process* model that addresses internal control systems. As noted in Figure 1.3, these perspectives on values are then overlaid with a set of leadership roles that are relevant to each model:

- The human relations model includes the mentor and facilitator role.
- The open systems model includes the boundary spanning skills of the innovator and broker roles.
- The rational goal model includes the directing skills of producer and director roles.
- The internal process model includes the coordinating skills related to the roles of coordinator and monitor.

While using the competing values framework leads to managerial roles that are similar to those in the Menefee framework, it places more emphasis on the performance of managerial roles in relationship to each other to reflect the complexity of administrative work. Since there is a continuous flow of different forces competing for the administrator's attention, managers find themselves working, consciously or not, to balance these competing demands in order to optimize the organization's effectiveness.

❖ MANAGEMENT FUNCTIONS

A final lens through which to view organizational processes and managerial work relates to a set of management functions needed for an organization to grow and survive. This framework is based on systems theory, in which an organization takes inputs from the environment (including funding, staff, and clients) and transforms them into service delivery programs and processes (e.g., information systems) to produce outputs (e.g., improved client and/or community functioning) (Katz & Kahn, 1978). Using the three subsystems of technical core, managerial system, and institutional system developed by Thompson (1967), Kettner (2002b) defines the technical core in terms of service provision, the managerial system of financial and human resources management, and the institutional system in terms of environmental relations.

Based on these systems concepts, Lewis et al. (2007) identify six major management functions, as illustrated in Figure 1.4.

The framework for the six functions involves the management of the organization's external environment, including a constant monitoring of the trends in the environment. This monitoring involves attention to political trends (e.g., welfare reform and the accountability

Figure 1.4   Management Functions

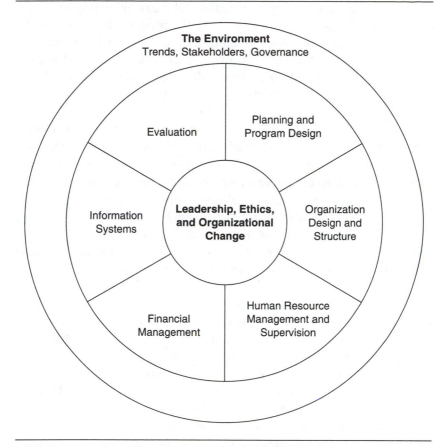

SOURCE: Adapted from Lewis, Packard, and Lewis (2007).

movement), economic trends that affect human services financing (e.g., unemployment and dislocation), social and demographic trends (e.g., the aging of baby boomers), and human services technology trends (e.g., the impact of Internet communications). The process of relating to stakeholders is another important aspect of managing the environment, especially identifying and addressing stakeholder expectations. Board relations and governance (as well as dealing with elected officials) are other aspects of managing the organization's environment. Some of the skills needed to assess the agency's environment include community needs assessments, marketing, and asset mapping.

The first of the six key management functions is planning. At the broadest level, managers and policy makers can use strategic planning to identify external opportunities and threats in the environment and assess internally the agency's strengths and areas for improvement in order to develop strategic directions. At the program level, data from needs assessments and asset mapping, coupled with knowledge of evidence-based practices and promising practices, can be used to plan and design new programs. Planning skills include the use of time lines, Gantt Charts, and PERT charts, as well as the capacity to engage in strategic planning.

The second management function relates to the organization design that is used to structure program and administrative units that are reflected on organization charts. The development and reassessment of decision-making and communication processes are critical design elements within an organizational culture related to promoting coordination and efficient organizational functioning. For example, are reporting relationships and roles clear, well understood, and appropriate? To what extent do the organizational structure and related systems facilitate effective coordination and communication across functions and programs?

The third management function involves an agency's human resource management system. Such a system ensures that all programs and positions are filled with competent, trained, and motivated staff. The specific human resource skills include job design and descriptions, recruitment (enhancing diversity), hiring, training, staff development, performance appraisal, discipline, and termination. Within the human-resource function, the supervision skills deserve special attention. To ensure that staff members are able to use their full capacities effectively, supervisors need to provide clear direction and guidance, demonstrate a capacity to motivate and monitor staff, and promote staff development and lifelong learning. Mentoring and coaching are other important aspects of the supervision function. Supervision issues often include the need to deal with inadequate job performance, work-family stress, and workplace impairments such as substance abuse.

The fourth management function relates to the financial management capacity needed to ensure that organizational resources are properly used. This function includes fund development (e.g., writing proposals for grants or contracts) and preparing and monitoring budgets. Financial statements and audits are essential tools to ensure the proper monitoring of funds. Irrespective of the nature of an organizational problem, managers need to be able to assess fiscal factors, to ensure that revenue streams are stable and adequate, that expenditures are within budget, and that accounting procedures are followed.

The fifth management function relates to the use of information systems to measure and monitor the implementation of all aspects of agency programs and processes. In human service organizations, information systems include data on client and staff characteristics, types and amounts of services delivered, outputs (e.g., the number of clients completing a job training program) and outcomes (e.g., the number of clients acquiring a full-time living wage job). The challenge in many human service agencies is developing and implementing an information system that adequately documents all aspects of the service-delivery program by clearly addressing program goals and objectives.

The sixth and final management function involves the evaluation of program implementation and results. The focus and methods of evaluation can address questions from staff, funding organizations, policy makers, or the community. Evaluations can focus on the process used to implement a service program, as well as the outcomes of such programs, with special attention to efficiency, effectiveness, and service quality.

While the organization's environment is an important context for agency operations, the critical element needed to connect the core management functions is agency leadership. Organizational leadership is essential to ensure that the organization accomplishes its stated goals and objectives, in addition to functioning in ways consistent with its mission and organizational values. The leadership challenge is to ensure alignment among all the organizational functions and processes, especially the alignment between individual employees and organizational goals. A key aspect of leadership is guiding organizational change and improvement that can result, in part, from being alert to the internal and external opportunities to improve organizational functioning. Another key aspect of managerial leadership is the balancing of staff needs with the needs of the organization. The ethical dimensions of managerial leadership often involve the capacity to articulate clear ethical principles and to ensure that these principles are followed throughout the agency.

Using the Conceptual Frameworks

While the context for the cases in this casebook includes the managerial roles of leadership, analysis, or interaction (see Figure 1.1), the chapters are organized by the major management functions described above. In essence, the leadership roles relate to the strategic and visionary management of external and internal environments, while the analytic roles focus on the adequacy of human, financial, and information resources through careful planning, implementing, and monitoring of organizational systems. The interactional roles involve the maintenance of ongoing communication, staff support, and managing change in order to improve the quality of organizational processes and outcomes.

In summary, different situations in organizational life call upon different roles and functions. Over time, managers acquire the practice wisdom to recognize which management roles are required, as well as the related functions that need to be performed. The role perspective is especially useful in determining the specific managerial behaviors that are needed. The systems perspective underlying the management functions is very useful for locating and assessing specific problem areas. The competing values framework provides a context for recognizing the need for balance and trade-offs in the process of planning, managing, and evaluation.

In using case-based learning, both instructors and students can select roles and functions that seem most relevant to a case, discuss their shared or divergent perceptions, and identify principles that can be used in practice. As described in the next chapter, instructors can select cases for classroom use based on specific learning objectives and one or more debriefing frameworks. Cases may also be used as part of an examination for a course or as an end-of-program comprehensive examination to assess the capacities of students to integrate knowledge and skills by applying their analytic abilities to a case situation (Packard & Austin, in press). And finally, the three conceptual frameworks presented here (managerial roles, competing values, and management functions) all offer unique perspectives and provide a context for the analysis and debriefing of a case.

❖ SUMMARY

We began this chapter with the identification of some of the uses and benefits of case-based learning. We then presented three conceptual frameworks that can be used to frame and analyze the cases: (1) the managerial roles managers perform, (2) the competing values that underlie an organization's competing priorities, and (3) the management functions related to organizational processes. Finally, we noted factors that may suggest the best framework to use for particular learning needs, and we suggested some of the ways in which cases can be used.

2

Case Assessment
and Debriefing

A teaching case, especially a complex one, can leave a student or even an experienced manager overwhelmed with details and without a clear indication of where to start. While the three conceptual frameworks described in Chapter 1 provide a structure for how to place a case within the context of management practice, a diagnostic checklist can provide a structure for developing an analysis of the case. For example, medical professionals use diagnostic categories to screen patients for minor and major symptoms prior to forming a comprehensive assessment. They do so by performing the following procedures: checking vital signs, observing and feeling parts of the body, listening to lungs and heart, asking about medications or allergies, etc. A similar process of assessment is needed to make sense of the organizational factors in a teaching case.

Without the same degree of structure and standardization as a medical professional, an experienced administrator uses a mental checklist that can also check the vital signs of an organization. In searching for additional information and areas needing special attention, a simple checklist could include: environmental factors, current plans and commitments, available information for evaluation, and the availability of financial and human resources. Figure 2.1 provides an example of an

Figure 2.1   Case Assessment Checklist

I. Organizational Environment and Leadership
___ Issues regarding public policy or board policy?
___ Issues in the leadership behaviors of top management?
___ Issues reflecting ethical dilemmas?
___ Issues in the practices of other organizations that might relate to competition?

II. Planning and Coordinating
___ Issues related to the presence or absence of an agency strategic plan?
___ Issues related to the demographics of the client populations being served?
___ Issues related to the agency's stage of organizational development (recently established, struggling, or established organization related to growth or contraction)?
___ Issues related to the structure of the agency, such as reporting relationships, changing roles and responsibilities, resource allocation, coordination, and communication?

III. Program Design and Evaluation
___ Issues regarding the use of service delivery technologies related to changing client needs?
___ Issues related to program design emerging from new research findings or evidence-based practice?
___ Issues related to service outcome measures or methods of dissemination?

IV. Financial and Information Systems
___ Issues related to the adequacy or appropriateness of information systems related to computer resources, administrative data, or output/outcome measures?
___ Issues related to financial management related to program revenues or expenditures, cost benefit analysis, or accounting controls?

V. Human Resource Systems
___ Issues related to staff qualifications, performance evaluation, recruitment, and training and supervision?
___ Issues related to the quality of working life related to salary and benefits, working conditions, autonomy, growth opportunities, or employee rights and due process?
___ Issues related to staff diversity such as valuing diversity, staff-client demographics, personnel policies, or discrimination?

assessment checklist to identify possible issues and information needed before problem solving and decision making begins.

Just as a medical professional can quickly screen for basic information prior to ordering a comprehensive battery of tests, a well-trained or experienced manager can also quickly identify the type of information needed to engage in a problem-solving process. While conducting a comprehensive problem analysis may not always be necessary, issues that appear to be simple may benefit from a complete analysis, in order to identify underlying causes that may need to be addressed. For example, dealing with an employee who has been habitually violating a policy or procedure (from lateness to not completing job duties) may involve a simple modification in supervision or the application of disciplinary procedures. On the other hand, a more comprehensive assessment may indicate that there are agency procedures needing attention (e.g., the lack of a well-defined performance appraisal and discipline process). Such an assessment may even indicate that employee behaviors are part of a larger issue of morale, climate, or even inadequate staff training.

With the use of a checklist, a student or manager assessing an organizational situation is better prepared to analyze problems and develop strategies to address them. Building on the three conceptual frameworks noted in the previous section, the checklist provides a useful foundation for considering the debriefing frameworks described in the next section.

❖ CASE DEBRIEFING

Beyond the content-specific questions found at the end of cases, instructors also have an opportunity to promote case-based learning through different case debriefing strategies. Several strategies are identified and illustrated in Figures 2.2 to 2.6 and can be used by individual students or by groups.

The first debriefing strategy on *managerial problem solving* views the case in the context of a manager needing to address an issue as if it had arrived in his or her mail (e-mail or snail mail) or had emerged in a staff meeting. Most managerial problem-solving strategies are a variation on the components noted in Figure 2.2. The steps in this debriefing strategy flow in a cycle, whereby the response to each step leads to the next step until finally returning to the first step on problem identification that seeks to address issues identified in the final step on monitoring and evaluation. While instructors may approach managerial problem solving in a different way, these six steps reflect the common components of most problem-solving frameworks.

Brody (2005), in his management textbook, has designed a debriefing strategy that features the *analytic and interactional aspects* of case analysis. He introduces the *ethical dimension of decision making* and the way staff members interact with each other to address problems. An illustration of these interactional aspects, as well as the analytic dimensions, is shown in Figure 2.3.

A debriefing strategy that features the process of *executive coaching* can provide students with yet another way to discuss a case (Bloom, Catagna, Moir, & Warren, 2005). This approach is based on the capacity to develop help-seeking behaviors. Seeking consultation, supervision, or mentoring often involves questions that are reflective in nature. Developing insights into one's own cognitive and affective domains is as

Figure 2.2   A Managerial Problem-Solving Strategy

Step 1: *Problem Identification,* in which the manager is encouraged to gather multiple perceptions of others (staff) with regard to how to define or frame the problem.

Step 2: *Identify the Underlying Assumptions* that are often buried in the problem definition (e.g., lack of support or funding to address this issue; it would take too long to address this problem; no one really cares to resolve the problem; we would never get the director's support for a change), as well as the implicit or explicit values that operate within the agency's culture (e.g., client services are our top priority; staff feedback is expected and valued).

Step 3: *Structuring the Involvement of Key Stakeholders* to gather perceptions of the problem and their motivations to address the problem.

Step 4: *Developing Three Viable Options* to address the problem by identifying the pros and cons of each option.

Step 5: *Selecting One of the Three Options* and developing an action plan for implementing the option over time (e.g., who should be involved, what resources are needed, what is a realistic time frame).

Step 6: *Monitoring and Evaluating* the option selected in terms of specifying the criteria by which the selected solution could be evaluated three to six months from the launch of the implementation process. (The goal is to identify what is working and what is not in order to start the problem identification process all over again.)

Figure 2.3   The Analytic and Interactional Dimensions of Case Analysis

I. Analytic Dimensions
   a. How does the problem/situation impact the entire organization? What are the short- and long-term implications? Can the problem be reframed to create a win-win situation?
   b. How can key stakeholders embrace/grasp the complexity of the problem? What are the root causes?
   c. What is the best way to assess the trade-offs in exploring alternative approaches? What are the strengths and weaknesses of the options?
   d. How can participants distinguish between decisions that must be made expeditiously and those that require "going with the flow of events" (muddling through) or "watchful waiting"? Is more information needed to solve this problem?
   e. How can participants plan ahead to deal with the problem but still be open to change along the way? What new problems may occur, and what contingency plans could be made?

II. Interactional Dimensions
   a. What is the best way to capture/consider the perspectives of different stakeholders?
   b. How can participants be open and honest with others in the organization as well as with themselves?
   c. How would participants determine that the decision(s) reached were based on fair play? Are there existing precedents that should be followed or reconsidered?
   d. How would participants aggressively pursue the true nature of the problem/ situation (e.g., searching for information, asking challenging questions, and conducting intense and robust discussions)?
   e. How would participants determine if the key players cared enough to make tough decisions? Do the decision makers need to work to be bold enough to make a decision that may be unpopular?

Figure 2.4   Help-Seeking Behaviors Related to Analyzing Teaching Cases

Step 1: What aspect of the problem(s) presented in the teaching case is most perplexing to you?

Step 2: Which actions taken in the case are least familiar to you (unsure of how you would actually carry out the actions)?

Step 3: What type of advice/consultation would be most helpful to you?

- Can you identify the areas in this case where you feel least confident or where you lack sufficient experience?
- Do you need additional information, and where might you find it?
- Which aspects of the case represent areas where consultation with others might improve your understanding of this case?
- What kind of feedback would be most useful to you in terms of the ways in which you analyzed this case?

Step 4: With whom might you consult to explore different ways of approaching the situations in this case?

- How might follow-up consultation address your concerns about this case?
- What type of mentoring or coaching would you find most useful in terms of expanding your own managerial skill set related to the issues in this case?

important for managerial practice as it is for effective clinical practice. It involves moving past ambivalence about seeking help from others because of: (1) a fear of appearing ignorant or incompetent, (2) a concern about being unclear about the advice being sought, (3) a lack of competence about how to gather and make use of alternative perspectives, (4) a fear that more advice will simply add confusion, and/or (5) a belief that asking for advice takes too much time. There are probably many other reasons for not seeking help. Figure 2.4 illustrates an array of questions that can be used to debrief a case from the perspective of the case analyst.

The debriefing framework related to *strategic issues management* is defined as a process of identifying strategic issues in a case and developing a plan for addressing them. Each of the following steps is described in Figure 2.5: (1) issue identification (a condition that needs attention), (2) goal setting (specifying change goals in the form of outcomes), (3) intervention planning (goal-related change activities), and (4) evaluating the intervention plan (gathering data and reflecting upon outcomes). The conceptual foundation for each of these steps is described in more detail in Packard and Austin (in press).

Finally, a debriefing strategy that is more relevant to the *policy practice dimension* of decision making is useful for managers involved in a policy implementation process (Hill & Hupe, 2002). For Brock (2003), the focus of the case analysis process is on the impact of new policies on organizational missions as they relate to opportunities and constraints,

Figure 2.5   Strategic Issues Management Approach to Case Analysis

1. *Key Issues*: Assess the organizational and administrative situation with supportive data. Include a list and description of key issues and problems. Also note organizational strengths and how these may be relevant to the issues. Discuss *the top 3–4 issues*, including why they need attention and the effects they are having on the organization. Use relevant theories, administrative principles, and research to support and elaborate upon your analysis.

2. *Major Goals*: List *immediate and long-term goals* for a change plan, in priority order, with rationales for each goal. Relate these to the top identified issues and problems listed above.

3. *The Plan*: Describe your *intervention/change plan* for the accomplishment of each change goal. Describe specific strategies, techniques, or activities to be used. Include your rationales for each, and how the activities will be evaluated. Use relevant theories, administrative principles, and research to support your plan.

4. *Evaluation*: Describe how you would *evaluate the outcomes of your intervention*, using any relevant program evaluation or other research methods. Be specific about the design and process for each element. These should relate to the above assessment, goals, and intervention plan.

as well as to short-term and long-term objectives. An adaptation of Brock's framework is noted in Figure 2.6.

Use and Organization of the Casebook

While some cases in this book are presented in the third person, most use a first-person perspective. Generally, a reader can assume the role of the administrator or supervisor in the case and imagine how she or he would assess the situation and then develop a plan of action. Alternatively, the reader can play the role of a consultant invited by the agency's executive to do an assessment and suggest recommendations.

The organization of the cases in the following chapters corresponds with the elements of the managerial functions framework. The cases focus on multiple administrative concepts and principles because they represent real practice situations. Each case was assigned to a particular chapter based on the editors' perceptions of the key issues in that case. Within these chapters, the cases are generally ordered in increasing complexity. In nearly every case, there are secondary issues as well. For example, the more complex case entitled "The Cabal" is located in the chapter on agency governance because of the board's role in overseeing the work of the agency's chief executive. However, this case also raises issues about financial management and supervision (a bookkeeper's misallocation of discretionary funds, presumably without the executive's knowledge).

Figure 2.6   Policy-Oriented Case Analysis

Step 1: Assessing Problems and Risks

- What are the most important components of the situation (prioritized)?
- What factors led to the situation?
- What are the risks to the organization and those associated with the actions of others?

Step 2: Assessing Impact on Organizational Mission and Legacy

- How might the organization's mission be affected by the problem/situation?
- How does the organization's external environment impact/influence the problem?
- How might this situation affect the organization's future/legacy?

Step 3: Identifying External and Internal Actors

- Who can help address the problem, and who might interfere?
- What might be the motives and interests of both sets of actors and how might they be addressed?
- What kind of power or influence is held by each set of actors, and how might it be exercised?

Step 4: Identifying Opportunities and Constraints

- What might be potential improvements in organizational processes?
- What are the opportunities to build working relationships with internal and external stakeholders?

Step 5: Identifying Outcomes and Related Strategies

- What are some of the key aspects of successful outcomes?
- How do the outcomes move the organization toward the organization's mission?
- How might opposition to the outcomes destabilize the organization?
- How might the outcomes strengthen the organization's capacity in the future?
- How do the outcomes make use of available tools, address current organizational constraints, and make use of available time for implementation?
- What strategies are needed to implement the outcomes (a plan with prioritized action steps, a timeframe, and an assessment of needed resources and support)?

Step 6: Identifying the Manager's Short-term and Long-term Objectives

- What are the short-term objectives to successfully address the problem and set the stage for long-term objectives?
- What are the long-term objectives, and how might the current situation affect future success/accomplishments/goals?

SOURCE: Adapted from Brock (2004).

The managerial functions have been organized into six chapters. We begin at the broadest level: governance, dealing with the environment, and organizational structures. Next, we present cases involving agency leadership and ethics issues. Subsequent chapters address issues of planning and program design; financial management and information systems (including evaluation); human resource management and supervision; and, finally, a chapter addressing organizational change and organizational dynamics such as organizational culture.

Chapter 3 begins with the big picture. It includes cases on agency governance (working with boards of directors), managing the environment, and issues of organization design and structure. Many of these cases highlight the tensions regarding the respective roles of board and staff. There are no clear answers or solutions when considering an executive's discretion in issues ranging from program philosophy to the appropriateness of various fundraising expenditures. An executive director also needs to manage the fine line between board "meddling" and its legitimate involvement in policy development.

Chapter 4 includes issues of leadership and ethics in the agency setting. The extent to which a manager's leadership style should be participative and empowering is a common issue in organizations. These cases also raise ethical issues, from staff theft to the mismanagement of funds.

Chapter 5 focuses on planning and program design. Topics range from the temptation to acquire problematic grant funds to deciding how to allocate limited resources. At the program level, managers often need to make adjustments in programs without compromising the program's integrity.

Chapter 6 addresses the two key organizational systems of financial management (including fund development) and management of information (including program evaluation). Fund-development issues range from getting the board involved in fundraising to dealing with the expectations of prospective funding sources. When expenses exceed revenues, difficult budgeting choices (e.g., increasing fees or cutting staff or services) must be made. The cases on management information systems focus on documenting the need for services and determining what data should be collected to monitor and evaluate program progress and outcomes.

Chapter 7 focuses on human resources management and supervision. The issues raised in these cases range from inappropriate communications between staff and board members to working with a union regarding performance appraisal and termination. The supervision cases deal with gaining worker compliance with agency accountability expectations (e.g., paperwork) and the challenge of managing, including answering to one's immediate supervisor.

Chapter 8 features cases on organizational dynamics and change. In some cases, crises force an agency into organizational changes. In others, new executives see opportunities for organizational improvements and introduce methods to create change. One of these is a comprehensive case study of a county human services agency that provides many examples of successful organizational change strategies and tactics.

Each chapter includes more complex cases featuring multiple issues involved with organizational change. The first challenge in these multi-issue cases is identifying the key issues out of an abundance of detail. There may be an overriding issue that needs particular attention because it represents a crisis or because it affects other issues. After issues are identified, sorted, combined, or prioritized, considerable analysis is needed to determine what should be done to achieve desired outcomes, including the consideration of options and the identification of roles to be played by those involved in the case. Of course, there are no correct answers, although some options are likely to be more successful than others. There is no single debriefing framework that can address all the issues.

One approach to case analysis is to: (1) determine if all the available information is accessible (see checklist in Figure 2.1), (2) select the debriefing framework most appropriate for the case situation, and (3) identify the conceptual framework that can facilitate the greatest learning following the case analysis. Each case ends with debriefing questions specific to the case that may be used for debriefing and discussion. Also included for each case is a suggested debriefing framework. Of course, an instructor may use any of the debriefing frameworks on a particular case or others not included here.

While case-based learning provides one approach to educating future and current practitioners, other forms of experiential learning should be noted. For example, the practices of observing and reporting on group decision making outside the agency, as well as comparing organization charts from different agencies, provide learners with a more individualized learning experience. In order to provide suggestions for additional experiential-learning experiences, a set of classroom-based exercises is noted at the end of each of the case-based chapters.

The matrix at the end of this chapter (Figure 2.7) lists each case in order. Columns indicate specific case subjects. Two Xs in a box indicate the primary subject. A single X indicates subjects that are also present in the case. Of course, readers may disagree about some of these designations. They are provided as general guidelines, especially for instructors searching for cases that incorporate particular issues. The top of the matrix also indicates relevant chapters in three current human services management textbooks (Brody, 2005; Kettner, 2002a; Kettner, Moroney, & Martin, 1999; Lewis, Packard, & Lewis, 2007) that parallel the conceptualization of management functions used here. Those books—or others—can be used to provide conceptual and empirical underpinnings for case analysis as well as relevant practice wisdom.

❖ SUMMARY

Using the management functions framework described in Chapter 1, we provided an assessment checklist to use in assessing cases prior to engaging in problem solving and/or decision making. Since managerial decision making involves critical thinking skills, five debriefing frameworks were described. Any one of them could be used to address a case. The debriefing frameworks include: (1) managerial problem solving, (2) analytic and interactional aspects of ethical decision making, (3) help-seeking behaviors related to consultation, (4) strategic management, and (5) policy-analytic decision making.

We concluded this chapter with a description of the subsequent chapters in the casebook, beginning with specific cases reflecting the organizational environment and governance and concluding with cases on organizational change. Given our approach to framing cases by using three conceptual frameworks of managerial practice and five debriefing strategies, case-based learning can be an effective way to educate future managerial practitioners. This learning approach can help such students explore their assumptions and perceptions while applying their acquired knowledge and skills to the complexities and uncertainties of contemporary human service organizations.

Figure 2.7 Matrices of Case Topics

Chapter 3: Matrix of Case Topics

Case	a. Governance b. Environment c. Structure			a. Leadership b. Ethics		a. Planning b. Program Design		a. Financial Management b. Information Systems c. Evaluation			a. HRM b. Supervision		a. Organizational Change b. Organizational Dynamics	
	a.	b.	c.	a.	b.	a.	b.	a.	b.	c.	a.	b.	a.	b.
Chapter 3. *Governance, Environment, and Structure*														
Relevant Chapters from:														
Brody (2005)	20			1		2	3, 4	12–16			7, 8, 11	10	4	5, 9, 17–19
Kettner (2002)		3	4	2, 6				8	7	14	5, 6, 9–11	12, 13		1
Kettner, Moroney, & Martin, (2008)			3–5			2	6–8	10, 11	9	12, 13				
Lewis, Packard, & Lewis, (2007)	2	2	5	11	11	3	3	8	9	10	6	7	4, 11	4, 12
Governance														
3.1 Meddling Trustees	XX				X			X			X			
3.2 KidsCan	XX			X										
3.3 Dorchester House Board of Directors	XX			X		X								
3.4 The Perfect Storm	XX				X						X			
3.5 Poor Leadership Boundaries	XX			X							X			X

(Continued)

Figure 2.7 (Continued)

Chapter 3: Matrix of Case Topics

Case	a. Governance b. Environment c. Structure			a. Leadership b. Ethics		a. Planning b. Program Design		a. Financial Management b. Information Systems c. Evaluation			a. HRM b. Supervision		a. Organizational Change b. Organizational Dynamics	
	a.	b.	c.	a.	b.	a.	b.	a.	b.	c.	a.	b.	a.	b.
Chapter 3. *Governance, Environment, and Structure*														
Environment														
3.6 The Cabal	XX													
3.7 The Cost of a Tuxedo		XX					X	X				X		
3.8 Choosing a Director		XX				X		X						
3.9 Collapse of the Coalition		XX				X				X				
Structure														
3.10 Merging Colossal and Grassroots Agencies			XX											X
3.11 Poor Interdepartmental Communication or Competing Service Ideologies			XX						X					
3.12 Whose Interests Are Being Served?			XX			X								X
3.13 Greenvale Residential Treatment Center			XX	X		X		X			X			X

NOTE: XX = Primary subject; X = Secondary subject

Chapter 4: Matrix of Case Topics

Case	a. Governance b. Environment c. Structure			a. Leadership b. Ethics		a. Planning b. Program Design		a. Financial Management b. Information Systems c. Evaluation			a. HRM b. Supervision		a. Organizational Change b. Organizational Dynamics	
	a.	b.	c.	a.	b.	a.	b.	a.	b.	c.	a.	b.	a.	b.
Chapter 4. *Leadership and Ethics*														
Relevant Chapters from:														
Brody (2005)	20			1		2	3, 4	12–16			7, 8, 11	10	4	5, 9, 17–19
Kettner (2002)		3	4	2, 6				8	7	14	5, 6, 9–11	12, 13		1
Kettner, Moroney, & Martin, (2008)		3–5				2	6–8	10, 11	9	12, 13				
Lewis, Packard, & Lewis, (2007)	2	2	5	11	11	3	3	8	9	10	6	7	4, 11	4, 12
Leadership														
4.1 Empowering Staff: Real or Imaginary?		X		XX										
4.2 Caught in the Middle: Mediating Differences in Gender and Work Style				XX							X			
4.3 To Talk or Not to Talk				XX	X									X

(Continued)

Figure 2.7 (Continued)

Chapter 4: Matrix of Case Topics

Case	a. Governance b. Environment c. Structure			a. Leadership b. Ethics		a. Planning b. Program Design		a. Financial Management b. Information Systems c. Evaluation			a. HRM b. Supervision		a. Organizational Change b. Organizational Dynamics	
	a.	b.	c.	a.	b.	a.	b.	a.	b.	c.	a.	b.	a.	b.
Chapter 4. *Leadership and Ethics*														
4.4 Agency Director Uses a Personal Coach to Address His Leadership Style				XX										X
4.5 Founder's Syndrome	X			XX	X	X		X						
4.6 Executive Leadership				XX		X		X						
4.7 Marian Health Center				XX		X		X	X		X		X	
4.8 Mosaic County Welfare Department				XX		X	X	X	X				X	
4.9 Project Home				XX		X		X	X			X		X
Ethics														
4.10 Damage Control					XX									
4.11 Philosophy vs. Economics					XX			X						
4.12 What? Me Worry?					XX			X						

NOTE: XX = Primary subject; X = Secondary subject

Chapter 5: Matrix of Case Topics

Case	a. Governance b. Environment c. Structure			a. Leadership b. Ethics		a. Planning b. Program Design		a. Financial Management b. Information Systems c. Evaluation			a. HRM b. Supervision		a. Organizational Change b. Organizational Dynamics	
	a.	b.	c.	a.	b.	a.	b.	a.	b.	c.	a.	b.	a.	b.
Chapter 5. *Planning and Program Design*														
Relevant Chapters from:														
Brody (2005)	20			1		2	3, 4	12–16			7, 8, 11	10	4	5, 9, 17–19
Kettner (2002)		3	4	2, 6				8	7	14	5, 6, 9–11	12, 13		1
Kettner, Moroney, & Martin (2008)		3–5				2	6–8	10, 11	9	12, 13				
Lewis, Packard, & Lewis (2007)	2	2	5	11	11	3	3	8	9	10	6	7	4, 11	4, 12
Planning														
5.1 Mallard County Private Industry Council						XX								
5.2 Be Careful What You Wish For						XX								
5.3 Decision on Resource Allocations						XX		X						

(Continued)

31

Figure 2.7 (Continued)

Chapter 5: Matrix of Case Topics

Case	a. Governance b. Environment c. Structure			a. Leadership b. Ethics		a. Planning b. Program Design		a. Financial Management b. Information Systems c. Evaluation			a. HRM b. Supervision		a. Organizational Change b. Organizational Dynamics	
	a.	b.	c.	a.	b.	a.	b.	a.	b.	c.	a.	b.	a.	b.
Chapter 5. *Planning and Program Design*														
5.4 Rational Versus Political Decision Making		X				XX		X						
5.5 The Achievement Crisis at Girls Works						XX		X			X			
5.6 Cutbacks and Performance Pressure			X	X		XX		X						
5.7 Hillside Community Center		X	X	X		XX	X			X			X	
5.8 Empowering Staff to Advocate for Chicano/Latina Clients						XX								X
Program Design														
5.9 Banksville Human Services Center	X			X			XX	X						
5.10 Massive Retrenchment			X	X			XX	X						
5.11 Productivity and Performance				X			XX	X	X					
5.12 Responding to Changing Client and Community Needs		X				X	XX		X					

NOTE: XX = Primary subject; X = Secondary subject

Chapter 6: Matrix of Case Topics

Case	a. Governance b. Environment c. Structure			a. Leadership b. Ethics		a. Planning b. Program Design		a. Financial Management b. Information Systems c. Evaluation			a. HRM b. Supervision		a. Organizational Change b. Organizational Dynamics	
	a.	b.	c.	a.	b.	a.	b.	a.	b.	c.	a.	b.	a.	b.
Chapter 6. Financial Management and Information Systems														
Relevant Chapters from:														
Brody (2005)	20			1		2	3, 4	12–16			7, 8, 11	10	4	5, 9, 17–19
Kettner (2002)		3	4	2, 6				8	7	14	5, 6, 9–11	12, 13		1
Kettner, Moroney, & Martin (2008)		3–5				2	6–8	10, 11	9	12, 13				
Lewis, Packard, & Lewis (2007)	2	2	5	11	11	3	3	8	9	10	6	7	4, 11	4, 12
Fund Development														
6.1 Should We Accept the Gift?								XX						
6.2 Changing the Ground Rules	X							XX						

(Continued)

Figure 2.7 (Continued)

Chapter 6: Matrix of Case Topics

Case	a. Governance b. Environment c. Structure			a. Leadership b. Ethics		a. Planning b. Program Design		a. Financial Management b. Information Systems c. Evaluation			a. HRM b. Supervision		a. Organizational Change b. Organizational Dynamics	
	a.	b.	c.	a.	b.	a.	b.	a.	b.	c.	a.	b.	a.	b.
Chapter 6. *Financial Management and Information Systems*														
Budgeting														
6.3 Showdown						X		XX						
6.4 Improving Cash Flow								XX						
6.5 Desperate for Program Funding								XX						
6.6 Painful Choices						X		XX						
Information Systems														
6.7 Measuring Performance						X			XX					
6.8 Information Services Overload									XX					
6.9 Evaluating a Strategic Plan for Children's Services						X			X	XX				

NOTE: XX = Primary subject; X = Secondary subject

Chapter 7: Matrix of Case Topics

Case	a. Governance b. Environment c. Structure			a. Leadership b. Ethics		a. Planning b. Program Design		a. Financial Management b. Information Systems c. Evaluation			a. HRM b. Supervision		a. Organizational Change b. Organizational Dynamics	
	a.	b.	c.	a.	b.	a.	b.	a.	b.	c.	a.	b.	a.	b.
Chapter 7. *Human Resource Management and Supervision*														
Relevant Chapters from:														
Brody (2005)	20			1		2	3, 4	12–16			7, 8, 11	10	4	5, 9, 17–19
Kettner (2002)		3	4	2, 6				8	7	14	5, 6, 9–11	12, 13		1
Kettner, Moroney, & Martin (2008)		3–5				2	6–8	10, 11	9	12, 13				
Lewis, Packard, & Lewis (2007)	2	2	5	11	11	3	3	8	9	10	6	7	4, 11	4, 12
HRM														
7.1 The Case of the Missing Staff											XX			
7.2 Client-Centered Administration or Organization-Centered Administration?					X						XX			
7.3 Union Headache											XX			X
7.4 The Influence of Religious Beliefs					X						XX			

(Continued)

Figure 2.7 (Continued)

Chapter 7: Matrix of Case Topics

Case	a. Governance b. Environment c. Structure			a. Leadership b. Ethics		a. Planning b. Program Design		a. Financial Management b. Information Systems c. Evaluation			a. HRM b. Supervision		a. Organizational Change b. Organizational Dynamics	
	a.	b.	c.	a.	b.	a.	b.	a.	b.	c.	a.	b.	a.	b.
Chapter 7. *Human Resource Management and Supervision*														
7.5 Growing Pains										X	XX			X
7.6 Challenges on the Line					X						XX			
7.7 Selecting a Clinical Director for Friendly House	X				X						XX			X
7.8 Fire a Competent CFO?								X			XX			
Supervision														
7.9 SOS in DHS: A Problem of Motivation												XX		
7.10 Deteriorating Performance of a Supervisee												XX		
7.11 Helping Supervisors Manage Their Staff												XX		
7.12 Supervising Five Case Managers												XX		X
7.13 Supervisory Leadership				X								XX		

NOTE: XX = Primary subject; X = Secondary subject

Chapter 8: Matrix of Case Topics

Case	a. Governance b. Environment c. Structure			a. Leadership b. Ethics		a. Planning b. Program Design		a. Financial Management b. Information Systems c. Evaluation			a. HRM b. Supervision		a. Organizational Change b. Organizational Dynamics	
	a.	b.	c.	a.	b.	a.	b.	a.	b.	c.	a.	b.	a.	b.
Chapter 8. *Organizational Dynamics and Change*														
Relevant Chapters from:														
Brody (2005)	20			1		2	3, 4	12–16			7, 8, 11	10	4	5, 9, 17–19
Kettner (2002)		3	4	2, 6				8	7	14	5, 6, 9–11	12, 13		1
Kettner, Moroney, & Martin (2008)		3–5				2	6–8	10, 11	9	12, 13				
Lewis, Packard, & Lewis (2007)	2	2	5	11	11	3	3	8	9	10	6	7	4, 11	4, 12

(Continued)

Figure 2.7 (Continued)

Chapter 8: Matrix of Case Topics

Case	a. Governance b. Environment c. Structure			a. Leadership b. Ethics		a. Planning b. Program Design		a. Financial Management b. Information Systems c. Evaluation			a. HRM b. Supervision		a. Organizational Change b. Organizational Dynamics	
	a.	b.	c.	a.	b.	a.	b.	a.	b.	c.	a.	b.	a.	b.
Chapter 8. *Organizational Dynamics and Change*														
8.1 Implementing Organizational Change as a Newcomer				X									XX	
8.2 Diagnosing Managerial Practice in a Budget Crisis				X									XX	
8.3 How Are We Doing?						X				X			XX	
8.4 Jefferson Hospital		X		X		X		X					XX	
8.5 Thurston High School		X		X			X		X				XX	X
8.6 The Leadership Challenges in Transforming a Public Human Services Agency		X	X	X		X	X	X	X	X			XX	X

NOTE: XX = Primary subject; X = Secondary subject

3

Governance, Environment, and Structure

❖ GOVERNANCE

CASE 3.1   Meddling Trustees

Walter has been hired as the new executive director of the Falmouth Agency, whose function is to work with released convicts and help them make the transition into the work world. Walter is a dedicated professional who has considerable experience in this field, but as a new director he now has to deal with a board of trustees that presents him with numerous problems. Here's what he has to say:

I have worked, in a limited way, with a board of trustees before, since my past positions involved being in administration but not the head of the organization. I can easily handle administrative issues, but my board is causing me lots of headaches. I want to proceed in such a way that I can help them do their job of governance without their unduly interfering with my job as director. Given the individual agendas of the various trustees, this is indeed a tremendous challenge.

First, they think the previous administration did a poor job of managing the finances, and they want to establish a search committee for finding and hiring a good chief financial officer (CFO) who would report directly to the board on financial matters. I'm wondering how I can convey to the board that as executive director and Chief Executive Officer, I should take responsibility for hiring (and firing) all members of my staff, including the CFO. If the CFO reports directly to the board, thus bypassing me, then my role as CEO will be seriously impaired.

Second, one of the trustees is upset that the services provided to his son were inadequate, and he has told me that he wants me to fire three staff members who worked with his son because he thought they were incompetent. I can appreciate his being upset, but I've looked into the situation and I've determined that staff acted properly. They've always had excellent evaluations. Still, I'm not sure how to handle this disgruntled trustee, who has been a major donor and who is insisting that I take disciplinary action against the staff members.

Third, another trustee, who has had some experience in public relations, now has time on her hands. She keeps coming in unannounced, wanting to work with our public information staff on our publications. My staff tells me that her ideas are not helpful but they don't want to offend her.

Fourth, one of the board members has asked that the catering for an agency special event be handled by her daughter. She says she's worked hard in the past on our special events and now wants this favor in return for her time and effort. It's true that she's worked diligently and given terrific leadership. I'd rather not alienate her, but I don't see how we can give her daughter special treatment, especially since her prices are higher than our regular caterer.

Finally, one of the trustees is a rental agent, and at the last board meeting he proposed that we consider appointing a committee to look into moving into new office space. Clearly, this is looming as a conflict-of-interest situation, and I've got to figure out how to nip it in the bud.

Discussion Questions

1. What specific steps should be taken to address each of the five situations?

2. What kind of discussion might the executive director have with the chairperson to help the chair actively work with board members to fulfill their roles in more appropriate ways?

3. How can trustees be helped to understand their roles in relation to those of the director?

4. Sometimes boards of trustees develop a code of ethics that can guide their individual and collective actions. If you think this is

a good idea, what elements would you recommend be included in such a code of ethics?

Suggested Debriefing Framework: 2.3 Analytical and Interactional Aspects

CASE 3.2   KidsCan

KidsCan, Inc., provides counseling and tutorial services for adolescent boys and girls with mild to moderate emotional and learning problems. Similar to many executive directors and board members of nonprofit organizations, Greg McKay, the executive director of KidsCan, Inc., was not aware of the underlying board recruitment problems and dynamics, or how he and his board members may have contributed to certain board performance issues.

Like most nonprofit organizations, KidsCan expected its board members to help solve problems, represent the organization in the community, develop and use important contacts, serve on committees, and help raise money. Notwithstanding some difficulties in seeing these expectations fulfilled, Greg was concerned about a "faction" of board members who had spotty attendance at board meetings, did not stay for entire meetings, did not accept committee assignments, did not make financial contributions, and did not attend special events. Greg reported that he had made four attempts to rectify board member commitment and performance concerns.

Attempt 1

Basing his attitude on his reading and on workshops he attended, Greg believed that the root of the problem was that board members did not really know each other. He reasoned that if the relationships among board members were enhanced, they would feel a stronger commitment to each other, leading to greater board member participation and follow-through. To achieve this end, Greg focused on the development and implementation of a board retreat that would encourage board member interaction. What happened was that some board members did not show, and some left early.

Attempt 2

In his second attempt, Greg opted to try a couple of the good tips that were shared at one of the workshops he attended at the statewide

SOURCE: Block (2004).

membership association of nonprofit organizations' annual conference, "Improving the Nonprofit Organization: Achieving Collaboration Through Leadership and Example." Specifically, Greg tried to improve board member attendance by increasing the different ways the board would be notified of board meetings. The idea was based on a marketing strategy about getting the "product" name out a certain number of times before people really pay attention to the message.

Two weeks before the meeting, a written notice and a materials packet were mailed. Three days later, Greg e-mailed the board members with a reminder. Around the same time, Greg's executive assistant called each board member by phone to ask if he or she had received the mailed packet. If the board member could not be reached directly, a message was left with an assistant or on the member's voice mail. The message included a reminder of the meeting day, date, and time.

Attendance did not improve as a result of these extra notices.

Attempt 3

Greg received a promotional brochure in the mail reporting favorable outcomes for organizations all over the United States and Canada who used a set of commercially produced board-training videos with accompanying workbooks. Greg invested in the package, convinced by the brochure's testimonial from a board chair: "I could not believe the improvement in the board's attendance and participation. I was so encouraged that I took out my checkbook and agreed to serve another term."

After reviewing the videos and workbooks with Dr. Anne Miller, the KidsCan board chair, the two decided that they would show one segment of the video at the start of every board meeting and then encourage a fifteen-minute discussion among board members using the outline from the workbooks.

The outcome was that two board members left the room while the video was playing in order to make cell phone calls. Following the video, very limited dialogue was exchanged among board members.

Attempt 4

Greg read in the workbook and heard on one of the videos that the board chair's role was more important than just facilitating board meetings. The message described the board chair as "being in charge" and needing to demonstrate that "leadership starts at the top." Greg believed that if Anne took her role more seriously, the other board members would follow suit.

Instead, after the board chair reviewed the video, she realized that she could not live up to the expectations that were presented. Anne resigned.

Discussion Questions

1. How has Greg misdiagnosed the problems with the board? What are the actual underlying problems?

2. What can Greg do to prevent these problems from occurring in the future?

3. What could Greg do as a leader to motivate board members?

Suggested Debriefing Framework: 2.2 Managerial Problem Solving

---

CASE 3.3   Dorchester House Board of Directors

Introduction

On New Year's Day, Virginia Markson, executive director of Dorchester House, spent three hours telephoning the members of the settlement house's board of directors to extend season's greetings. This was the first time since she was promoted to the chief executive office a year and a half ago that she had made such an attempt to win over the board members. She had spent much of her job tenure frustrated and bewildered by the director's lack of interest and involvement in Dorchester House—except as barriers to change.

Dorchester House is a 72-year-old settlement house in Chicago's Hyde Park. Situated in the heart of a racially mixed university neighborhood, Dorchester House was founded to provide social services to everyone in the neighborhood and to help strengthen a sense of community. The original constitution in 1907 established the settlement house "as a center for social, educational, and civic improvement to be carried on in conjunction and association with the people residing in the neighborhood." Dorchester House now offers programs to children, senior citizens, and current and former substance abusers, and students of theater and crafts from all over Chicago.

Recently, Martin Kona ended a 35-year career as executive director of Dorchester House. Kona, an influential member of the community,

---

SOURCE: Updated from Greenberg, E. (1978) under the supervision of Professors T. P. Ference and J. A. F. Stoner. Institute for Not-for-Profit Management, Columbia University.

in many ways *was* Dorchester House. A long-term staff member said of him, "Mr. Kona treated us all as if we were his children." During his administration, his pet project, the Theatre Arts School, developed city-wide prominence. The day care center, senior citizens' center, crafts programs, thrift shop and summer camp programs were well established. Other programs had disappeared due to lack of interest, and the physical plant was in disrepair. Over the years, the settlement house had moved away from the community involvement that had been its hallmark at the beginning of the 20th century.

Ten years ago, Kona hired Virginia Markson, a young therapist with a master's degree in social work, to direct Dorchester House's Senior Citizens Counseling Program, including psychiatric outpatient services. In response to government funding, Dorchester House was able to expand these services and the number of persons served. When Kona announced his retirement, he told Virginia Markson that the board of directors had, upon his recommendation, selected her as the new executive director.

Virginia Markson recently remarked to a close friend, "I was surprised that the board wanted to hire me. I really had very little contact with them as the counseling center director. Once a year, all the program directors were asked to present reports at a board meeting. We were brought into the room, and Mr. Kona introduced us to the board members, who were not introduced to us. We presented glowing reports, were thanked and were promptly escorted from the room. Kona later told us how we did. Actually, I was executive director for over two months before I could associate most of the members' names with their faces."

The appointment of Markson, a comparatively young person with no prior experience in management, was received with some surprise in the community. Markson later explained, "It took a lot of encouragement from Martin Kona and John Belfer, the secretary of the board, and from my husband to persuade me to take the job."

Kona was out of town for most of the transition period following his resignation announcement. He did not take the time to introduce Markson to the board members or to his contacts in foundations and government agencies. However, he did give her some advice: "It's a good idea to play up to the board members. I usually call each member once a week and take him or her to lunch every month. I also send them all gifts from the House on their birthdays, anniversaries, and at Christmas."

The Board of Directors

The board of directors of Dorchester House consists of 14 men and 10 women. They are a homogeneous, wealthy, and politically conservative group. Potential members are recruited from among the social peers of the present directors; the minutes of the meetings do not indicate any in-depth examination of anyone nominated. The nomination committee meets spontaneously during the actual board meetings. Jovial comments such as, "I can't remember if I'm on that committee or not," can be heard whenever the question of a new prospect arises. The chairman of the nominating committee has held his position for close to 15 years.

Most of the directors do not live in Hyde Park, and five or six have never even visited the settlement house. Meetings are held downtown in the Loop, in the offices of the board president. Absenteeism is extremely high; meetings average eight to ten members. Although some members never attend meetings, there is no mechanism for removing board members. For some members, it is clear that the House serves as a pet charity. In other cases, membership on the board reflects a tradition passed on from one generation to the next; other members see Dorchester House as a social stepping stone.

The majority of the board members have served for over 35 years. The youngest member is 40, while the oldest is approaching 80. There are ten active members of the board: four women and six men. The four active female members include a well-known stock broker, a chemist/ patent attorney, and two vice presidents of large corporations. Three women "in good standing" have not been to a board meeting in five years, and the involvement of the remaining three is sporadic.

All of the male members are extremely wealthy, and many sit on other nonprofit boards. They display a sense of fiscal camaraderie. The four officers are the most active members of the board. The chairman, Stuart Winship, recently retired as chairman of the board of a large Chicago utility. Winship is a powerful, dynamic leader who commands respect by his very presence. He never initiates policies or suggests programs; rather, he sees his role as the "father of accountability." He takes his responsibilities quite seriously, and seems deeply troubled if there are any difficulties with the settlement house.

The board president, Robert Ames, heads his own publishing firm. John Belfer, the secretary, is a lawyer. The treasurer of the board, Richard Winship, is, at 40, the youngest board member. Also the son of the chairman, Richard Winship is vice president of a large bank. Michael Burton, who heads the nominating committee, owns a number of television stations and communications centers throughout the country.

Other board members include a 60-year-old man who has never worked, as well as a vice chancellor of a university who moved away from the city two years ago but still retains his seat. Another member, who attended only the first meetings held after his appointment to the board two years ago, is quite famous in the area of nonprofit institutions. The remaining men are all board chairmen and presidents of their own firms.

Virginia Markson remarked to a friend, "I'm really puzzled about the board members. None of them are personally involved in any of the agency's programs. What's more, most of them don't even give us any money! There are never spontaneous visits, requests for tours, or reviews of services. Since most members seldom set foot inside the facilities, they are unaware of the need for repairs. On very rare occasions, three or four board members will attend an event that has been sponsored by the board, but only after much coaxing on my part. Since board members are so detached from the House's actual service delivery, their suggestions are often impractical and unrealistic.

"They are not known to praise, but they are quick to criticize. They usually criticize by comparing us with the achievements of other settlement houses when they get publicity in the national press."

The Executive Director and the Board

In discussing her first year and a half as executive director of Dorchester House, Virginia Markson expressed a continuing concern with regard to her relationship with the board of directors:

"I now feel comfortable with the staff and the operations of the House, but I'm still uncertain about dealing with the board, and I'm afraid this could hurt our programs. I'm not Martin Kona and never will be, but I keep getting the feeling that the board compares me with him. Several members told me that they miss Kona.

"Most of the members are distant and aloof, at least with me, although I suppose I might be partially responsible for that. I thought that I could win the respect of the board by my work, not by currying favor with them—as Kona suggested I do. I thought my methods would work, but the board members don't seem to notice when I'm doing well. I wonder if Kona was right.

"I also worry about what the community thinks about me, and how that might affect the House. Kona was *the* director of Dorchester House. I just don't know what they think about me.

"I do feel comfortable with John Belfer, the board secretary. Maybe that's because he came up through the ranks and didn't inherit his wealth like everyone else on the board. Unfortunately, John doesn't play an active role in board meetings."

John Belfer has been on the board of Dorchester House for six years. Belfer had a particular interest in the Senior Citizens

Counseling Center's programs, and had worked closely with Virginia to secure government contracts for the center. It was this association that led Belfer to encourage her to accept the Director's position when Kona retired. As Belfer remarked, "I've had more of a chance than most of the board members to get to know Virginia because of the work we did together. I've always found her to be capable and intelligent, and she was certainly aggressive and confident in pushing for her programs.

"When Kona retired, I urged her to take the job. She really cares about the House and wants to do a good job. She seems to have had some difficulties in working with the board, however. Her presentations at meetings have been thorough, but stiff and rather formal. Stuart Winship told me recently that she had not initiated any direct contacts with him during her first year as executive director. This may have been a mistake. Stuart is not the kind of man to volunteer advice, and yet his continued involvement is critical to the House.

"The board doesn't meet regularly and, in the past, meetings were called only when one of the officers wanted to talk about something that was bothering him or her. For the good of the House, the executive director has to be more active in bringing issues to the board. I think Virginia has come to see this, and she has told me that she now initiates meetings with Stuart to give him regular reports on the House's activities. I think her initiatives have helped her relationship with him, and that's important because Stuart can sway a vote without voting himself. Her eyebrows still pop up when he calls her 'kiddo' or 'baby' at a meeting, but he has been supportive of her efforts.

"Virginia also works well with Dick Winship. Dick, however, always defers to his father and won't take an independent stand. Unfortunately, Stuart is thinking of resigning and retiring to Europe next year, and Virginia does not get along well with Bob Ames, our president. I can understand this—Bob is not easy to deal with, and he and I have tangled frequently. Bob's a true aristocrat; he is condescending towards the entire staff, including Virginia."

"He refers to them as 'hired help, who should know their place.' Last year he rejected a proposal for a new pension plan saying, 'Anyone who works for a nonprofit organization deserves what he gets.'"

Conclusion

A few days after her New Year's calls, Virginia Markson echoed the words of Bob Ames as she talked with some friends. "Maybe I got what

I deserve. Dorchester House has big problems—we're in debt, the building desperately needs repairs, I don't know if we're meeting the needs of the community, and staff morale is low. But I spend most of my time worrying about the damned board. What should I do about them?"

Discussion Questions

1. What should be the purposes and functions of the board of Dorchester house?

2. Is the board's membership appropriate to fulfill its functions? If not, what criteria should be used for future board members?

3. What should Virginia do about her current board members? Can any of them adapt to new expectations, or should they leave the board?

Suggested Debriefing Framework: 2.3 Analytical and Interactional Aspects

CASE 3.4   The Perfect Storm

My name is Rob Gander and even now as I tell my story, three months after I've been fired, I am still shaking and tremendously upset about what has happened. It's still hard for me to believe that after all I've done for the agency, I'm out of a job—all because of people who betrayed me.

For seven years, I was in charge of a family shelter and treatment program. When I began with the agency it had a budget of $1 million, and during my tenure I was able to draw in over $3 million annually. Not bad for a grassroots organization. I expanded our program to include counseling, job readiness, the GED, and a housing department. We developed a day care program that now receives about $300,000. Through my efforts, we obtained grants from the county, the state, and the federal government. The staff went from 20 to 90. I even arranged to buy our building with money that we had available from our fund balance. We were then able to remodel the building by developing the skills of men in our program that they can later use to obtain jobs. Clients really felt good about coming into our renovated building.

I was also proud of supporting our staff, many of whom were themselves one notch above being homeless persons or on public assistance. I've helped them find housing, encouraged them to get more education for themselves, and arranged to give them training in mental health, drug addiction, and child care.

With all of these positives going on, I guess I was not aware of the storm clouds that were looming and that eventually resulted in my being struck by lightning. Two things—one that affected my relationship with the board leadership and the other that emerged from my dealings with a staff member—converged to make the perfect storm.

About a year ago I ran into difficulties with the board president because he wanted me to use his construction company to renovate our building. I said I appreciated his offer, but it would be better if our clients carried out this responsibility. Besides, it might be construed as a conflict of interest for him to do this. Grudgingly, he agreed, though after that our discussions always seemed to have an edge, and I knew he harbored resentment. Our board's vice-president, a member of our community, was also upset with me, but for a different reason. He worked as a city utility worker and seemed jealous of the salary I was making. He thought my last raise was much too high, even though other board members supported the raise because I had brought in so much additional income to the agency. My salary was in line with those of other nonprofit executives administering similar agencies.

The situation with a staff member triggered a major confrontation with my board. We had hired this staff member because, though she was rough around the edges, she was from the community, and we thought she would have empathy for our clients and their families. I realize now that she was experiencing her own problems—her husband had recently left her with two young children—and this may have been one of the contributing factors to her hostile, negative attitude toward clients. About five months ago, she almost got into a fistfight with a female client. I insisted that she apologize to the client and reprimanded her for her unprofessional behavior. A month later, when I learned of another episode in which she shouted at a client, I said I wanted to see her in my office. My intent was to give her another warning. However, before her appointment with me, she called the board president, saying that I made her feel uncomfortable and that she had refused my offer to have a date with her. As I learned later, she claimed sexual harassment. I believe, as I look back on the situation, she made a calculated decision to take preemptive action so as to prevent my possibly firing her.

Unfortunately, her scheme worked. The board president and vice president met with other members of the executive committee without me and decided that I could no longer stay with the agency. They said they feared that the publicity would greatly harm the organization and they arranged a quiet meeting with me to discuss how I could leave. I was so angry at the injustice of what was happening that I thought about filing a lawsuit for wrongful termination, but then realized that I could not afford the cost of a lawsuit. Besides, my relationship with the board had been poisoned, and they offered me a good deal to leave quietly, without fanfare.

Since leaving three months ago, I think almost every day about how the board leadership had a vendetta against me and used the staff member's unsubstantiated claim to terminate me, but when I look in the mirror, I feel right about who I am. Those who know me best—my wife, my friends, and my professional colleagues—are aware that I operate with the highest ethical standards. I am still wondering, however, whether I should have fought my dismissal.

Discussion Questions

1. What could the executive have done, if anything, to prevent the build up of antagonism with the leadership of his board?

2. What safeguards might be undertaken to prevent unfair accusations? Assuming Rob is telling the truth, what steps could he have taken to prevent the board from taking action without due process?

3. If you were a trustee and sensed that a power play was taking place, what could you do to ensure a fair process?

4. Should Rob have challenged the decision? What could he have done to marshal his defense?

Suggested Debriefing Framework: 2.3 Analytical and Interactional Aspects

CASE 3.5   Poor Leadership Boundaries

The Charles Space and Science Center (CSSC) has existed on the West Coast for over 100 years. The old center was outdated and did not have the capacity to attract the public. Their new facility in the Oakley hills opened in 2000 with a new organizational focus: offering public exhibits and teaching while continuing to spotlight astronomy and other sciences.

Problems in the organization first started during a leadership transition between CEOs. The previous CEO was an older man, a good friend of many board members, and had been with the organization for many years. The new CEO, Alex, was a highly qualified younger woman from Holland. Alex was hired to take the agency in a new direction following two years of financial failure after the opening of the new building. Alex was hired in 2002. For the next two years, she struggled to create a new relationship between the board and many of the longtime volunteers (many of whom were major donors and/or spouses of board members).

Since the opening of the new building, many board members had treated CSSC like their personal clubhouse. They would use the facilities for their personal use, hold private events in the exhibit halls and use the center's storage area for their own equipment. Board members would come into Alex's office at CSSC without an appointment and tell her how she should be running the organization. Board members and certain volunteers were also given keys to the entire building, including the administrative offices. Volunteers were often asked to temporarily take over staff positions without being given proper contracts or training. In general, there was no clear, firm leadership; the organization was being run as if it were the board's hobby instead of a revenue generating business.

This situation occurred and the behaviors of the board were tolerated because of the lack of the clear leadership boundaries that the former CEO had had with the board. Many of the board members, had worked tirelessly to create and raise funds for the new building and as a result felt entitled to certain privileges. Poor hiring practices also contributed to this problem: instead of conducting extensive searches for the best astronomers, teachers, and business people, the board instead decided to hire volunteers, friends, and amateur astronomers from the area. The poor staffing and volunteer decisions were also a problem during 2003, when CSSC had to downsize due to fiscal concerns. The staff members that were laid off were still allowed to volunteer. Many of these people were permitted to keep their keys to the facility and maintained a sense that they were still staff and deserved to give input into the daily functioning of the organization.

This breakdown of leadership boundaries and structure also occurred because there was a lack of long-term strategic planning before Alex was hired. CSSC's new building was created to be a teaching center, a science center, and an exhibit space. The board relied too heavily on its own network instead of consulting museum professionals, and, as a result, there was a lack of planning and design expertise. The building design was not conducive to large exhibits. It was not built for easy passage for people who use wheelchairs, nor was it designed to have revenue-producing venues (such as large conference spaces or a portion that could be transitioned easily to accommodate a private party). CSSC is now in the process of completely renovating the building to remedy these problems, only four years after it was built.

The poor judgment exercised by the board has had a dramatic impact on the staff, volunteers and revenue production. Staff felt disempowered by the board having too much control over daily operations. Alex's power was also lessened by the board's intrusion. It was very difficult to make the needed changes in the organization. Volunteers were affected by not having clear boundaries around staff versus volunteer roles. Revenue was affected by not hiring the right people initially and also by the physical structure of the building. Bill Cormier, the volunteer services coordinator, was also affected by all of the above forces. He was working with a group of volunteers who were not accustomed to operating within a structured environment. He had no financial resources because of the drastic budget cuts that had happened before he became an employee. Some of the volunteers felt entitled to special privileges because their spouses were on the board. Staff members were overworked and morale was low.

The board's poor boundaries and their inability to make objective decisions about CSSC have created a difficult situation for the new CEO. Alex is stuck between needing to please and impress the board members while still doing what is best for the organization. Her ability or inability to create an organizational culture based on professional–leadership boundaries will decide the future of CSSC.

Discussion Questions

1. What policies and procedures should Alex propose to put necessary parameters on the board members' involvement with the agency?

2. What should Alex and Bill do in the human resources area to ensure proper and adequate staff and volunteer coverage of required activities?

Suggested Debriefing Framework: 2.2 Managerial Problem Solving

❖ ENVIRONMENTAL RELATIONS

Case 3.6   The Cabal

For two years, I have been on the board of trustees of an organization that has been doing a great job of providing home-care services for people with disabilities. We have been able to obtain new funding from the county, and, from what I can determine, our clients really appreciate our services. Tonight, however, I have been called to attend a special meeting to decide the fate of our director. The executive committee has been meeting in special sessions for the last two months and the board meeting tonight is to decide whether or not our director should remain. I am concerned that a cabal of the officers is trying to push out the director.

Our new board president is opposed to keeping him and the rumor is that he wants to replace him with a candidate of his own choosing.

Apparently, some executive committee members have lost confidence in the director because of recent events. These trustees have been concerned that our director has caused conflicts with other agencies involved with people with disabilities. We are in a natural competition for funding, but our director may have been overzealous in pushing for funding at the expense of other agencies. Those agencies, in turn, have been disparaging our organization. I happen to like the idea that our director is a fighter for what he believes in, but I could understand that our agency needs to be a team player in our community.

Of more serious concern is a situation of financial mismanagement. We discovered recently that the bookkeeper, presumably without the director's knowledge, decided to allocate $90,000 of special board discretionary funds (raised through board-sponsored events and private solicitations) to programs that received reduced funding from the state. She was well intentioned in wanting to preserve these programs and save staff jobs, but this should not have occurred without board authorization. Our director denies that he was aware of this, and I believe him. Still, he should have been more on top of the situation.

On the positive side, I'm aware that our director is a leader on the national scene, and is former chairman of the National Council of Disabled Persons. He is charismatic, intelligent, and the staff seems to like his leadership style. Most importantly, he has kept the budget balanced and has successfully written numerous proposals for funding.

I'm concerned that at tonight's meeting, the board will hear slanted reports from the executive committee whose members have interviewed competing agency directors and are likely to give biased accounts. They may be starting from the belief that he should be fired and are then finding facts to rationalize their decision.

Discussion Questions

1. What are the pros and cons of keeping this director?

2. If you were this trustee, what could you do to sway the opinion of others?

3. Financial mismanagement is a serious charge. What should the executive director have specifically done differently to prevent this from occurring?

4. What should be done now to address the financial problem?

Suggested Debriefing Framework: 2.4 Executive Coaching

Case 3.7   The Cost of a Tuxedo

I'm a trustee of an agency for homeless women and children. Tonight I have to make a very difficult decision about our CEO. Here's the situation:

Three years ago we hired John Davone, a person who is experienced in running a program like ours. During his tenure, he has worked diligently and competently to expand our program. He's been very successful in obtaining grants; now, however, we're at the point where these grants are declining. We're aware that we have to find other ways to raise revenues. Our board members are genuinely committed to the work of the organization, but we need to expand our connections with people who could provide us with additional income. We told John that he must make more contacts with corporation heads and wealthy people in our community. We've encouraged him to expand his network by joining the chamber of commerce and becoming active on committees of United Way so he can meet business and professional leaders. We even gave him a special executive budget account so that he could take businesspeople out to lunch. He's told us that he has identified people who might become interested in joining our board, and we were hopeful that he could continue his networking opportunities. He's reported that as a result of his growing community contacts, several people have indicated being open to serving on a fund resource development committee.

Three weeks ago, John reported at our board meeting that he and his wife had attended the Red Cross Ball and as a result met several business leaders and their spouses who indicated an interest in our organization. We were pleased, at the time, that he was taking this initiative.

As of yesterday, the positive attitude that we had felt toward John changed 180 degrees. Our local newspaper headline screamed, "DIRECTOR OF POVERTY AGENCY SPENDS LAVISHLY." Apparently, the reporter had gotten a report on our expenses for the last three months. She didn't say where the information came from, but I assume that the leak may have come from someone connected with our accounting department. The article described, in detail, John having lunches and dinners at the most expensive restaurants, purchasing costly gift items, buying expensive tickets to professional basketball games, and, what upset me the most, purchasing a tuxedo.

Last night at an emergency meeting with the executive committee of the board, John responded to every allegation. He didn't deny any of them. Instead, he stressed that in every instance he felt he was following the mandate of the board to reach out to wealthy prospective board members or donors. He thought he was following our sentiment of "to get money, you have to spend money." All the money, he explained, was spent on meals or gifts to prospective donors. Grudgingly some members of the executive committee said he had a good point and that the board did indeed encourage him. Some of them even said that his purchase of the tuxedo was in keeping with his having to be part of "high-society events." But there were other concerns raised that made members of the executive committee feel that we needed to meet as an entire board to determine a course of action.

Here's what concerns me the most: John may have been well intentioned in following what he perceived to be the sentiment of the board. But I think he went too far. Now that we have suffered this negative publicity, we have to consider what is best for the organization. I'm very concerned that the bad publicity will make John the kiss of death; that is, those people with financial means we want to attract to our organization will now be turned off. I expect heated discussion tonight about what we should do.

Discussion Questions

1. Given the board's encouraging John to connect with people of wealth, what are the pros and cons of the board keeping John as the executive?

2. Were there ways that John could have met the board's requests to network with wealthy individuals that might not have resulted in such negative publicity?

3. If the newspaper had not printed the article, would his purchases have been an issue for this board?

4. What guidelines might have been established in anticipation of the consequences of the board's request to reach out to business and professional people?

5. Assuming that the board makes the decision to keep John, how should the organization handle the newspaper's interest in a follow-up story?

Suggested Debriefing Framework: 2.3 Analytical and Interactional Aspects

CASE 3.8   Choosing a Director

Our faith-based national organization started 20 years ago as a small Methodist agency providing volunteers and small amounts of money ($2,000 to $3,000) for needed community projects. It began in Chicago and spread to 10 other large metropolitan areas like Akron, Los Angeles, Houston, and Boston. Now we're at the point of raising about $750,000 annually. Though we've had inquiries from other Christian denominations about helping with fundraising, our board has wanted us to remain identified with Methodist congregations. These projects involve tutoring programs, rehabilitating housing, volunteering, working with substance abusers, and assisting the children of people with AIDS.

We're now at a crossroads—as we are about to replace our executive director, who is retiring. Our two top candidates represent two different directions for the organization and the board is struggling with a decision. Richard is a candidate who represents the position of maintaining the status quo, that is, preserving what we are now doing. He recently resigned as a Methodist minister, saying he wants to become more involved in social issues. He is attracted by the idea of working with an organization like ours. We've made inquiries about his qualifications and experience, and we found him to be well respected and admired by those with whom he works. We've told him that our current director has an annual salary of $60,000 and he thought this would be acceptable.

The second candidate, Michael, represents a major change for the organization. Currently Michael is in charge of resource development for a large Catholic social services agency in a large metropolitan area. He is a young, energetic man who is highly committed to what we're doing and wants to greatly expand our horizons. He thinks we ought to be more ecumenical by including other Protestant denominations, as well as Catholic, Jewish, Muslim, and Hindu congregations who want to work together on inter-denominational community projects. With a master's degree in nonprofit management, Michael would bring a professional tone to our organization and significantly expand our fundraising efforts. He envisions that we would eventually expand our work to 30 cities.

Several of our board members, including me, are excited by his vision for the organization. We recognize that in this highly competitive world we'll either have to grow or die. Our donor base is aging and our charismatic founder is no longer able to provide guidance. In considering the two candidates, Richard clearly represents what we have been doing. Michael represents a significant forward-looking change, but he also presents financial issues we would have to surmount. He wants a salary 50% higher than what we are now paying. In addition, he wants to hire a high-level fund developer and administrative staff assistant. He thinks he'll be able to bring on graduate students to assist in the office, and they will need good supervision.

Our risk is that to hire him and his proposed additional staff we would have to incur an additional $120,000 expense annually. He's aware that we have a board endowment fund from which we have determined to only use the interest and not the principal. He's asking us to consider our taking money from the principal to pay the additional expenses for him and his new staff. He is confident that he will be able to obtain external support from foundations and business corporations within the next three years to support our additional expenses. Some trustees, on the other hand, are not so sure this is a gamble we want to take. Further, some trustees are balking at his expansive vision of our becoming more ecumenical. Frankly, I don't know where Michael gets the confidence that he can achieve his vision for the organization, but he is willing to put his job on the line if he doesn't succeed. He clearly is willing to take a risk. The question is, are we?

Discussion Questions

1. If you were Michael in this situation, what kind of assurances could you give the board that might tip them in your direction?

2. If you were Richard in this situation, and you knew your competitor was arguing for a broader vision, what assurances could you give for the future viability of the organization by maintaining the status quo?

3. If you were a member of the board, how would you vote and why? How might your own personal style and background affect your decision?

4. Suppose the board is considering updating its strategic plan. What are the pros and cons of undertaking this endeavor before hiring a new director?

5. What additional information should be gathered to make an informed decision on the strategic direction of the agency?

6. Suppose it's a year later, and Michael has not shown progress toward raising the external support. What action, if any, would you take if you were on this board?

CASE 3.9 Collapse of the Coalition

For the past two years, my organization, Employment Now!, has participated in the Jobs Coalition, a group of employment-training organizations, including Vocational Services, Metropolitan Ministerial Association, and the Urban Employment Agency. My agency provides supportive services, such as bus fare and day care vouchers, as well as two weeks of specialized training in interviewing skills and employee responsibilities. All of the agencies focus on low-income persons who had been on public assistance before they came to the program and now face termination because of the length of time they have been enrolled with us.

The Jobs Coalition was formed because a $2 million contract was made available to us if we would coordinate working together. My agency, like the others, was given $500,000 to provide support services, training, and job finding. Although the funding was to be performance-based with a contract stipulating specific milestones that we were each required to achieve, in reality not much attention was given to performance. The Jobs Coalition seemed more concerned with obtaining money for agency partners and gave only lip service to achieving outcomes. For example, we were supposed to achieve an objective of 70% of enrollees completing the intake and training process. Moreover, we had an additional objective of having over 60 % of those who completed training obtain jobs. I'm proud to say that my agency continually met the contracted objectives. Several of the others did not, but there was no consequence for those who fell below the threshold.

In the first year, the Jobs Coalition received a high number of referrals from various county offices, but this past year the referrals have dropped off dramatically. As a result, we are not able to meet our quotas. The county administrators are beginning to seriously question whether the Jobs Coalition should continue. I think they are right to raise questions, but my partners blame the county for the lack of referrals. When we've talked to the county offices, they say that the Jobs Coalition is not getting jobs for people, so why should they make referrals? I think they are right to challenge us for our poor performance.

The Jobs Coalition is beginning the process of contracting with the county for a third year of funding. Although the money has been a huge benefit to our agency, I am beginning to wonder whether our organization should remain in the Jobs Coalition. Yes, it would be in our financial best interest to continue, but I'm concerned that there could be a day of reckoning. The reputation of our agency could be greatly diminished because of the continuing poor performance of the Jobs Coalition. I dislike the idea of giving up a lucrative contract. Several of my board members are also questioning whether we should be giving up this golden opportunity in light of our limited resources

Discussion Questions

1. What are the short- and long-term consequences of participating (or not participating) in the Jobs Coalition?

2. What are the pros and cons of continuing with the Jobs Coalition for the third year? How do you come out on this issue? Explain.

3. If the organization were to continue, what data and outcome measures should be included in the contract for program evaluation purposes?

Suggested Debriefing Framework: 2.6 Policy Practice

❖ STRUCTURE

CASE 3.10 Merging Colossal and Grassroots Agencies

The two executives of the mental health agencies operating in the same community have decided to meet, at the requests of their respective boards, to determine the desirability and feasibility of merging the two organizations. A major decline in mental health funding has prompted the county's mental health board to encourage the two agencies to merge. They serve comparable populations—both are located on the city's west side; both have a similar mission of offering mental health services to improve the quality of life for the people in their community. If we could tune in to the inner thoughts of each executive director, this is what we would learn:

(Colossal Mental Health Agency:)
"My agency has an annual budget of $2 million. We are well respected in the community and have, over the years, attracted high-level professionals, including attorneys and businesspeople, to serve on our board. They are committed to raising one third of our budget through annual giving and special events. My board likes the idea of expanding, but only if we can assume major control. I am concerned that if we were to merge with the Grassroots Mental Health Agency, we might lose the involvement of some of our major donors who like to rub shoulders with high-level professionals on our board. On the other hand, if we merge, the mental health board will see us in a favorable light. And a newly merged agency will be eligible for a 10% fund increase. I like the idea of eliminating competition in our geographic area. We could potentially attract $200,000 more in state dollars for expanded services; staff could be used more efficiently; staff duplication could be reduced; and there is a good likelihood that the synergy between the two operations could produce expanded services and outcomes."

(Grassroots Mental Health Agency:)

"My board has asked me to explore the merger because we are going to have a hard time surviving and meeting the needs of the clients we serve. Yes, I can see a real advantage in being part of the Colossal Mental Health Agency because of its strength and position in the community. We are, after all, an agency with a budget of only $200,000, and we are limited to serving a fraction of the people that the Colossal Mental Health Agency serves.

There could be a real advantage to our people being able to draw from the influence of the Colossal Mental Health board. On the other hand, there are significant cultural differences between our organizations. Colossal is far more elitist than we are. It is accustomed to having businesspeople move quickly on issues, whereas we like to take our time before making decisions. Our board is composed of mostly grassroots members who are very much committed to our community and who will likely be very uncomfortable, even intimidated, by the Colossal board, as well as by having to give up some autonomy in a merged organization. Moreover, I think the cultures within the two staffs are different. We operate with more of a consensus, but I've heard from Colossal's staff members that, because of their size, there is a more bureaucratic, top-down style of decision making. We'd also have to make difficult administrative decisions about which staff to let go in the merged operation. For example, we will not need the same number of accounting and management information staff. I know that I will have to take a deputy role in the new organization, and though this bothers me slightly, I think that this would be manageable because I could learn a lot from Colossal's executive."

Discussion Questions

1. How would you assess the trade-offs involved in considering the merger?

2. Are there compelling considerations that would lead the two organizations to merge?

3. Do you see any way of overcoming the disadvantages by the administrators of the two organizations?

4. If the two organizations decide to pursue the merger, what kinds of exploratory questions should be raised that could result in a successful integration of the two organizations?

5. If you were the directors of Colossal or Grassroots, what would you recommend to your respective boards? Why?

Suggested Debriefing Framework: 2.6 Policy Practice

Case 3.11   Poor Interdepartmental Communications or Competing Service Ideologies?

One of the largest problems at my first-year field placement, the Office of AIDS (OA), was a lack of communication between the departments within the OA. There are two departments, the care and treatment department and the education and prevention department.

On numerous occasions, I have heard management and line staff members from both departments mention that there was little communication and information exchange between departments. Indeed, one of my suggested duties (while I was interning) was to develop a method to increase interdepartmental communication. Although the problem was recognized, there were never any measures carried out to alleviate the situation.

The care and treatment and education and prevention departments shared office space and held monthly staff meetings together, so it would seem that this problem could be easily overcome. However, some link was missing in the communication because the issue would come up time and again. It was not a physical gap that separated the two departments and blocked communication, but rather a difference in ideologies.

Much of the communication breakdown stemmed from differing opinions as to what the priorities of the Office of AIDS should be, as well as the uneven distribution of funding between the two departments. The care and treatment department received twice as much funding as the education and prevention department. There was a clear view of the importance of each issue in the mind-set of the federal government as represented by the priorities for the allocation of funds. The education and prevention department thought that more money should be allocated to their department in order to slow the spread of AIDS, while the care and treatment department thought that the money would be spent more wisely on those who were already suffering from the disease.

The lack of communication could be seen in the way each department scheduled its meetings on conflicting days, the lack of teamwork on projects, and the lack of knowledge sharing. There was also a lack of knowledge about the programs and goals of other departments.

When I discussed the disparity of the allocations with the manager of the care and treatment department, she was not aware that the disparity between the particular ratios of the allocations was so extreme. When this issue was brought to her attention, she agreed that prevention measures were extremely important and should be addressed—not only because of the impact the lack of prevention measures was having on the community, but also because it meant that even more people might get HIV, requiring even more funding to treat those people.

Because of the frustration that was caused by perceived ideological differences about where the money should be allocated, the teams did not communicate as effectively as they could have. I believe that these frustrations would block communication because staff members who thought the funding distribution was unfair would become disgruntled. I don't think the department supervisors ever met to discuss the problem exclusively or ever decided what measures to take on the matter.

Discussion Questions

1. Should the communication problem be addressed directly, or are there underlying problems that should be addressed first? If so, what are they?

2. Assuming that the two departments need to work together, what should be done to improve this situation?

Suggested Debriefing Framework: 2.2 Managerial Problem Solving

CASE 3.12   Whose Interests Are Being Served?

The following events took place in a family service agency providing domestic violence and sexual assault services in a small rural county. The client population consisted primarily of women and children. Services included crisis intervention and response, emergency and transitional shelter services, individual and group counseling, court and social service advocacy, prevention education, and information and referrals. The agency structure consisted of an executive director, two program managers, 13 staff, approximately 25 volunteers, as well as a five-member board named the "Guardian Council."

Agency History

The agency's services enjoyed a 25-year history in the community. Two and a half years prior, however, the agency that provided such services closed due to mismanagement by the former board of directors. For several months after the agency closed, volunteers maintained a crisis line for counseling, information, and referrals. Five months later the agency reopened its doors, with a newly formed Guardian Council, executive director, and staff. At least three of the new agency's staff had worked for the former agency, but they had left due to the management crisis in the former agency. The executive director of the new agency left after one year at the new agency, feeling pressure from a lack of experience. Subsequently, a new executive director, who offered 17 years of management and executive directorship experience in a successful human service agency, was hired.

Management Dilemma

A staff retreat was held to assess progress on a strategic plan developed just over one year ago. During the meeting, breakout sessions were arranged, in which agency values were discussed. Back in a full-group session, participants generated a list of agency values. Next, the facilitator outlined the agency tasks and the staff/board/volunteer positions having primary responsibility for each. Because this was a small, newly formed agency with a small budget, most of the agency maintenance and administrative duties rested with the executive director and the two managers, who also shouldered a small to moderate caseload. The staff took on most of the caseload, and everyone shared responsibility for answering phones and responding to walk-ins during office hours.

One of the young staff members who had been employed with the previous agency suggested that instituting a flat organizational configuration by dismantling the present hierarchical structure might better serve clients. She argued that such a structure might better fit the agency's values of equality, feminism, and empowerment of vulnerable populations, such as women and children who have experienced domestic violence and sexual assault. She gave an example of an agency that provided similar services, in which the executive director and other managers and staff rotated duties, sharing fiscal, administrative, and direct-service responsibilities. Her suggestion also included a more equitable pay structure between current staff and management. This staff member had volunteered her efforts, along with another staff member and several of the current board members, to provide services while the agency was closed. She was subsequently also involved in discussions about opening the new agency. She mentioned that the idea for instituting such a structure had been discussed at these agency formation meetings, but it had never been implemented.

Subsequent dynamics and unspoken viewpoints emerged from this suggestion. Some staff, volunteers and board members were interested in further examining this idea, while others felt it was unrealistic. The executive director expressed her skepticism, saying that with 17 years of experience she was not ready to take a cut in pay. However, she and others felt that expressing negative feedback to this idea might make them appear as if they were protecting their own self-interests, diminishing the values the organization proclaimed it adhered to. It was also believed that the staff member making the suggestion was attempting to assert her own self-interest to obtain higher pay and greater responsibility. There had been several incidents prior to this indicating the employee possessed a negative attitude and attempted to undermine the work and/or authority of others, primarily through gossiping.

Discussion Questions

1. How would theory regarding organization design and structure help inform this analysis?

2. What would be an appropriate structure for the proposed flat configuration, given its size of programs, and values?

3. In light of the structure you propose, what decision making, communication, and coordination processes would you suggest?

Suggested Debriefing Framework: 2.2 Managerial Problem Solving

CASE 3.13   Greenvale Residential Treatment Center

The Greenvale Residential Treatment Center (GRTC) provides educational, residential, and clinical services to approximately 100 at-risk boys with emotional and behavioral difficulties severe enough to interfere with remaining in their schools, homes, or communities. The clients, ranging in age from 7 to 18 years, typically have disorders related to aggressive, withdrawn, or self-injurious behavior. GRTC staff work with these clients in the context of three primary programs. A day school helps students improve academic and social skills, develop more appropriate behavior controls, and enhance self-esteem. A clinical department provides diagnostic evaluation, individual and group psychotherapy, and case management. A residential department oversees various types of residential treatment facilities, including the management of three campus houses and a few scattered off-campus houses. The residential program involves the creation of a therapeutic milieu, in which group interaction, behavioral control, consistent daily routines, and the teaching of social skills combine to support individual development.

The three departments—education, clinical, and residential—are each managed by a department head. The departments are simultaneously separated and integrated in their operations. The separation is geographical, with the activities of each department occurring in particular

SOURCE: Adapted from Kahn (2005, pp. 113–125).

areas of campus, and temporal, as clients move from one area to another during their days and nights. The residential department is responsible for clients before and after school, during which the education department is responsible. The clinical department is responsible for clients at specific, relatively limited points during the school days, when therapy, medication, or case management is required. Child-care workers staff both the residential and the education departments.

An administrative team of five oversees the departments and ancillary services. It also sets the strategic direction of the agency. The five administrative staff members consist of:

- Executive director—works with external constituencies
- Director of programs—oversees the daily operations of the residential and education departments
- Director of clinical services—supervises the operations of the clinical department
- Director of administration—oversees client movement into, through, and out of the agency
- Business manager—responsible for all financial aspects of the agency

Interdepartmental Disintegration

The three departments—education, residential, and clinical—exist mainly in the form of sub-groups. Staff members identify more strongly with their departments, programs, houses, shifts, and informal cliques than they do with the agency as a whole. Several boundaries exist between the groups, creating isolation. Each department's culture, physical location, various working shifts, and different approaches to clients reinforces the isolation. In addition, each department pursues its own agenda. This is partly a function of disciplinary differences, as each department operates on a different set of principles rooted in beliefs about the best way to serve clients. The departments share goals, but each holds different beliefs about how to achieve those goals. The educational department focuses on behavioral outcomes. The clinical department focuses on the cognitive and emotional process of past and present events. The residential department focuses on teaching life skills and fostering peer relations.

While each of these foci is clearly integral to the ultimate development of GRTC's clients, the differing beliefs and premises translate into a struggle whereby each department (and corresponding treatment philosophy and practice) seeks to dominate the agency. Staff members routinely disparage members of other departments. They blame one another and are routinely disrespectful to other departments' members. Rather than inquire about their experiences, perspectives, and approaches in specific situations, they circulate rumors or confront them in a bullying or disrespectful fashion. Often, they simply ignore one another.

The lack of integration among the three departments can be seen most strongly in the relationship between the three department heads. The system was designed on the premise that the heads would be the primary integrating mechanism. Ideally, they would confer, advocate, and struggle toward consensus as a daily practice. Unfortunately, this does not happen. The clinical department head withdrew from the advocacy process, leaving the heads of the residential and educational departments to battle more publicly for prominence in the agency. These two women did so with a vengeance, taking every opportunity to diminish the other's stature. The agency is rife with rumors about their latest battles, waged publicly in administrative meetings and privately through back channels. Their battles are treated largely as interpersonal—they simply "can't get along" or "hate each other." The education department head is widely perceived as "ambitious," and the residential head as "a bully." These women act in ways that help confirm such projections.

Led by their department heads, staff members are quite territorial in their relationships with one another. In protecting their own territory, they neglect to maintain a common ground on which agency members can meet and work through issues. This is most obvious in the context of treatment teams. The teams are composed of representatives from each department who meet weekly to create and evaluate treatment plans for each client. These team meetings are poorly attended and poorly functioning. Members push their own department-based perspectives and agendas. Team members are rude and aggressive towards one another, accusing rather than inquiring about one another. Staff members continue interacting with clients based on their own departmental perspectives, rather than implementing decisions made during treatment meetings.

The three departments have created their own working culture that often differs from their counterparts. The residential department is the strongest, mainly because they have the most staff. It is characterized by anger and resentment towards the agency. Its staff members feel unappreciated. These sentiments are fueled by the department head, who routinely voices her grievances against the other departments.

The education department consists primarily of special-education teachers who are steeped in the realities of teaching students who feel inadequate, inferior, and anxious. The education department head feels she has dealt with the other two department heads for too long, and she presents herself as a long-suffering victim. This attitude creates a staff that is largely cynical about the possibility of changing agency dynamics.

The clinical department is composed of trained therapists, mostly social workers. Clinical department staff members display a lack of energy. Therapists rarely join with one another, spending much of their time in their offices with clients. The department head tends to ramble on, skipping from one tangent to another, and only occasionally helping to connect department members to one another. Due to high amounts of paperwork, the clinical staff constantly feels unable to get on top of their work. This fosters anxiety, depression, and anger; and it prevents them from focusing on and completing specific tasks.

These three cultures create inconsistency in their collective treatment of clients. In the case of a child acting disruptively in class, a teacher might put him in "isolation" once he was back in the residence, but the residential staff might ignore this decision because they distrust the teacher's motives and rationale. Or the residential staff might ask for support from teachers or clinicians in helping with the transition into the classroom and be rebuffed by teachers who say they need to finish preparing for class.

The absence of an integrated therapeutic model leaves a void in the agency that is filled by a continual power struggle between departments. The department heads fight over scheduling; staffing patterns; movements of clients into, through, and out of the agency; or just for the sake of fighting. They fight publicly with their respective staff standing by and urging them to fight louder. They fight in an attempt to have one program head become the single champion whose focus (academic, therapeutic, or social skills) can cancel out the others and relieve them of the necessity of integration.

Discussion Questions

1. What should the executive director do to address the conflicts within the administrative team?

2. What should be done about the conflicts and other problems among the three departments?

3. What theories of organization design (structure, decision making, and communication processes) could inform the analysis of this case? Is a redesign appropriate? If so, what should a new design look like?

4. What principles of organizational change leadership could be used to address these problems?

Suggested Debriefing Framework: 2.2 Managerial Problem Solving

❖ CHAPTER EXERCISES

Understanding the external environment of an agency is critical to effective management, along with the need to periodically restructure services to address changing client demographics and funding streams. In the area of governance, it is critical to be able to assess the political dynamics of group decision making. In addition, it is equally important to begin to understand an agency's formal structure by analyzing the organizational chart, especially the scope of its programs and its authority structure. The following exercises are designed to enhance one's skills in assessing the dynamics of governing boards and the role they play in an agency's external and internal environment.

Exercise #1: Observing and Reporting on the Regular Meeting of an Elected Board of Public Officials (City Council, County Board of Supervisors, School Board, etc.)

This activity involves collecting information prior to classroom discussion and could build upon several of the themes found in the governance and external environment cases. The following are some guidelines to enhance the discussion process.

Guidelines for Documenting Observations About a Public Community Board Meeting (School Board, County Board of Supervisors, City Council, etc.)

Using the following guideline, describe a meeting and the role of the person providing staff support (school superintendent, county manager, or city manager). Since a meeting is a mini-version of a group process with a beginning, middle, and end, give particular attention to: (1) the committee/meeting process, (2) roles played, (3) meeting/committee context (including the community and organizational influences), and (4) group efficiency and effectiveness. Documents such as agendas, handouts, and minutes of previous meetings may be used to augment the analysis. The description of the meeting could include the following items:

I. Meeting setting (name of group, stated purpose of meeting [agenda], date and time of meeting, names and formal roles of persons present and absent [where possible], name of person who called the meeting and method of notification, opening and closing hour of the meeting)

II. Student goals and perceptions (why was this meeting selected, expectations regarding outcome, name of staff person or lay leader consulted before or after the meeting to understand the nature of the meeting).

III. Events
   A. Pre-meeting period: Describe anything pertinent that occurred prior to the beginning of the meeting from the entry of the first person until the formal opening of the meeting. Note the pattern of arrival and group activity during this period.
   B. Meeting period: Describe the role of the chairperson; summarize the substance of the discussion (who said what to whom), the role of the staff, the action taken at the meeting (if any) and future plans noted explicitly at the meeting. Note whether there were any relevant presentations by outside or guest speakers.
   C. Post-Meeting Period: Describe anything pertinent that occurred immediately following the formal closing of the meeting. Comment on the pattern of departure.

IV. Sharpening observation skills with questions to help describe the meeting.
   A. Process Questions
      1. How was leadership displayed in the group?
      2. What was the group's capacity for solving the problems?
      3. What was the scope and intensity of participation?
      4. Were there examples of conflict or hostility?

   B. Task Questions
      1. What decisions were made and how did they evolve?
      2. To what extent did the group digress from the agenda?
      3. How was the carryover from the previous meeting sustained?
      4. What next steps (responsibilities) for action were identified?
      5. What was the extent of spontaneous involvement?

   C. Context Questions
      1. What possible community factors could be impacting this group?
      2. What possible organizational/agency factors could be impacting this group?

Exercise #2: Comparative Analysis of Organization Charts

This classroom exercise is based on the availability of organization charts that students might acquire as part of their field placement or workplace. The exercise is based on small groups of students describing their respective organization charts and developing a comparative view of their similarities and differences. This shared analysis builds upon the cases related to understanding and modifying the structures of human service organizations.

**Exercise #3: Building a Grid for a
Board of Directors Nominating Committee**

This classroom exercise involves students in developing a grid for assessing the appropriateness of a board of directors for an agency of their choosing. While the grid could be constructed in different ways, one approach is to identify a list of demographic characteristics for one axis (age, gender, race/ethnicity, wealth, etc.) and to relate the other axis to expertise/experience (occupation, business sector, nonprofit sector, religious sector, geographic region, etc.). Once the grid is built, students could consult with their fieldwork supervisor to learn how many of the boxes can be checked based on the composition of the existing agency board. Then they could share the results with the group that helped to develop the grid. This experiential exercise parallels the work of thoughtful agency nominating committees seeking to nominate new board members in relationship to those already serving, as well as representatives who might relate to new and emerging issues facing the agency.

4

Leadership and Ethics

❖ LEADERSHIP

CASE 4.1   Empowering Staff: Real or Imaginary?

A youth organization in Big City was getting ready to hold a "Youth of Color Organizing Summit." The Youth Leadership Group had decided to hold the summit at a school in Harley, since they had done outreach at the school and the adjacent housing project in the past and thought this would be a better location to recruit youth of color than the upscale neighborhood where their agency was located. The staff facilitators of the leadership group, Program Director Carmen and Jen, a line worker, strongly endorsed the youth group's decision. However, it turned out that the executive director, Lisa, strongly felt that Harley would not be a safe location for the Summit and that the Youth Leadership Group had not adequately partnered with youth groups in Harley to justify holding the event there.

During one of the Youth Leadership Group meetings, Lisa announced her concerns about safety and the lack of partnering with local community organizations. In an emotional exchange, several of the young people disagreed with Lisa, stating that they had long been collaborating with the high school and had personally been invited by the principal and student groups to hold the summit there. Others explained that it was a relatively safe area of Harley and that it was an ideal place to recruit low-income youth of color. Jen urged Lisa to accept the youths' decision, which they had developed through a long and arduous consensus-building process. Lisa insisted that the location was dangerous and that the organization could not afford to hire security guards. She added, "This will never fly with the board." Finally, Lisa agreed that she would approve the location, but only if they got more local youth organizations to endorse the event and did extensive research on the crime rate and safety issues in the area.

When Carmen and Jen later discussed the issue in private, Jen complained that Lisa did not seem to respect the views of the clients and staff and that she might be using the board as an excuse for boycotting the location. She urged Carmen to use her position as program director and her close relationship with Lisa to arrange another meeting with Lisa and the youth group, and possibly also with the board, to discuss a solution. Carmen was afraid to raise the issue again with Lisa and thought Lisa would never let them talk directly to the board anyway. However, she was confident that if they adequately addressed the safety issue and partnered with local youth groups, Lisa would definitely approve the location.

Over the next few days, several members of the leadership group dropped by and volunteered to get endorsements from local youth groups and research the safety issue. Soon the group had a long list of endorsements from a variety of local youth groups, including religious, cultural and activist groups, project residents, the Harley Youth Council and even a local politician. They documented that the crime rate in the area was lower than in most other low-income neighborhoods in Big City, and that the annual block party in the housing project had been taking place peacefully for decades. They even recruited several security guards from the school and the projects to volunteer for the event, along with two police officers from a community policing agency.

Confident that Lisa would now approve their plans, Jen and several youth group members approached Lisa with their findings. To their great surprise, Lisa still refused to approve the location, stating that the work they had done was still inadequate and she was still concerned about the response from the board. The young people were upset that Lisa had made them do all this research and outreach work, yet she still rejected their plan all the same. Some of them openly vented their anger. One youth even asked Lisa: "What do a bunch of rich, fat, white board people know about Harley and about what we're trying to do with this event?" Lisa said that she was sorry for any hurt feelings she might have caused, but that she would never let them hold the event in Harley and that she had actually already decided on another location. At the next leadership group meeting, Carmen, Jen and the group came to a consensus that they had exhausted their options and that they would just have to go along with Lisa's plans. Soon after that meeting Lisa announced that the summit would be held in the upscale business district of Big City.

Long after the event, the relationship between the youth group and Lisa continued to be tense. Carmen and Jen continued to be upset with Lisa, and Lisa continued to be upset with them. Lisa never let Carmen or Jen facilitate any of the youth groups again.

Discussion Questions

1. What would be effective leadership behaviors in this situation and what leadership theory could be used to explain those behaviors?

2. Should Carmen and Jen just put up with the continuing tensions with Lisa or should they do something? If so, what could they do, considering that they are subordinate to Lisa?

Suggested Debriefing Framework: 2.3 Analytical and Interactional Aspects

Case 4.2   Caught in the Middle: Mediating Differences in Gender and Work Style

Health Outreach Alliance is a nonprofit organization that works to increase access to health care for low-income families and individuals by building community coalitions and conducting community outreach efforts. HOA was established in 1992 by four founders. With their professional expertise, ties with the community and a large grant from the Wellness Foundation, these founders built HOA into a reputable and effective health advocacy organization. All founders except one have since left the agency and are no longer involved in any capacity. The fourth founder serves as executive director and is still closely tied to the agency and its mission.

The agency has a central office in Big City and a field office at the other end of the state. The executive director, program director (second in command), and three program teams (each comprised of four staff members) work from the central office in Big City. The focus of the central office is program development, coalition coordination, and state policy advocacy. The field office employs two staff members. It focuses on field advocacy and community organizing around the efforts of the central office. The executive director, program director, and field advocates are men, while the remainder of the staff are women, a majority of whom are young (late twenties to early thirties).

Over the past few years, HOA has experienced high staff turnover. Internal conflicts have increased, and program team leaders are expressing increased job dissatisfaction. The conflict lies primarily between the team leaders and the ED. The program director has managed to maintain a highly communicative relationship with both the ED and the team leaders and often serves as the mediator to the best of his abilities.

The team leaders feel that the ED repeatedly oversteps his boundaries. They sense that he does not trust their abilities to do their jobs successfully. The ED has interrupted meetings being facilitated by the team leaders and has criticized their work in inappropriate settings. According to the team leaders, the ED often overrides decisions and "steps on their toes." The team leaders would like to have more ownership of their projects and receive more encouragement from the ED.

The team leaders are convinced that this is largely a gender-related issue—that the ED doubts their capabilities and performance because they are young women. Although the field advocates in the field office are of similar age and experience level as the team leaders, the team leaders believe the ED is more supportive of the field advocates' ideas and efforts because they are men.

Not surprisingly, the ED, committed to HOA, wants to be involved in all aspects of its decisions and developments. HOA is his baby, and he is personally and emotionally vested in its success and reputation. Experiencing founder's syndrome, the ED is resistant to the changes occurring within the structure and to the focus of HOA. The ED also feels that his expertise and experience in the field, and his relationships with the community and agency affiliates, are an asset to HOA and should be used rather than overlooked. In response to the team leaders' claim that the conflict is a gender issue, the ED asserts that he is just as involved with the projects of the field advocates.

The program director is very aware of the conflict between the ED and the team leaders and approaches staff meetings and discussions with extreme discretion. Although he greatly values the experienced input and guidance of the ED, he recognizes that he is often overbearing and too critical of the team leaders. At the same time, however, the program director feels that the team leaders have become too sensitive and take constructive criticism too personally. Regardless of whom he finds responsible for the conflict, he is aware that the communication problems need to be addressed and the organizational structure needs to be modified.

Within the last three years, the three highly qualified women team leaders have left HOA. Each of the three leaders claimed that lack of autonomy and confidence from the ED was largely to blame for leaving the organization. The ED acknowledged that his involvement influenced their decisions to leave, yet he refuses to accept significant responsibility and admit that there is a deep-rooted problem that needs to be addressed.

The program director feels it is a lose-lose situation and that the ED and team leaders will never see eye-to-eye. The program director has attempted to ease the conflict by opening up lines of communication. Bimonthly meetings involving the ED, the program director, and the team leaders were arranged to allow time and space for dialogue. However, both the ED and team leaders are stubborn, unwilling to see the other's point of view. After the fourth meeting, the program director realized that the meetings were only creating more tension and awkwardness. Meetings have therefore been discontinued, and any efforts at conflict resolution have come to a stand still.

Discussion Questions

1. Are there further actions that the program director could take that might improve the situation?

2. How could the executive director change his style, while still ensuring that his expertise, experience, and relationships with outside groups are effectively used?

Suggested Debriefing Framework: 2.2 Managerial Problem Solving

CASE 4.3 To Talk or Not To Talk

In the early years, the Open Door Family Shelter was a modest operation in the basement of the United Church. Sybil, the current executive director, was working as a secretary for the pastor and kept leaving the basement doors accidentally unlocked. The homeless began coming in, and the church was persuaded to raise funds to open a permanent shelter. Despite its humble beginnings, the Open Door is a thriving nonprofit shelter with three locations in the city.

Even though she knows there are problems in other parts of the agency, Jenny Gunn enjoys her job as site manager for Queens Street. She is confident that Queens provides superior service—staff turnover is low, permanent housing placements are improving, and staff morale is high.

Naturally, work is far from perfect. In particular, Sybil has no experience in direct service and her on-the-job management "training" is a challenge to endure. However, over time, Jenny has developed a good working relationship with Sybil and has stopped counting the weeks until Sybil's retirement. While Jenny has considered leaving the shelter, members of the board of directors actively encourage her to stay, and she intends to stay as long as the personal and professional relationships are rewarding.

The Turning Point

One afternoon while Jenny is finalizing a report, Kelly, the most senior staff member, knocks on Jenny's door. She and Kelly have been with the shelter from the nascent stages; Jenny decided to pursue a management position, while Kelly remained in direct services. Jenny welcomes the opportunity to chat with Kelly and invites her into her office.

Kelly looks nervous and says that she wants to talk as both a friend and co-worker. She tells Jenny that there is growing dissatisfaction with the management at Open Door. For example, at the Woverleigh shelter, the program manager is verbally abusive to residents. At the Green shelter, the supervisor will not schedule African American women on day shifts. At Queens, the ever-changing shift supervisors create a strain on the staff. Furthermore, there are problems with scheduling, staff development, and respect for the residents. The workers from the shelters have tried to convey these systemic problems to Sybil, but nothing has changed. Kelly informs Jenny that at tomorrow's all-staff meeting, the workers want to discuss these concerns. Kelly asks Jenny to help facilitate the conversation and convey the depth of these problems to the executive director. Jenny thanks Kelly for her honesty and assures her that she will do everything she can.

At the all-staff meeting, tensions are running high. Sybil wants to move through her agenda, but Sarah from Woverleigh and Anita from Green are polite but firm about discussing their concerns. Sybil asks Sarah and Anita to schedule a private meeting to continue the discussion, but Sarah and Anita assert that this response is inadequate. Jenny intervenes to say that the issues appear urgent and that Sybil should strongly consider adding this discussion to the agenda. Sybil is visibly angry with Jenny, and she remains steadfast that the topics will be discussed at the next all-staff meeting. About half the attendees walk out of the meeting, and the rest of the staff appear distracted for the duration. At the conclusion, Jenny approaches Sybil to discuss the confrontation, but Sybil is curt and says that she has another meeting to attend. She adds that the site managers can debrief tomorrow at the already-arranged management meeting.

The next day Jenny notices that Kelly and the rest of the Queens Street staff are acting oddly. She asks Kelly if there is anything she can do, and Kelly says that the two of them need to find a time to talk later. After her shift, Kelly does not drop by Jenny's office. Instead, she calls her from home. She informs Jenny that yesterday's meeting was Sybil's last chance to address the problems. The staff is tired of the disrespect and have decided that the only way to make Sybil listen and create long-term change is to unionize. Kelly says she values Jenny's friendship and asks her to keep the conversation in confidence. Jenny tells her that she will consider her request. Kelly replies that she hopes Jenny will do what is right and abruptly hangs up.

Jenny half-heartedly continues working for the next two hours until the site-manager meeting. At this meeting, Sybil and the other two site managers will finalize a presentation for the board of directors meeting that evening and debrief on the all-staff meeting.

Discussion Questions

1. How would you describe Sybil's leadership style? In what ways is her style a good fit or a bad fit with staff in this work setting? Use relevant theories in your analysis.

2. Is there any way that Jenny can convince Sybil that she should change her leadership style? What recommendations should Jenny make?

3. How could Jenny raise this issue with Sybil without creating more defensiveness and resistance?

Suggested Debriefing Framework: 2.3 Analytical and Interactional Aspects

Case 4.4 Agency Director Uses a Personal Coach to Address His Leadership Style

By the summer of 1997, one year into implementing our strategic plan, I realized that an additional element should be added to the effort to change the agency. With the support of my officers, I began using a personal coach who helped me see how my leadership style affected various stakeholders and how I might change my behaviors to model the new directions laid out in our plan. After 20 years in the role of executive director in several different cities, it was not easy to begin a process of self-assessment with the prospect of changing my established behavior pattern. In order to make sure that I was not an obstacle to the major stake-holders engaging fully in the change process, I needed to determine how the lay and professional members of the agency perceived my support, the extent to which I demonstrated my ongoing appreciation for their efforts, and the extent to which I was modeling unhelpful behaviors.

Once the coach was retained, she suggested using some candid, confidential interviews with three stake-holder groups (the board, staff, and members/clients) in order to develop some baseline data. The coach and I developed a series of open-ended questions for an interview of no more than an hour, as well as a list of possible respondents, including those who I knew were critical of my work. Sample questions included: (1) What in this agency do you think needs improving?, (2) How would you describe the executive director's work style, including listening skills?, (3) What barriers do you see in working with the executive director?, and (4) What suggestions do you have to help the executive director improve his effectiveness?

The results distilled by the coach were organized into three areas needing attention: (1) Personal style (stakeholders not always certain that their views were heard; observed occasional displays of impatience and anger by the executive director), (2) Accessibility/visibility (need for executive director to do more management by walking around [MBWA] among staff to demonstrate a more visible and caring style; similarly, more visibility among member/client populations), and (3) Management teamwork (more attention to strengthening the management team, including more connection between the strategic plan's goals and objectives and the traditional work of the departments). In each of these domains, the coach helped me focus on simple changes in behavior that she could help reinforce. In addition, key staff and board officers were given permission to monitor my efforts to change some of my behaviors and to let me know if old habits resurfaced. A diagnostic update on how I am doing with my learning agenda is included in my annual performance review with the officers. While much has improved over the past year, it's definitely hard work to change ingrained and comfortable habits.

While this coaching experience was extremely helpful to me, it became clear that I also needed to address the larger job of changing the organization's culture. To that end, I reached out to yet another coach.

Discussion Questions

1. With the limited amount of information presented, what might be some specific activities that could address the three main issues of personal style, accessibility/visibility, and managerial teamwork?

2. Is hiring another coach the best way to address the task of changing the organization's culture? What other strategies may be appropriate? Should the board encourage the executive director to resign?

Suggested Debriefing Framework: 2.2 Managerial Problem Solving

CASE 4.5   Founder's Syndrome

In 1994, two young medical school students began to cultivate the idea for Youth Aware after volunteering in the juvenile halls of West Coast City. Kiran and Jen redirected their energy while in medical school, postponed their research indefinitely, and served West Coast City youth in detention. In 1998, Youth Aware became an official 501(c) 3 not-for-profit organization. Kiran and Jen both completed their M.D. degrees that year but also were awarded seed funding to follow their passion of serving adjudicated and incarcerated youth. While Jen maintained a role in the organization, Kiran took the reins. She rallied together a board that would support her. For the next few years, Kiran drove the organization. She did over 90% of all the fundraising. Her story was easily sold to foundations; namely, a physician who could easily earn a six-figure salary had found greater value in serving youth who had been caught up in the juvenile justice system. The organization received attention in a number of publications. *UTNE Reader*, a progressive magazine with international readership, featured Kiran and the organization. To this day, one can still find articles about Kiran and the organization she founded.

The organization grew to seven staff members who operated three core programs: (1) volunteer counseling inside a detention facility, (2) an internship stipend program for transitioning back into the community, and (3) a health outreach program to educate youth. The staff included:

- Kiran. As the founder and executive director, Kiran provided a clear line of authority, consistency, and predictability that comforted the staff. However, she also created a situation in which staff were dependent on her vision and direction and took very few risks.

- Michelle. An intelligent young woman with promise, she was brought on board as office manager.
- Chantal. Hired as a development director, she did not have much experience but was thought to have much potential.
- Gaylon. Gaylon ran the program for interns who helped out around the office and counseled them with problems related to their probation officers, their girlfriends, or their parents.
- Hasan. He ran the program at the juvenile detention facility, Log Cabin Ranch, that focused on stress reduction and increasing inner awareness. Hasan worked about 10 hours a week. He was never in the office, but he contributed insightful comments in staff meetings.
- Byron. Byron ran a health outreach program that educated youth on health issues, especially those that affected communities of color. He also encouraged youth to get screened for specific health problems.

The board of directors was also largely dependent upon Kiran's leadership. This very caring group of nine individuals who felt strongly about the need to serve disenfranchised population included:

- Bob. This soon-to-be-outgoing board chair had retired from a career as a real estate attorney. He devoted his Saturdays to working with youth at the detention facility.
- Jeff. One of the younger members of the board, Jeff was interested in moving into the position of board chair. He was a senior manager at a software company, and he, too, volunteered time at the detention facility.
- John. A banker, John tended to stay on the sidelines of any decisions or discussions but did attend most meetings.
- Cynthia. A certified public account, Cynthia was a relatively new addition to the board. She was quickly moved into the role of treasurer.
- Audrey. A public defender active in the community, Audrey was known for being a strong advocate of juvenile rights.
- Kitty. Kitty was the most connected to potential individual donors and small family foundations.
- Jasmine. An ordained Zen minister, a published author, and an activist who had somewhat of a master status among meditation practitioners, particularly those of color, Jasmine led meditation talks throughout the country. She was added to the board to

guide and add expertise to the organization's focus on inner awareness, especially in the detention facility.

- George. The only board member who was actively involved in social services, George had directed an organization serving similar clientele in another city. However, he has been unavailable to attend or participate in board meetings.

This group was guided by Kiran's charisma. In many ways the board was accountable to Kiran, rather than the other way around.

The Transition

As time went on, Kiran refocused her energy, and it drifted away from Youth Aware. She redirected her energy to focus on her two new daughters, the book she was writing, and teaching. She searched for the right person to fill her shoes, but the perfect person never materialized. The funding was getting thin. A last-ditch effort resulted in a replacement for Kiran in December 2005, but when Jasmine looked into Youth Aware's financial status, it seemed that there was no money to pay the potential successor for more than the first month. The new hire was aborted.

The organization stumbled along, and in April 2006, with the organization on the brink of collapse, Jasmine stepped in as leader. This new leader was also charismatic, possibly more so than Kiran. She was young and intelligent. Most of all, she was powerful. Her power came not only from her intelligence, but also from how she carried herself. She had an acute awareness of her own strengths and paid little attention to the things that did not interest her. Even though Jasmine refused the title of executive director and opted for the title of president and director, she placed herself at the decision-making apex of the organization and was forced to fill the gaps created by the absence of an executive director. She did not have time for the director role and was not particularly interested in it. This was because she ran an additional organization in another city that focused on inner awareness and taking action on insights gained from inner-awareness practices. With a perpetually full plate involving both organizations, she devoted one day a week to her personal meditation, leaving fewer than eight hours per week for Youth Aware.

Between April and August 2006, three staff members departed (Michelle, the office manager, went on to graduate school; Chantal, the development director, moved to the east coast; and Byron, the health outreach program coordinator, was fired). With a near 50% staff turnover, Jasmine decided to hire Judy, a volunteer at the detention facility. Judy was a familiar face to many of the youth and was hired to develop and coordinate a volunteer program and maintain some continuity for the youth amidst the staff turnover.

Jasmine convinced the board—now including founder and former executive director Kiran—to hire an organization and strategic change consultant. She assured the board that she would raise the additional funds for the consultant's fees. Jasmine recommended Dee Taylor. Dee was a personal friend and inhabitant of Jasmine's residential community, sharing a large home with others. She was retained for a three-stage plan that totaled $47,000 over nine months. Since the board fully trusted Jasmine, no steps were taken by board members to check any of Dee's references.

Since Jasmine was not stepping in as an active executive director, Youth Aware sought to fill the void created by the departures of Michelle, Chantal, and Kiran by posting an ad on CraigsList, Idealist, and other job posting sites for an operations manager. The posting made it clear that the organization was in a period of transition and offered a flexible work schedule and the opportunity to work with one of the "foremost thinkers on social change" and an "effective strategic change consultant." The full-time job description included the following responsibilities and time expectations: financial/legal management and reporting (5 hours per week), fundraising development and coordination (14 hours per week), relationship and communications management (7 hours per week), human resources management and supervision (2 hours per week), office and operations management (4 hours per week), volunteer and stakeholder relationship oversight (2 hours per week), and ongoing contact with co-workers (6 hours per week). The organization was flooded with resumes, but many applicants were not qualified. After narrowing the top 12 down to a few finalists, Jasmine and Dee concluded that if the person selected in September worked out, they would want that person to become the executive director at the end of the year.

Lawrence was hired quickly, less than three weeks after he submitted his application. He was a recent MSW graduate of a management and planning program and had experience developing and running programs that served a similar population. The staff seemed to like his optimism, his willingness to take charge, and his interest in creating a team environment. The staff members were ready to work with someone who would take charge because Kiran had been largely absent for the last six months, and Jasmine was unavailable to them.

Multiple Issues

As a board member, Jasmine, like other Youth Aware board members, did not have a clear understanding of the organization's operations.

With Kiran no longer manning the ship, Jasmine began to ask questions and educate herself about the youth being served. One of Jasmine's first surprises was that the closure of the Health Outreach meant that only 13 youth were being served by the entire agency.

Financial Condition

As the new Operations Manager, Lawrence was now in the office daily, and some of the organization's primary issues began to reveal themselves. With no one at the helm of Youth Aware, no one was really paying much attention to the finances. Despite a limited paper trail, no transactions had been properly recorded since May. After a search for all the financial information, it became clear that the primary issue was to determine the financial status of the organization because no one on the staff or board knew anything about Youth Aware's finances. Lawrence realized that the organization's bank accounts were either in the red or dreadfully close to it. After he alerted Jasmine, she was able, within 24 hours, to secure a $35,000 no-interest loan. The loan check was deposited immediately, but due to its size, a hold was placed on the funds. The organization was in the red, and checks began to bounce, generating fee notices for insufficient funds exceeding $1,000 for the overdrawn account.

Lawrence realized that the organization spent about $30,000 a month and only served approximately 10 youth at any given time ($20,000/month for salaries and benefits, approximately $5,000/month for the consultant, $2,000/month for intern stipends, and $2,800/month for office rent). Then when he looked at the revenue side of the organization, he found extensive use of restricted funds for other purposes. For example, in 2006, the organization had received approximately $150,000 from five foundations to run the health-outreach program that had been defunct since January 2006, when Byron left the organization.

The lack of record keeping or dates on any documents made it unclear as to which foundations had provided the funding. Many of the interim reports to the foundations were due on September 20th (Lawrence's first day), yet the program was not operational and had not been for any part of the year for which these funds were designated. The biggest problem was that these restricted funds had been spent. Jasmine's goal was to develop a program that would meet the objectives proposed but to do so without spending any money. The annual budget for the upcoming 2007 fiscal year was approximately $350,000, but the organization had only raised $140,000 ($50,000 from individual donors and another $90,000 from two additional foundations, one related to Kitty's contacts).

The grant proposals that brought in the funds for the health outreach program on file were not well written (unclear outcomes) and this was generally true of all the proposals requesting program funding. It was clear that the money flowed in because of Kiran's charisma and the relationships she had established, rather than as a result of the integrity of the proposals submitted. Kiran had sought out money from foundations where she had developed relationships, mostly in the medical arena. This appeared to pull the organization in different directions; the mission statement varied depending on the foundation's guidelines, but Kiran was able to hold the course and direct the organization's programs and its staff. The proposals offered little in the way of program description other than the one-page flyer used to recruit interns to work for a $10-plus-per-hour stipend.

Lack of Leadership

Youth Aware's financial predicament reflected its lack of active leadership and board accountability. The staff needed active and steady leadership. While a charismatic leader had created the organization and rallied the board and staff around her, both board and the staff were placed in supporting roles. They were followers, rather than decision makers, leaders, or partners in the organization's mission. This dynamic disempowered the staff as they became accustomed to supporting the leader. It would take time to change the organization's culture.

Neither leadership nor oversight was forthcoming from the board of directors. Their involvement in Youth Aware had been minimal. Both Kiran and Jasmine had adopted the philosophy that the board should not be informed of problems unless there was a specific plan to fix them. Board member advice was rarely sought and the board had become accustomed to confirming and not determining future directions. The level of board meeting attendance had been very low. Only two board members (Bob—the current chair—and Kitty) appeared at the first board meeting after the new operations manager (Lawrence) was hired; (board members Jeff and John called in with regrets). As they waited for Jasmine and a quorum to arrive, Dee arrived and took the opportunity (created by Jasmine's absence) to initiate a frank discussion of the financial crisis. Lawrence outlined the situation and noted that there was no money to make payroll the next day unless something miraculous happened. While the board members were impressed by the arrival of the $35,000 no-interest loan, they had not known that it was even needed and were under the impression that the organization was financially stable. Even though Dee wanted to discuss the feasibility of shutting down the organization, the board members made it clear that they were invested in the organization's continuation. Based on the chair's suggestion, each Board member present agreed to wire $1,000 to the organization's checking account the next day. This discussion was particularly difficult for one board member who had recently secured a $50,000 foundation grant for the organization, and she wondered how it had disappeared.

An emergency board meeting was set for the following week. All but one of the board members showed up. While a set of difficult questions for Jasmine to address was placed on the agenda, Jasmine quickly took the floor and spoke for 25 minutes on an array of topics that all hinted at solutions to the financial situation. She did not address the sources of the problems, the reasons for not involving the board, or a plan to get the organization out of the crisis. And yet all the board members, except one, seemed to be satisfied that she had a plan that did not require board involvement. However, Kiran (the founder/former executive director/current board member) continued to ask pointed and probing questions that Jasmine labeled as an attack. The other board members decide that Jasmine and Kiran should sort out their differences elsewhere. Further discussion was tabled for the next meeting.

Lawrence was confused by the continuing efforts to keep the board of directors in the dark. He was warned by Jasmine to be aware that an open discussion of the sensitive financial issues with the board could result in Kiran, the founder, becoming defensive as a result of being perceived as the one who had created the financial crisis.

Leadership Styles

Jasmine, the decision maker, was generally not very accessible. This lack of access made this small organization seem like a giant bureaucracy. Lawrence, along with everyone in the office, was at the bottom of the hierarchy. Jasmine made it clear that she had a plan for Youth Aware—but that plan was obscure. Jasmine would frequently state that she would follow through on things; for example, returning the call of a foundation staff member, completing some aspect of a financial document, or reviewing a proposal. However, due to her other commitments and priorities, she rarely completed the tasks and left others in the dark to determine whether a task had been completed.

The conflicting styles of leadership between Jasmine and Lawrence also prevented momentum from developing. Lawrence wanted to move the organization toward becoming a learning organization with a collaborative, team approach. The culture that had been established by Kiran and reinforced by Jasmine related to non-participatory management for both the staff and the board surfaced in both staff and board meetings. The board and staff meetings highlighted this issue. The way the staff meetings were structured did not allow room for the staff to *participate*. The meetings were focused on passing information with little room for questions and even less for contributing to the discussion. Each topic on the agenda was listed as an update (development update, strategic update, operations update, and program update). Questions could only be asked after all the updates had been completed. There was rarely time. Lawrence was told that he could not extend the staff meeting, and Dee resisted changing the format.

At one of the staff meetings, where neither Dee nor Jasmine was present, Lawrence decided to open up the format a little. Gaylon, who ran the internship program, noted that a culture of hesitancy had taken over the organization—staff waited for direction and was hesitant to proceed without direction. Lawrence, like other staff members, felt as though he were cut off at the knees, unable to address the future directions defined by Jasmine. He felt like an outsider. He saw no opportunity for his input to be used and felt like he shouldered all the responsibility of an executive director but none of the authority to make necessary changes. He decided that if Jasmine was not going to provide staff members with direction in face-to-face meetings, he would do his best to motivate them by developing a plan for specifying program objectives in order to begin developing measurable outcomes. He created a more realistic job description for himself and strongly advocated for Jasmine to define her role. He also encouraged staff members to update their own job descriptions. Lawrence began to contact foundations and to smooth the ripples created by a lack of communication.

Throughout his first three months on the job, Lawrence was working on a report to the board based on his experience and observations. He had decided that the situation was intolerable and that he would need to resign. However, he worked hard to craft the report in a positive way to help move the organization forward, rather than simply providing a litany of the organizations problems. The 12-page report included recommendations for the person who would replace him, focusing on the following areas: (1) defining a strategic direction for the organization, (2) fostering participatory decision making at the staff and board levels, (3) upgrading human resource policies and procedures, (4) upgrading program policies and procedures, and (5) upgrading financial policies and procedures. It was clear that the organizational culture that had been established would be difficult to change and that change would take time.

Epilogue

Three days after Lawrence resigned, those who remained on the board engaged in an executive session without Jasmine to provide a venue for an honest discussion about the current and future state of the organization. Lawrence was invited but declined. Dee attended and then resigned (due, in part, to the unresolved tension between her and Jasmine). The chair of the board called Lawrence the next day and told him that the board would find a way to oust Jasmine, close the organization, and then regroup. This decision surprised Lawrence, as it was not a direction that he had expected the board to pursue.

Discussion Questions

1. What issues should be addressed in mapping the organization's strategic directions for the future?

2. How could Lawrence, operations manager, have fostered more participatory management?

3. What should appear in an upgraded human-resource manual?

4. What specific program policies and procedures would you recommend?

5. What financial policies and procedures would you put in place and why?

Suggested Debriefing Framework: 2.5 Strategic Issues Management

CASE 4.6   Executive Leadership

Miranda County Human Services (MCHS) provides job training and employment skills for low-income persons, housing for needy families, job training, mental health case management, and a receiving home for children. The founder and CEO, Jim Offcliff, began the organization seven years ago, and it has been through his entrepreneurial enthusiasm and tremendous dedication that it has grown to a staff of over 100 and an annual budget of $3 million. MCHS has expanded from the local area to four counties in the region. There are currently a number of tensions facing Jim and his executive team. His team members include:

*   Stan Davis, manager of the housing program
*   Tom Rempp, director of the receiving home for children

- Leona Estrella, manager of the mental health case management program
- Karen Sowinski, the new director of finance and human resources

Jim, as a dynamic, hands-on manager, has clear ideas about how the agency should be operating and what it should be doing. At this time, he is resistant to one manager's ideas for shifting direction in a training program, and he has suggested to another manager that their receiving home should be eliminated and replaced by a treatment facility. He does not hesitate to comment on the below-standard performance of individual program staff members; but at the same time, his administrative director is concerned that Jim, in his entrepreneurial zeal, is neglecting important administrative systems, from finances to governance.

The Training Focus in Public Housing

Stan Davis is responsible for education and training programs for residents of a Public Housing Authority (PHA) that serves a population of 4,000. In the past, the federal agency funded general education programs for residents, but this past year they have pressured MCHS to focus on employment and training. This suited the PHA administration because they benefit from having residents concentrate on building trades related to maintaining properties.

To date, top management has insisted that residents only participate in this training category. Recently the city ran a Poverty Summit that revealed likely job growth for low-income employees in the next few years. Occupations included, for example, positions in hospitality (restaurants and hotels), health services (nursing/health aides), and light-manufacturing assembly. Stan Davis told the management team about the potential of these jobs and emphasized that they ought to consider providing training in these areas for 80% of participants. He said, "We should be providing training for where the jobs are." Stan found, however, that Jim was not only lethargic in responding to this suggestion, but after Stan persisted, he became downright hostile. Jim countered that they should focus on the agency's needs. In response to Stan's request to talk to people from Housing and Urban Development about expanding the participation in training categories, Jim said, "You can't talk with them."

Stan is faced with a dilemma. He's been with the agency for 10 years and likes his work. But now he feels tremendously frustrated. He sees great potential to help residents obtain jobs, but he believes that Jim's perceptions about addressing needs of the PHA are first and foremost.

Substituting a Receiving Home With a Treatment Center

Another member of the executive team, Tom Rempp, director of the receiving home, believes he gets along well with Jim because their strengths are complementary. Tom's style is to encourage staff participation; he sees the CEO as having a more directive, decisive, and strong-willed style. As Tom has put it, "When he gets an idea, there is no deterring him."

Yesterday, Jim met Tom in the hall and said that he'd had a brilliant idea the night before "that will put us on the map." He said, "You know how we've been running this receiving home for emergency placements for older children and also as a temporary placement for children who are difficult to place? I think we should close the receiving home and replace it with a treatment center for children with moderate emotional and behavioral problems. In doing so, we could reduce out-of-county placements in treatment facilities and save the agency money."

When Tom said the idea sounded interesting, Jim pulled him into his office and said he didn't want him to discuss this with staff because they wouldn't understand. Jim thought the agency should bring in consultants to help plan the program and then send the child care workers for special training. Tom simply nodded in agreement.

But afterwards, Tom thought to himself that Jim had really gone overboard this time, believing that this decision could be catastrophic. Jim has not suggested any funding sources for this initiative but appears to be confident that funds could be found. The agency has $3 million in reserves, but this money is funded through county tax levies and is earmarked for future services. If the next levy doesn't pass, the agency will be in real trouble, unless these reserves continue to be available. They are not a Medicaid-approved facility, so all costs would be absorbed by the county and by the agency.

The CEO thinks that the cost of running the treatment facility would be similar to the costs of the receiving home. Tom is not so sure that this is a valid assumption. Knowing how determined Jim is when he gets an idea, Tom doesn't think he can raise doubts with Jim without jeopardizing his own position. Tom recognizes a need for this kind of facility but doesn't think they are the right organization to meet this need. He believes Jim is on an ego trip and wants to make his mark on the world by leaving a legacy in a new building. He thinks that maybe Jim's tenure as a successful director is blinding him to the pitfalls of pursuing an idea that could have repercussions for many years to come. Ultimately, he wonders if Jim's growing arrogance and hubris, as Tom sees it, could financially ruin the agency.

Micro-Management in Mental Health

In the mental health case management program, program manager Leona Estrella is experiencing some micro-management from Jim. Having just gotten an earful from one of her staff about him, she is trying to figure out how to balance his aggressive style with her staff's needs. Apparently, the CEO has become very critical of Nancy, one of the case managers. She was a day late in submitting two of her thirteen case reports, and her grammar was substandard in several of her case notes. She has taken two days more than her sick-day allotment, and returned 15 minutes late from lunch last Wednesday. The director, who is concerned that Nancy has spent significantly more time on some cases than others, told her that she must strive to work more efficiently. Jim sent Leona a memo detailing Nancy's faults and wrote in red pen above it, "You should have caught these problems before they made it to my desk. I'm too busy doing your work. Do better next time!"

Leona has worked with the director for five years, and knows that he is a perfectionist and becomes angry easily when people don't perform to his expectations. She knows Jim's heart is in the right place. He wants to do the best for the clients, and he has done much to obtain funding for the department, despite widespread cutbacks. Recently, Jim told Leona about his concerns that the county funding agency is considering ways to cut funding for this program or put it out for bid with hopes of getting a lower-cost contractor.

But as a manager, Leona is also aware that he goes way overboard in his "encouragement sessions" with staff. Maybe it's because of the pressure he is under that he seems to be belittling staff constantly. Leona cringes when Jim calls them "brain dead" and says they are wasting taxpayers' money. He has begun raising his voice and getting all worked up over slight errors in reports from caseworkers. His hands-on, micro-managing style is rubbing staff the wrong way. Leona sees the staff as professionals who are overloaded and generally doing excellent work with difficult clients.

Leona believes that case managers like Nancy have to prioritize their time and that sometimes they do have personal situations and family emergencies that put demands on them. Jim does not seem to recognize this. Nancy told Leona that she is fed up with Jim and doesn't need aggravation anymore. She's threatening to quit. The agency's annual turnover rate is about 25%, and it's costly for the agency to continually hire and train new people. Several other staff members are considering quitting because of the pressure they are feeling. Leona feels that she has to do something to help create a better work climate, but the director doesn't take kindly to criticism. It's his way or the highway.

Private Entrepreneurialism Versus a Not-for-Profit Agency

In yet another department, Karen Sowinski, the new director of finance and human resources, has other concerns about the CEO. As Karen has said, "We're supposed to be a nonprofit organization, but he runs it as if it is his own private business. Yes, we have a board of directors, but it consists mainly of his friends and people he's handpicked. The board meets quarterly and rubber stamps his requests. When he's gotten into cash flow difficulties, he's put up as much as $20,000 of his own money and has gone to the bank for temporary loans. So far, the organization has been able to juggle the finances as we've grown, but I'm told there have been some scary moments. He refers to the organization as 'our company.' His style is to dream up great ideas and then somehow expect staff to pick up the pieces because he lacks the patience to pay attention to administrative detail."

Karen does acknowledge that, on the positive side, his entrepreneurial style has produced remarkable results in that the agency has gotten contracts with over 400 employers to hire people from their program. They are being touted as an exemplary model for getting job placements. Jim drives the staff crazy with his continuous demands, but the staff members who've stayed with the organization are ones who share his dedication to placing people in new jobs.

One of Karen's responsibilities as director of finance is the preparation of grant proposals. In this role, she needs to communicate to potential funders that the board is providing proper oversight over the governing of the organization. Karen sees that foundations are concerned that the agency's board does not include anyone who has financial expertise and that the four board members meet only quarterly. When she mentioned to Jim that the agency needs to shift from a fast growing entrepreneurial business to one that has sound administrative procedures, he seemed mildly interested but retorted, "If it ain't broke, why fix it?" Karen is afraid that while they are riding high now, they are "headed for a big crash as we expand without having proper systems in place, including board engagement."

The CEO's Perspective

As the agency's founder, and someone who has led its growth to a current budget of over $3 million, Jim is frustrated that his managers are not more attentive to his ideas. He feels that with his track record, staff should respect his judgments. Jim knows that he has a brusque style; but he believes that, overall, his approach is effective because he is only concerned about the success of the agency and about the quality staff performance necessary for achieving that success. Given all the pressures he and the agency are facing, he is beginning to reflect on how he may need to adjust his approaches, both toward staff and toward the direction of the agency.

Discussion Questions

1. Regarding Jim's criticism of staff, what could Leona say in private to him about helping the situation with her staff? Is he justified in his criticism of staff performance? If so, how can his concerns best be handled?

2. How can these managers, individually or as a group, use candor and honesty in raising their concerns with Jim in a way that they could be adequately addressed?

3. What are the impacts of Jim's behavior on the entire organization? Are there themes present in each situation that should be addressed in a coordinated way? What would you suggest if the CEO is willing to consider changes?

4. Considering the big picture, what are the strategic issues facing the organization? What steps are needed to ensure the agency's future viability? What, specifically, should be done?

Suggested Debriefing Framework: 2.5 Strategic Issues Management

CASE 4.7   Marian Health Center

Marian Health Center is a skilled nursing facility with 70 beds and 40 staff, whose mission is to provide quality health care to senior citizens. It is part of a not-for-profit organization providing comprehensive services to seniors. It is currently in a three-year rapid-growth and program-development process. The agency incorporated 40 years ago and was for many years closely affiliated with a Protestant church. There has been less emphasis on this over the past 10 years; however, the agency employs a chaplain who is an evangelical Christian. One of the agency's programs has developed a significant deficit, and there is increasing pressure agency-wide for cost cutting. An agency-level Long Range Planning Committee of executive and program managers, board members, and corporate staff has been meeting to update objectives for the coming year. Health Center staff members do not pay much attention to program objectives.

Historically, most of the patients have been middle- or upper-class retirees, almost exclusively white, who have had very good insurance coverage and financial assets. Recently the center has had increasing numbers of Medicaid patients. Medicaid payment does not quite cover daily costs for patients. Serving Medicaid patients is becoming more complicated because Medicaid in the state is increasing its HMO enrollments.

The director of the center reports to the chief operating officer, who is highly experienced in skilled nursing facilities (SNFs) and is aggressive regarding growth for the agency. He often makes decisions without consulting health center staff and is not highly regarded by them. Recently he became enamored of a new nursing-service delivery system which, if implemented, would radically change the duties of nurses and certified nurse assistants. He expects it will also lead to significant cost savings. The director has been very effective at marketing and generating admissions. Daily census averages 95%.

The center enjoys an excellent reputation for offering high-quality services. Increasing competition, especially from for-profit organizations, is impacting marketing efforts. The state has begun to require use of a computerized case record management system, which the program is not yet using. A recent site visit by state auditors documented weaknesses in client record keeping and personnel records. The medical records clerk for the past 10 years was recently replaced by a more energetic clerk who has taken the initiative to modify many of the record-keeping procedures. Recently, to save time, she signed a case document that should have been signed by the patient's physician.

Most of the staff members work in the nursing department. Directors of nursing and most of the registered nurses have been white. Licensed Vocational Nurses and Certified Nurse Assistants (nurse's aides) are predominantly Filipino. The Director of Nursing, who had been at the agency for 30 years, including the previous 10 years as director, recently retired. She was well-liked and tried to protect her staff from administrative interference from corporate staff. She freely granted overtime and let nursing staff manage their own schedules. She was replaced by a much younger registered nurse who had been a nursing administrator at a family-planning clinic, and who had no previous geriatric experience. She has implemented strict controls on the use of overtime. Staff members have recently greatly increased their use of sick leave, complaining about stress on the job. Two nurses resigned and have not been replaced. Uncovered shifts are being filled by using a temporary nursing service that costs 30% more than regular nurses. Recently there have been increasing complaints from patients and their families that nursing staff have been rude and unresponsive (e.g., not responding to patient call lights promptly). Nurses and certified nurse assistants believe that many patients are overly demanding and often request assistance just to have someone to talk to. There has been some tension between Nursing and Food Services regarding special patient eating requests, such as wanting to eat in their rooms rather than the dining area.

The COO has asked the health center director to implement the new staffing concept and to develop a plan for addressing other identified problems in the center.

Discussion Questions

1. How should the Health Center director deal with the expectations and ideas of the COO regarding the new staffing concept?

2. Using relevant theories, how would you assess the change in leadership style related to the Director of Nursing position? How should the new Director of Nursing address the problems here?

Suggested Debriefing Framework: 2.5 Strategic Issues Management

CASE 4.8   Mosaic County Welfare Department

The State of New Amsterdam Department of Social Services has recently finished analyzing the net effects of federal funds cutbacks. The governor's office was considering simply passing these cuts, estimated to be around 30%, directly along to the county offices. Five years ago, Sam Pacific was appointed commissioner of Mosaic County's welfare department after spending 20 years as a state legislative assistant and being very active in local politics. Since he became commissioner, the department's caseload has doubled, while the number of assigned caseworkers has slightly decreased.

Even though he is currently facing the problem of losing additional funds and staff at a time when caseloads are up, Sam considers this a good opportunity to "clean house" and "trim the fat." Sam has done everything he can to allay his staff's anxieties, including soliciting their opinions and encouraging full participation in all actions affecting them, but many remain concerned about their futures.

Upon arriving at work one Monday morning, staff members at the Mosaic County Welfare Department were astonished to receive the following note from the Commissioner:

SOURCE: Adapted from Crow and Odewahn (1987).

> MEMORANDUM
> TO: All Staff, Mosaic County Welfare Department
> FROM: Commissioner Pacific
> RE: Reorganization
>
> As you all know, our workloads have been increasing over the years. In an effort to serve our clients more efficiently, I am creating a new office for Program Planning, Analysis, and Development. It will be run by Al Henchley. He will report to Ken Monarchi of Administrative Services. Al worked with me on several projects when we were state legislative assistants, and I can assure you that he is a most competent and conscientious individual. He will be responsible for coordinating the programs of the Social Services and Public Assistance offices and will be assisting me with overall department planning and management. I am sure that you will find most useful his ability to provide you with extensive, current, and accurate information. This should help you to reduce duplicate payments, ineligibility, fraud, and waste, and generally help to improve the planning of caseloads and public assistance payments.
>
> Please welcome him aboard as enthusiastically as I do, and give him your full cooperation.

This memo is only one of a number of steps that Pacific has taken to make the best of this opportunity. One of the people that he has used in this process is Arnold Steward. Steward joined the staff as Sam's administrative assistant four years ago, having then just received his master's degree in social welfare. Young and enthusiastic, he got along well with many of the caseworkers at the office. Sam immediately made him his right-hand man, giving him general office responsibilities that included planning and monitoring operations, auditing and controlling activities, and implementing a management information system.

Two weeks before the memo was posted, Arnold had been given a new assignment. Sam asked Arnold to help him establish an aggressive and creative organization that could cope with the inevitable stress that would result from trying to improve services in the face of budget cutbacks. Arnold attacked this challenge by getting ideas from fellow staff members. He initially met with Chris Luby, the director of social services; and her two assistants, Karen Dolenz and Bertha Clancey. They noted that their division has lost two positions recently and that caseloads have doubled, and they expressed frustration that they are spending too much time helping staff fill out forms. The next day, Arnold met with administrative services staff, who said they could respond better to his requests for information if they had more staff and an updated computer system.

The following Monday morning, Alex (Al) Henchley arrived to begin his new job. His first act was to send a memorandum to all of the welfare department employees, in which he ordered all staff to submit to him their plans, schedules, and workloads to facilitate a better allocation of resources, including time, money, and people.

Over the next few weeks, Henchley received information from everyone and had to work late into the evenings to sort it all out. It seemed that as hard as he tried, he never had time to get through it all. He finally requested a meeting with Sam. He told Sam that he was getting overwhelmed with information, and that in fact much of it was client problem data which he found to be useless. Al suggested that, rather than rely on staff input on the new reporting and management system, he should himself draft a new system. Sam told him to prepare a draft for his review.

Over the ensuing weeks, staff expressed increasing frustration among themselves that Al had no understanding as to how things were done in their department. They were also bothered that directives from Sam and Al resulted in people not knowing from day to day what would happen next.

The following memo was circulated to all staff in the department.

MEMORANDUM
TO: All Employees, Mosaic County Welfare Department
FROM: Al Henchley
RE: Reporting and Management System

A little over two weeks ago, I requested comprehensive data from all divisions focusing upon: (1) division planning; (2) scheduling of activities; and (3) actual workloads. It is essential for me to obtain such detailed information so that it can form a basis for improved program planning and development. Furthermore, it will allow for more efficient allocation of resources. I have thoroughly reviewed the reports that have been submitted, and as result of this review, certain issues have become quite clear:

1. Management reporting is inadequate. Data formats are not standardized from division to division and, therefore, reports are fragmented, incomplete, and often conflicting.

2. In all program areas there is far too much emphasis upon reporting the details of individual client problems. Such information is valuable for social workers who work with the clients, but it is totally useless for my purposes.

3. There is a pressing and immediate need for an agency-wide reporting and management system to address the information needs of the Office of Program Planning, Analysis, and Development.

Given the above, I have developed a system that will use standardized forms specifically geared to meet my data needs. All staff will be expected to use this system in the reporting of activities, etc. Next week I will be meeting with all division heads in order to explain thoroughly how the system will work, staff responsibilities, and my expectations concerning these responsibilities. In turn, they will relay this information to their staffs. I expect that this system will be fully operating throughout the agency within 30 days.

Fifteen minutes after the release of the memo, division heads went to Arnold demanding that he tell Sam to order Al to stop making unrealistic requests.

Discussion Questions

1. Using relevant theories, how would you assess Al's leadership style? In what way is it appropriate and inappropriate for this situation?

2. Should Arnold try to get Al to change his approach or should he get his staff to go along with Al's plan? Given your choice, what specific steps would you recommend that Arnold take?

Suggested Debriefing Framework: 2.5 Strategic Issues Management

CASE 4.9   Project Home

Project Home is a social service agency that provides homeless children (aged 8 to 17) with responsible adult volunteers as role models. The agency staff includes the director, the fund-raiser, an assistant fund-raiser, office manager, social work supervisor, and the social workers as the primary caregivers of the matches made between volunteers and youth. Agency members work from a central office.

Project Home has been undergoing a difficult period in terms of both financial management and personnel. Staff turnover has been high. During a one-year period, four of six social workers, their supervisor, and the secretary left and were replaced (after considerable delay). The

SOURCE: Adapted from Kahn (2005, pp. 73–88).

assistant fund-raiser who left was not replaced. A senior social worker calculated that 14 social workers (of a staff of seven) had left in the preceding 28-month period. The turnover undermined consistent relationship with clients, many of whom slipped through the cracks left by revolving personnel. One social worker noted, "A lot of us get files that have been passing around and around." Another told of calling a volunteer who reported that his charge had been in the youth services lock-up for two years, which no one at the agency had known or recorded.

Director–Social Worker Relationships

The relationship between the director and social workers was marked by mutual animosity and the withdrawal of support. The director perceived the social workers as largely "irresponsible," unwilling to "take ownership of their work and their mistakes." He also perceived the social workers as out to get him. The social workers perceived the director as "cold" and "manipulative," caring more about numbers than about the children or the staff and unwilling to allow them to meaningfully participate in relevant decisions. The relationship was caught in a web of mutual perceptions, to the point that agency members were largely unable to see or believe evidence that contradicted their images of the other party. They became locked within self-fulfilling prophecies, behaving in ways that elicited from each other exactly the behaviors that confirmed their beliefs about each other. Interchanges between the director and the social workers, while few, were characterized by mutual frustration, bitterness, and withholding. In interactions between the two parties, the executive director often spoke abstractly and unemotionally, while the social workers spoke in terms of concrete immediacy and of their emotions.

The social workers reacted to the director in various ways. Some confronted him, trying to get him to understand and respond to their concerns and experiences. This was invariably unsuccessful. Over time, they became angry and sad. They retreated emotionally from interactions with the director. Most of the social workers at Project Home avoided interaction with the director, attempting to take care of their business with as little contact with him as possible.

Administrator–Social Worker Relationships

The relationship between the lower-level administrators (i.e., fund-raiser, office manager) and the social workers was marked by a gulf in which members of each group felt disrespected by, unheard by, and disconnected from members of the other group. The gulf was shaped by the perceptions that members of each group held. The administrators perceived the social workers as naïve; demanding; oblivious to the financial aspects of the agency; and irresponsible. At the same time, they perceived themselves as responsible; fiscally aware; and struggling to keep the agency afloat. For their part, the social workers perceived the administrators as caring more about numbers—grants secured, funds spent, clients served—than the youth the agency sought to serve. The social workers perceived themselves as being on the front lines of a struggle with difficult issues and having their time and energy wasted by administrators who demanded too much paper-work. These various perceptions led administrators and social workers alike to feel neither supported nor valued by the other.

Supervisor–Social Worker Relationships

The supervisor and the social workers liked and valued one another, while abdicating their roles of supervisor and supervisee. This abdication assumed a variety of forms, ranging from the supervisor not representing the social workers' interests to the administrators, to the social workers taking care of their supervisor without reciprocation. The interaction between the two was very habitual. The supervisor sat with social workers, listened to them, supported them, and was verbally appreciative of their work. Yet, her positive emotion was not often grounded in empathetic understanding. The supervisor did not fully take in and digest the social worker's experiences. She limited her intake by focusing on administrative rather than emotional issues. The supervisor abandoned the social workers by limiting her support for them, not helping create a sense of consistency, and not offering protection.

The social workers reacted in particular ways. They became self-sufficient, withdrawing from expressing their needs. They simplified the problems rather than work through the larger issues. The social workers found themselves offering care to their supervisor, giving her support but not receiving any in return.

Implications for Social Workers

The social workers sought to create meaningful attachments among themselves. They felt that they had little choice but to turn to one another for care giving. In doing so they cut themselves off from other parts of the organization that failed to provide adequate care giving, becoming care-givers for themselves as well as their clients.

This pattern is illustrated in a monthly group supervision meeting the social workers led for each other. The supervisor led these regularly scheduled meetings, but when she was unavailable the social workers facilitated their own meeting rather than have the executive director lead the meeting. The meeting contained the following interchanges:

Social worker 1:   What else?

Social worker 2:   It's been hard to get hold of the volunteers; they don't seem to get their messages or return my calls a lot of the time. It's frustrating.

Social worker 3:   I know what you mean. It is frustrating. It sometimes helps to leave messages saying exactly when they can call you, so you don't think they have to waste their time trying.

Social worker 1:   When you reach them, how do you find conversations?

Social worker 4:   Sometimes people don't offer much. I'm afraid to put words in their mouth. I don't want to feed them when we talk; I want them to talk on their own.

Social worker 2:   I know, it can get like pulling teeth. Sometimes it's important just to stay on the phone with them sometimes, just to build the relationship. After a time, it gets easier.

Social worker 3:   I think that's right. It lets them know that they have some place to go to when they need to.

Social worker 1:   I was thinking that it would be useful to flag some issues and how to deal with them. I was thinking about a mother who called me and was beside herself because the volunteer was letting her child sit on his lap and drive the car. What would you do with that?

Social worker 5:   The mother is the one who has to feel OK about her child's match. I would try to affirm and legitimate her perspective and hear what's going on for her.

Social worker 6:   (rising to close the conference room door) Can I ask about a case I have? It involves a sexually abused child who is not talking about it with his volunteer.

Social worker 1:   Let's help. What's going on?

In this meeting the social workers set up boundaries (requesting that the executive director be absent, closing the door), literally and figuratively creating the space in which to care for themselves. Within that space, they shared feelings and experiences. They explored issues and emotions. Together they worked on the task of caring for youths and volunteers and created a care structure for themselves. As the social workers re-entered the organization looking for direction, information, and resources, they did not find the same structure. They slowly began to look to each other more than to their nominal superiors. The social workers were caught in a bind. If they did not become self-contained they were bereft of care giving; when they did become self-contained they distanced themselves further from others. The social workers were, by and large, left relatively isolated in the agency. One social worker noted:

> "It's like all individual here. Everyone is out for themselves. That's in a sense how I'm functioning now; I have to take care of myself. There's no system to give back or get back from. There's no circle to join, nothing that I can be part of."

The isolation—the "nothing to be part of"—held implications for the social workers' work, burnout, and turnover. It was difficult for them to be emotionally present when they were tending to clients and coping with lack of support in their own agency. Social workers conducting constant reality checks with one another and devising effective strategies to deal with agency relationships were less present for their clients. Time spent huddling about how to deal with the latest perceived insult, administrative policy, or agency dynamic was time not spent with clients. Emotional energies expended in dealing with their isolation took them away from working with clients' more painful emotions. They withdrew from such difficult emotional work. They were late completing necessary documentation, unwilling to get involved in agency-wide activities, and slow to develop solutions to lingering problems. They traced such withdrawal to their treatment in the agency. One social worker noted, "I know that if I were receiving more I would be better here. There's a lot of potential that I have that isn't being nurtured here and everyone suffers."

Discussion Questions

1. How would you analyze the communication processes in this agency? What specific interventions may improve communications?

2. What conflicts do you see regarding role expectations? What could be done to address these conflicts?

3. What suggestions would you give the director to help him become an effective leader? Refer to leadership theories which support your analysis.

4. What could the management staff do to improve their relationships and support of the social workers?

Suggested Debriefing Framework: 2.2 Managerial Problem Solving

❖ ETHICS

CASE 4.10   Damage Control

As the county agency responsible for providing oversight for 60 day care centers, we are constantly monitoring them to see that they adhere to proper building codes, financial administration, and programmatic procedures. I am the administrator of the program, and a bombshell landed on my desk a week ago. I received an anonymous letter in the mail accusing four staff members from two different centers of taking food from their agencies, falsifying mileage reports, and stealing office supplies.

I'm faced with the dilemma of whether to take a strong position right now denouncing the accused staff of the two day care centers or take time to permit the administrators of these two day care centers to undertake a proper due process investigation. News reporters are calling me daily asking my position so they can report on the story and keep it in front of their readers. They want to know the names of the staff. Editorials are beginning to ask whether we have provided proper oversight. I know that if we denounce the staff, we would look good in the newspapers and to those who are demanding that something be done. On the other hand, I believe strongly that we need to conduct our own investigation, which will take some time. I want the children to operate in a safe environment, and I want to make sure that they have the proper role models. At the same time I don't want to have the staff wrongfully fired, which would surely invite lawsuits.

Discussion Questions

1. What are the pros and cons of suspending the accused staff, pending the completion of an investigation? Should any other immediate steps be taken?

2. Should the administrator consider closing the two centers until her investigation is completed?

3. Suppose it is determined that the allegations were unfounded, how should the administrator proceed with the staff?

4. What should the administrator's response be to media inquires?

Suggested Debriefing Framework: 2.3 Analytical and Interactional Aspects

CASE 4.11   Philosophy Versus Economics

As the executive director of a major nursing home in our community, I have decided to take a stand that is making me quite unpopular with my fellow nursing home colleagues. Most of our clients are Medicaid eligible, that is, their resources are so limited that we receive full reimbursement for their care. But about 10% of our clients have children who are financially able to contribute at least some portion of the costs of care. For example, a number of families are able to pay $50 a month, which we report to Medicaid and treat like any other resource, such as Social Security or pension. When we interview a family, we ask for financial information and make a determination with them about whether they would be able to pay for services. Because our reputation is so good, and because family members want the best care, we have usually found them to be cooperative in making a contribution.

Having learned of our procedures and policies, my colleagues have become very annoyed with me. They have argued at our professional meetings with me that our agency is the only one doing this, and that I am foolish for taking this approach. In fact, some of them have described how they have conducted annual contribution campaigns with family members to encourage them to make donations to their agencies, which then become additional funds for them to use. In other words, they get the money to use for their agency rather than have it subtracted from the Medicaid payment.

But I believe what we are doing is morally the right way to go about this. Some members of my board, however, are beginning to raise questions about whether my philosophical commitment is interfering with the potential economic benefits to the agency.

Discussion Questions

1. Is the director doing the right thing?

2. How would you explain the moral high ground the director is taking in this situation?

3. Suppose you were the director and you felt as strongly as she does, would you consider altering your position if your agency was faced with a budget shortfall?

Suggested Debriefing Framework: 2.4 Executive Coaching

CASE 4.12   What? Me Worry?

Yes, I have a problem—but I have solutions. If I've learned anything in the last 11 years, it's that somehow things have a way of working out. I used to worry, but I've decided that worrying doesn't accomplish much, especially when I can use my head to work my way out of problems.

We are in a temporary financial difficulty. I say temporary because I know we'll be able to work out the problem. The grant request for our tutoring and counseling program for released convicts was not renewed this year because of belt tightening at the federal level. We have an excellent program with outstanding staff, and it is essential that we preserve the program. My bookkeeper has informed me that at the rate we're going we will likely incur a $140,000 deficit by the end of the year, seven months from now. The reason I might be able to finesse the situation is that I know I have four viable options for dealing with our shortfall:

First, I could ask the board to draw money from the board-designated endowment fund. In the past, when we experienced minor deficits of a few hundred or even a few thousand dollars, the board accepted my request to use these reserve funds to make up the deficit. It's true that we only have approximately $700,000 in this fund, and this request would represent quite a chunk at 20%. The trustees are fairly inactive and haven't paid much attention to our finances, so I think I could slide this request through without much discussion. If they inquire, I could probably give them vague assurances that eventually we could replenish the funds taken out for this year.

Second, we could take the option of borrowing funds from the bank which would allow us to have a short-term fix for our financial situation. Although we don't have immediate prospects of paying back the loan, I could try to obtain a 10-year time frame so that we could pay it back gradually. I'm due to retire in three years, so this could be the next director's worry.

A third possibility is to arrange to use new grant money we anticipate receiving in July to apply toward this program. In the past I've been able to juggle funds from one grant to provide for another, and we've always managed to stay one step ahead of the game. I would just delay the start up of the new proposal and use the money for our current deficit. Then when new grant money hopefully comes in next year, I'll apply those funds to this year's grants. I know this sounds like robbing Peter to pay Paul, and my accountant is very uncomfortable with this, cautioning, "There could be a day of reckoning." I know it's tricky, but it has worked in the past and I know the future will somehow manage to take care of itself.

If none of these plans work out, I can always go to the board with a fourth option and say that they've got to be more aggressive in raising money through special events or personal solicitations. I know that they haven't been eager to do this in the past, but if they truly care about the organization, they're going to have to step up and raise the needed money. I'm a little hesitant to go to the board because they don't know of the shortfall and they might become a little upset with me. If I have to resort to this option, I'll merely tell them that I was trying to find the money through other means before concerning them.

So, that's why I'm not too worried. I've learned over the years not to take problems home at night, knowing that somehow or other things will work out. I'm really looking forward to my retirement in three years.

Discussion Questions

1. If you were this director and facing a $140,000 deficit, at what point would you alert your board of trustees? What would you say to them?

2. Based on the review of the pros and cons for each of the four options, which one(s) would you consider pursuing?

3. What other approach(es) might you consider in addressing this type of situation?

4. What should be the role of the board's treasurer and finance committee in monitoring the organization's budget?

5. What odds would you give that this director will be able to continue until his planned retirement in three years?

Suggested Debriefing Framework: 2.6 Policy Practice

❖ CHAPTER EXERCISES

While there are many self-assessment tools available for classroom use, three are described below:

Exercise #1

One instrument that captures both leadership skills and competing values is based on the work of Quinn and illustrated in the first chapter of Edwards and Yankey. By completing and scoring this self-assessment instrument, students in small groups are then able to compare and contrast their scores with each other.

Exercise #2

Building upon the competency model developed by the National Network for Social Work Managers (http://www.socialworkmanager.org/Standards.htm), their instrument has been modified to encourage students to rank order the items (#1 being the most important) in each of four clusters: knowledge base (ranked 1–9); personal skills (ranked 1–18); values (ranked 1–5); and technical skills (ranked 1–14) that are most relevant to their current learning needs.

I. Knowledge Base Cluster

Rank Order

Service Delivery Technology

1. ____ Service Delivery Technology. Understands the service delivery methods when providing leadership and management

Policy

2. ____ General social policy. Understands the local, state, and national policies that impact on the client group served by the organization

3. ____ Organizational policy. Understands the policies that govern the operation of the organization

Organizational Theory

4. ____ Organizational theory. Understands the theories that explain the development and operation of organizations

Political Process, Administrative Law, and Governance

5. ____ Political process. Understands the process by which local, state, and national policy makers are chosen and the process by which they make decisions

6. ____ Administrative law. Understands the local, state, and national laws and regulations that govern the operation of employers

7. ____ Governance. Understands the theory and methods that govern the internal control and policy making of organizations

Advocacy

8. ____ Advocacy. Understands the theory and practice of advocating for policy change at the agency, local, state, and national level and of advocating to fill the needs of particular individuals, groups, and communities

9. ____ The Community. Understands the demographics, resources, needs, and strengths of the community in which the organization operates

Quality Production

10. ____ Quality production. Understands theory and practice of outcome/results oriented work and total quality management

II. Personal Skills Cluster

Rank Order

Communications

1. ____ Oral communication. Ability to achieve desired outcomes through clear and succinct use of the spoken word

2. ____ Written communication. Ability to achieve desired outcomes through clear and succinct use of the written word

Collaboration and Negotiation

3. ____ Collaboration. Ability to form collaborative groups inside and outside the organization

4. ____ Negotiation. Ability to facilitate achieving agreement on activities and the conditions surrounding those activities among different people or groups

Team Work

5. ____ Internal teamwork. Ability to work within a team context inside the organization

6. ____ External teamwork. Ability to work within a team context outside of the organization

7. ____ Meeting management. Ability to achieve the goals of a meeting on time while soliciting the input and acceptance of all members of the group

Leadership

8. ____ Leadership. Ability to blend the expertise of others in a coordinated fashion in order to achieve the purposes of the organization

9. ____ Bold and creative personal leadership. Ability to inspire excellence in program development and staff and organizational performance

Entrepreneurship

10. ___ Having an entrepreneurial attitude. Willingness to take calculated risks that may result in gain to the organization, but may also result in loss

11. ___ Involvement in the political process. Actively engaged in the choosing of elected officials through voting and other means and take an active interest in the making of social policy

Cognitive and Emotional Maturity

12. ___ Conflict resolution. Ability to achieve a widely accepted solution to a dispute without recourse to formal processes

13. ___ Group dynamics. Ability to observe and understand the interactions of members of a group and act on that understanding to guide the group to meet its objectives

14. ___ Collaboration. Ability to form collaborative groups inside and outside the organization

15. ___ Tolerant of ambiguity. Ability to remain in ambiguity until such time that the information and resources necessary to the resolution of an issue are available

16. ___ Thinking critically

17. ___ Being future oriented

18. ___ Ability to handle situations of great complexity

III. Values Cluster

Rank order

Commitment

1. ___ Commitment to clients. Support meeting the needs of clients within the purview of the services offered by the organization

2. ___ Commitment to the work. Support of the work and the organization that transcends personal desires

3. ___ Commitment to the profession. Acting upon the social work values of social justice, equity, and fairness

Identification

4. ___ Identification with the employer. Having knowledge of the organization and a loyalty to the mission of the organization

Advocacy

5. ___ Advocacy position. Taking an advocacy position and being an activist on important social justice issues as well as specific issues of importance to clients, staff and the organization as a whole

---

IV. Technical Skills Cluster

Rank order

Health and Human Services

1. ___ Specialized fields. Knowledge of the skills necessary to deliver the services of the organization for which one works

Organizational

2. ___ Program planning. Ability to develop formal goals, objective, and methods for achieving program initiatives

3. ___ Coordinating. Ability to bring together disparate groups and individuals to carry out specific tasks in an efficient and effective manner

4. ___ Decision making. Ability to determine and state clearly decisions required by one's position

5. ___ Human resources management. Ability to hire, train, develop, and place the appropriate individuals in the appropriate jobs while following organizational policy

Business

6. ___ Marketing. Informing those who could potentially make use of the products of the organization as to the availability of those products and increasing the share of these products provided by the organization to customers

7. ___ Strategic planning. Facilitating the development of strategic plans and business plans

8. ___ Accounting. Understanding of and ability to use standard accounting methods

9. ___ Resource development. Ability to identify and access resources

10. ___ MIS. Ability to be an informed consumer of management information systems data

11. ___ Budgeting. Ability to develop realistic and usable details of projected income and expenditures

Evaluation

13. ___ Evaluation/research. Ability to be an informed consumer of evaluations and research findings and conduct agency based program evaluation

14. ___ Statistics. Ability to be an informed consumer of statistical information

Exercise #3

A third leadership exercise relates to an array of management roles identified by Menefee (2000). Based on Menefee's description of each of these roles on the following pages, rank order the roles in each of the three role sets (leadership; interactional; and analytic) with 1 being the strongest down to 3 or 4 as the role needing to be improved or strengthened.

Leadership Roles

_____Boundary Spanner

_____Innovator

_____Organizer

_____Team builder

Interactional Roles

_____Communicator

_____Supervisor

_____Facilitator

_____Advocate

Analytic Roles

_____Resource Administrator

_____Evaluator

_____Policy Practitioner

Definitions of Managerial Roles

Leadership Roles

1. Boundary-spanner: Managing relationships, networking, influencing others to foster interorganizational relationships, developing partnerships, and integrating service delivery systems.

2. Innovator: Capacity to forecast trends in the external environment and develop alternative and innovative strategies for responding to these forces.

3. Organizer: Capacity to arrange and structure the work of an agency to optimize the use of human and material resources (includes delegating and staffing), in order to continuously modify internal structures, processes, and conditions to adapt to external—often turbulent—environments.

4. Team builder/Leader: Building coalitions and teams (interagency, intra-agency, interdisciplinary, etc.) by organizing and enlisting

groups to ensure service availability and effective agency operations, with special attention to group maintenance and task functions of meeting management.

Interactional Roles

5. Communicator: Exchanging written and verbal information, making formal presentations, and keeping internal and external stakeholders continuously informed through the extensive use of technology.

6. Advocate: Representing the interests of individuals and groups by lobbying, testifying, and fostering relationships with public officials and community leaders.

7. Supervisor: Directing and guiding the delivery of agency services while attending to the socio-emotional needs of staff through the use of coordinating, supporting, and consultant advising activities needed to motivate staff, coordinate workloads, set goals and limits, provide corrective feedback, and monitor work processes and outcomes.

8. Facilitator: Enlisting others in accomplishing the vision, mission, and goals of an agency or community coalition by enabling, orienting, training, and empowering others through modeling methods for collaboration and coordination that can change and strengthen organizational culture.

Analytic Roles

9. Resource administrator: Managing efficiently and effectively the human, financial, informational, and physical resources needed by agencies related to fundraising, grant writing, marketing, media relations, and performance management.

10. Evaluator: Capacity to conduct needs assessments and program evaluations related to the agency's impact on client populations and community needs, based on a strong understanding of research methods, as well as a capacity to supervise/contract specialists in regard to continuous quality improvement and outcome assessment.

11. Policy practitioner: Capacity to develop/formulate, interpret, comply with, and influence public policies, as well as the capacity to understand and articulate to staff the full range of policy implementation issues and challenges.

5

Planning and Program Design

❖   ❖   ❖

❖ PLANNING

Case 5.1   Mallard County Private Industry Council

Mallard County Private Industry Council (PIC) staff members are perplexed and anxious. PIC trustees have recently begun to call for a strategic planning session to take stock; figure out what is happening in the employment and training arena; and set some new directions. A new ball game with new rules has left the PIC in an ambiguous position.

Funded principally by grants under the federal Job Training Partnership Act (JTPA), the Mallard County PIC has plodded along for years, doing a solid if unspectacular job of training eligible "disadvantaged" participants and getting them placed in jobs. Federally determined performance standards are regularly exceeded. Most staff members are good at—and dedicated to—what they do.

By conventional standards, the PIC is a model agency. But in a time when job training is sorely needed at the local level in order to meet the needs of a rapidly changing economy, Congress is cutting JTPA funding, while seriously considering the creation of a more comprehensive national employment and training system.

Discussion Questions

1. Where PIC will be in the new system once the dust settles is currently unclear, but, in the meantime, does it make sense to continue delivering the same programs in the same way?

2. If not, what should be changed, and how can an anxious and defensive staff be encouraged to participate fully in determining a new direction?

Suggested Debriefing Framework: 2.4 Executive Coaching

CASE 5.2   Be Careful What You Wish For

The Life Skills Agency (LSA) serves autistic children in a tri-county area. It was founded 15 years ago by families of autistic children who had received no counseling intervention, life-skill training, or socialization in their own homes or local schools. Sam Moore volunteered to help these parents organize a voluntary campaign and was later hired as the administrative director to build up the program.

As services, costs, and clients grew, Moore lobbied county, state, and federal education departments for five years to change the law. He also wanted to create and fund a developmental disabilities education division that would expand to offer services for adults, knowing that the children they now worked with would eventually need adult services. Moore and his parent advocates succeeded in accomplishing their early goals. Now the LSA has a board of dedicated child-development experts, committed parents, and business professionals. Recently, during a strategic planning retreat, the LSA board affirmed that its mission is to expand educational and life-skill training for autistic children through adulthood. Moore had hoped that the board would consider broadening the definition to include other vulnerable populations, especially children and adults with mental illnesses, but most board members preferred keeping the narrower focus on the autistic population.

Last week, an anonymous potential benefactor telephoned Moore with an offer of an apartment building in a middle-class suburb with 30 units of efficiency suites for use as low-income housing, specifically for vulnerable adults. The wealthy benefactor made it clear that while some of the potential residents could fit those served currently by the agency, she did not want to limit the residents only to those who were autistic. The donor herself had had a severely depressed adult son who had committed suicide, and she saw this building as a memorial to him. While the acceptance of the building would push the organization to expand its mission to include adults other than those who were autistic, Moore was excited about the offer. Moore had wanted to expand the organization's target population, but even this was beyond his wildest dreams.

Tonight, in the emergency meeting of his board, Moore excitedly told his board of the building, estimated at a value of $5 million. With proper renovation and on-site supportive services, it would make an excellent permanent home for disabled, mentally ill, and homeless persons. Moore advocated, "These people have nowhere to go except the streets or under the bridges and I believe we have an obligation to help them."

Members of the board were apparently not as enthusiastic as Moore. Art Lewis, for example, argued, "Even if this kind of housing service project were to serve the autistic population, which it probably won't, how could we possibly afford to operate something of this magnitude? Where are we going to get the money to operate this building?"

Moore countered, "Our potential benefactor has offered matching funds when we are ready to renovate the building. She is confident that she can get people from the building trades to provide their labor free or at a discount. I see this as a wonderful opportunity to expand the vision of our agency. So many children with autism, without help from agencies like ours, end up in institutions or become homeless. This also is a chance to broaden our support for those who might otherwise become destitute."

The board president, Don Pomeroy, observed, "How can we be sure that this so-called benefactor isn't using this for an easy tax deduction? Could this be a building she's looking to unload?"

Mrs. Hawkins, another trustee, expressed concern. "Our focus is on educational and skill development for children with autism. If we try to take on housing for adults, we're in a whole different realm of work. I'm afraid this could end up being a drain on our resources."

Speaking in favor of the idea, Jessica Berg, an attorney, stated: "Aren't we really trying to help people integrate into the community and help them live more independently? These apartments are about teaching them independent living skills, forming support groups, and keeping out of jail. I believe our purpose should include helping vulnerable people become responsible adults."

Bob Streeter, a tax accountant, asked, "What about costs and funding?"

Moore responded, "The building would normally cost $500,000 to renovate for the disabled, but, I think, with contributions from the building trades, we could achieve a cost of about $200,000. I envision that a three-year capital campaign could easily raise the money needed from our donor base. I think we could interest the U.S. Department of Housing and Urban Development in providing ongoing operational funding. The benefactor is willing to contribute an additional $1 million in equities to our organization if we accept her offer."

Discussion Questions

1. What are the pros and cons of accepting the offer and modifying the organization's mission—or adhering to the mission and rejecting the offer?

2. Taking on this project would clearly require the executive and the board of trustees to shoulder extra responsibilities and divert time and energies from their current mission, services, and programs for children with autism. What do you think about this?

3. What do this executive and board need to consider regarding their capability of raising the capital funds? What scenarios (including a possible shortfall) might occur in the next several years? How would the organization respond to these worst-case scenarios?

4. Why do you think Sam Moore is advocating so enthusiastically in favor of this new opportunity?

5. What are the pros and cons of different possible options? What's your viewpoint?

Suggested Debriefing Framework: 2.6 Policy Practice

CASE 5.3   Decision on Resource Allocation

As a result of a lawsuit filed by the Coalition for the Homeless, the city of New Bosco is now faced with having to provide homeless shelters for single men and women and for families. New Bosco was initially reluctant to settle the case but finally agreed to allocate resources for these various homeless populations. Until the lawsuit occurred, the city had been providing a few limited shelters, but most of the resources had gone into services, such as mental health and substance abuse counseling, child care, and employment training. Now, with the settlement of the lawsuit, the social services administrator has to make decisions about dispensing a finite amount of money. The city has allocated $1.2 million for homeless services and housing, but this budget is strained beyond its capacity to meet the needs of those the agency is committed to serving. For example, in order to set up shelters for families, new bathrooms and new cooking facilities have to be installed.

The administrator is faced with difficult choices: If she puts more money into the shelters, she will have less money available for services. Compounding her dilemma is the prospect of having to make a decision about which of the target populations—men, women, or families—should be allocated more resources. If she puts more money into the single male adult groups, she could probably serve many more people than if she allocated funds to homeless families, since these families require many more services. Allocating funds to serve single adults could result in getting them out of their homeless situations because counseling and job training could help them become more self-sufficient. Her pragmatic nature tips her in favor of providing more housing and services for the 550 single adults, as there would likely be immediate pay-off for the investment. Her sense of values, however, directs her to provide services for the 240 needy families who need shelter and services to meet their many needs, but who are unlikely to become self-sufficient in the near future.

Discussion Questions

1. What information should be investigated and facts considered that could influence how you would resolve this dilemma?

2. After reviewing the pros and cons of providing for single adults versus needy families, what factors would you give the most weight to?

3. What values or assumptions might operate to determine how you would make your decision?

4. What options do you see?

5. What solutions would you recommend?

Suggested Debriefing Framework: 2.6 Policy Practice

CASE 5.4   Rational Versus Political Decision Making

As the director of senior services, I am responsible for administering 20 independent centers that provide recreation, meals, and transportation services for senior citizens. About five years ago, one of our major centers, located in a public-housing facility, had to be closed because the public-housing authority needed the space for other essential services. We hurriedly arranged with a local church to provide an alternative location. Until last year, the program was working well, but then we ran into rough times financially. Because of cutbacks at the local and federal levels, we were unable to provide the necessary funding for this particular program. This center is more costly than our other centers: We have to pay the church $30,000 annually for rent, which amounts to about 20% of our budget. This cost, plus other expenses, has to be subsidized through United Way funding and our own individual fundraising efforts involving private solicitations and special events.

Our problem is compounded by the unfortunate reality that the program is substantially declining. In this particular downtown location, not many new seniors are coming into the program, and fewer of the former participants are attending. We've tried many ways to attract people through flyers and special events, but apparently the demographics are changing; seniors, when they can, move out to the suburbs. Those who remain are becoming increasingly frail and find it increasingly difficult to attend.

This year, our budget is one of our worst in many years. Our United Way funding has decreased. Despite efforts to raise money through our annual campaign, our overall budget is 12% smaller ($240,000 lost from a $2 million budget). I'm going to have to make serious cuts in administration costs, and I'm going to be forced to eliminate the least productive of our senior centers. This center is costing $150,000, yet it serves only 40 people. I cannot justify keeping it open in light of our looming budget deficit.

Although it is completely rational for me to make the decision to cut out this program, I am faced with certain political realities that transform this decision into a dilemma. The pastor is politically connected, and he was instrumental in our obtaining a sizeable community development grant from the city that permitted us to renovate the senior center. It's quite possible that our cutting this program would cause him to oppose our next community development grant. In addition, one of the active women in our program is the mother of the local councilman who has been instrumental in our obtaining city funding. Our overall budget is quite dependent on public funding, so I have to be mindful of the political repercussions of my decision. I know that closing this center would stir up negative media publicity and could ignite a firestorm among senior advocates.

I've been inclined to put off the decision because, as I weighed the financial issues against the political issues, I was at an impasse—until today. In this morning's e-mails, I received a note from the church's bookkeeper saying that the church has decided to raise our rent from $30,000 to $40,000 to keep up with the inflationary costs of running the church building. Is this a sign to me to make my decision?

Discussion Questions

1. Initially this director did not want to make a decision while she balanced economic and political considerations. If you were she, would you now be ready to make a decision? If so what would it be?

2. Before making your final decision, with whom would you confer?

3. Supposing you decide to cut the center, what options might be considered for the 40 people who have been served?

4. What might the repercussions be of closing the center, and how would you deal with them?

Suggested Debriefing Framework: 2.2 Managerial Problem Solving

CASE 5.5   The Achievement Crisis at Girls Works

Agency Description, History, and Current Status

Girls Works, a girl-centered nonprofit founded in 1958, provides a multitude of enrichment programs for underserved girls and their families throughout a large West Coast county. The organization promotes girls' growth and development; nurtures their academic and athletic potential; and imparts confidence and self-esteem. Girls Works is an affiliate of a national organization.

The agency offers academic enrichment (including literacy, math, science, and college preparation), leadership, and health and sexuality programming, as well as affordable counseling services, to over 7,000 young women and their families every year. Most of its clients are low-income, with 56% coming from households earning less than $30,000 annually, and 52% coming from single-parent families headed mostly by women. The Girls Works constituency is 28% Latina; 23% African American; 12% Caucasian; 10% Asian American or Pacific Islander; and 27% other ethnicities.

Girls Works' most notable programming accomplishment is its continuum of services, including a set of four after-school and summer programs that supplement girls' education from kindergarten through the end of high school. From the GIRLStart literacy program serving kindergarten through second grade, participants graduate into the Watch Out World (WOW!) literacy and fitness program for third grade through fifth grade; from WOW! they enter the Sports, Technology, Academics, Responsibility, Service (All STARS) middle-school program;

and from All STARS, girls complete the Girls Works continuum in the four-year Eureka! (a math, science, and college preparation program).

In 1998, Girls Works embarked on a strategic plan. The plan included four main goals:

1. Increase the intensity of services by creating a middle-school program that will complete a "continuum of service" model to offer summer and after-school programs from kindergarten through high school.

2. Increase services in Oak Town by adding two more literacy programs and one more economic literacy and sports program.

3. Open a site in Oak Town.

4. Be seen as an expert advocate for girls.

In 2003, the Board completed a business plan to support the strategic plan goals. This plan specified the following:

1. Create an infrastructure to support growth—create an executive management team, hire 20 new staff, and increase board membership.

2. Develop a program plan and a timeline for growth. This includes increasing services from 3,000 to 5,000 girls in the continuum of service as well as increasing the budget from $3.3 million to $5 million.

3. Raise money to support growth; implement a planned giving program.

To date, the organization has made significant progress. All goals in the strategic plan have been met. The middle-school program is up and running in three Oak Town schools. Two more literacy programs are in place and one economic literacy program will start in September 2006. Girls Works secured a new site at a park in Oak Town, and services began in February 2006. In 2003, Girls Works completed a research project that documented the needs of girls in the county. This received much press coverage. Girls Works now has dedicated a staff to marketing and public relations.

The business plan's progress has been positive, as well. The new management team is in place, and staff has increased from 55 to 75. The board has recruited three new members. The program plan and timeline have been adhered to, and 4,000 girls are being served through the continuum. This year, our budget is projected to reach $5 million. The planned giving program has started. It has five new members who have made a commitment to include Girls Works in their wills.

Girls Works is an extremely successful nonprofit organization, run by an executive director who has led the agency for 29 years. She has dedicated her life to the organization, and she has developed it from a budget of less than $1 million to one of nearly $5 million and from 7 employees to nearly 80. In the 1970s, the organization offered after-school programming at a small rented house—today, the organization owns a large headquarters and offers programs at 40 school sites. In addition to the hard work and talent of the ED, this immense growth can be attributed to one family's generous contribution. After the family reviewed the organization's 2003 business plan for growth, they committed to giving $2 million a year for five years. With strong leadership and a large donation, it was exciting for the organization to continue moving forward.

Girls Works has made progress in implementing the business plan for the past three years, increasing services and agency capacity. But as her 30th anniversary is approaching, the executive director has decided to retire in a year. The implications of a retiring ED are many, especially with a multi-million–dollar gift that is halfway through the five-year commitment and with no plan to backfill the gift. The agency has urgent decisions to make on its already over-taxed situation.

During the course of implementing its business plan, Girls Works has increased its services for girls, which in turn has increased demands on all departments in the organization—including administrative, fundraising, and facility needs. The business plan did not take into consideration the weight of the increased services on departments outside of programming. In this crisis, many issues need to be addressed while the drum beat of daily work must continue.

The Challenges Ahead

Challenge #1: Human Resources. The increase in staff has brought technology and space-planning issues to the forefront (purchasing a server, buying and upgrading computers and printers, making staff cubicles smaller, etc.) This amount of growth significantly affects staff—both concretely (smaller workstations) and psychologically (the agency is large so we should get more training, have more opportunities for promotion, and offer more competitive salaries, etc.). Additionally, as the number of staff grows, more personalities are involved, and, therefore, more policies need to be established. Some personnel policies were created for all employees, such as the dress code. Some policies were left up to departments.

The amount of work increased for the Fund Development department. The workload each team member carries is extensive, but manageable. In the past, each development employee worked on multiple types of duties (a graphics person managed the database; all the staff shared responsibilities for the main fundraising event, etc.). No single person had specific expertise in any one area. There were no formalized training plans. Two years ago, each staff member's job duties became focused on a particular area to increase knowledge and capacity (events, database, marketing, and grant writing). Staff members received internal and external training, and the quality of work increased significantly, but some team members feel the jobs have become too focused. For many staff, this is their first job since graduating from college. They are exploring their occupational interests and want and need significant training. Once staff members learn their new functions, they get restless. They either want a promotion, or they look outside the organization for new jobs. Staff turn over, on an average, after approximately two years.

Girls Works hired a firm to map the personnel structure and determine appropriate job levels and salaries across all departments. All staff salaries that were determined to be below the median level were raised. Due to the lack of excess budget monies, none of the other staff members received an annual salary increase. The mapping process also allowed the fund development department to develop a hierarchical system that leaves some room for advancement; however, the outcome does not provide a comprehensive solution to the problem of job satisfaction. As compensation for no salary increases and narrow job definitions, some staff members have requested more involvement in service delivery (one staff member is offering a poetry class for the summer; another joined the summer running club). Staff members who are not interested in working directly with the girls have asked for flexible work hours. Because of these perks, the issue of entitlement has begun to spread around the team—since they work hard and didn't get salary increases, then they are entitled to other work benefits.

Challenge #2: Budgetary Issues. Girls Works is committed to the wonderful family benefactors whose contribution supports 40% of the budget. The family asked Girls Works to expand specific programs into additional sites and has designated their gift as general operating funds with the understanding that specific programs will continue to be offered and grow as outlined in the business plan. As a result of this growth, management realizes that they have outgrown their headquarters. After analyzing the revenue and expenses, the senior management team determined which budget items would be cut. They know that, in the future, they will need to discuss which programs most strongly align with the mission and which programs are doing well—great evaluations and attendance.

As Girls Works follows its business plan and grows its academic achievement programs, staff members are noticing that there are two competing priorities. Girls Works has always focused their programs on motivating girls and increasing their self-esteem. With the intense focus on academic achievement, the curriculum is less focused on the soft skills related to motivation and self-esteem. This issue may align with the budget issues and is yet to be addressed.

It must be noted that Girls Works offers a counseling program to community members (including families, men, boys, and children in the foster-care system.) Some feel that this successful program, with over 11 licensed clinicians, does not strongly align with the mission. Yet, in some fiscal years, this program has helped supplement the agency budget. In other years, however, programs for girls supplement counseling services.

Challenge #3: Leadership—Fund Development Issues. The fund development department is concerned about replacing the $2-million-a-year commitment. The department needs support from the board to raise the funds. It is considering hiring a major gifts staff to assist in increasing current contributors' donations. Time is running short.

Board of Directors. When the agency was in its infancy, its amount of policy and fundraising work was adequate for its modest board of local small-business representatives. With the increase in fundraising needs, however, the board needs people with high-level access and influence in the community. Recruiting board members has been a focus within the past year. Cultivating new board members, and then having them cultivate donations takes a lot of time.

Executive Director Succession Planning. After 30 years of service, the executive director will be leaving. This type of transition is not easy for the organization or for the ED. It may be a struggle to transfer donor relationships from the ED to current staff or a new ED.

Next Steps. With the significant number of issues presenting themselves— succession planning, an overtaxed agency with quick growth, and a large donor gift expiring soon, the board of directors felt they needed a new strategic plan to help guide their next steps. Girls Works received a grant from a large foundation to assist with succession planning and strategy setting.

Discussion Questions

1. What might be the prioritized goals for a strategic plan that would address the identified challenges?

2. What would be a list of action steps needed to begin achieving goals?

Suggested Debriefing Framework: 2.2 Managerial Problem Solving

CASE 5.6   Cutbacks and Performance Pressure

The Heartland Community Center (HCC) started as a multipurpose community center serving an inner-city, low-income neighborhood. From its small original site, it has grown over the years to include professionally staffed programs at seven sites throughout the county. Its current programs include:

- A senior center offering a day care program, bingo, educational programs; and support groups, including bereavement programs.
- An employment-development program, with decentralized services in seven multi-service centers, providing job-interviewing skills, child care, and substance-abuse counseling.
- An outpatient behavioral health program.

The senior center, once highly regarded, has suffered from recent funding cutbacks and deterioration in service quality. The employment development program has experienced significant growth over the years and currently offers a full range of services. However, recent decreases in client demand have forced cutbacks and raised issues of further program changes or retrenchments. The behavioral health program, after 15 years of effective functioning, is now performing below state standards. It is at further risk because the state is moving to performance-based contracting, basing payments upon outcomes which may be difficult for the agency to achieve.

Troubles in the Senior Center

After major federal funding cuts in recent years, the senior center has been limping along. Because the city itself has had to cut back services, it no longer can provide this senior center with janitorial services. Adding to the agency's woes, the senior center director recently died, and the new director has discovered equipment theft and major personnel problems.

The new director is desperately trying to keep the center going; but, unfortunately, the agency is not even meeting minimal standards of health and service provision. The adult day care program does not have a nurse, afternoon program activities are nonexistent, and the agency is unable to provide transportation because it cannot pay its drivers. The remaining staff members are overworked and complain of being exhausted.

The city that funds the program will be faced with sanctions from the state if it continues to let services deteriorate and permits it to remain out of compliance with state requirements. For this reason, the city is struggling with the decision to possibly discontinue funding for the senior center. The city recognizes that this is an agency that serves an inner-city population, one that has valiantly struggled to provide quality services with limited and declining resources. The agency executive team has been discussing other options, including consolidating or even eliminating some services so that it can give proper attention to other services. For example, it could give up adult day care, and maybe even give up home delivery meals so that it could preserve the social-activities program. This would allow HSSC to retain a skeletal staff and provide very limited but quality programming.

Centralizing Employment Development Services?

In the employment development program, services have grown since the early years of welfare reform, and they are now decentralized in seven multi-service centers around the county. These centers provide job-interviewing skills, child care, and substance-abuse counseling. Through these centers, people can receive direct service or have access to services from a nearby agency. Staff members also provide case management and brief counseling.

Due to recent reductions in the large numbers of people originally served, the agency has decided to provide services to other populations, such as seniors and the disabled, in the centers. They have had to make major staff reductions to accompany the reductions in clients. Managers are now thinking that with the reduced number of clients, it may make more sense to consider a more centralized approach. This would mean making the current downtown office the main headquarters for services that were formerly provided in the seven centers. That would result in 6,000 individuals coming to a central office to receive services that could help them enter the employment market. This is especially important as more people reach their time limits on public assistance and need very special follow-up, either to get them into a job or to help them through services and resources.

To deal with this urgent situation, management formed a task force to identify the pros and cons of decentralized versus centralized services. Here is their report in an abbreviated form:

Decentralized Service Delivery
Pros:

1. Provides one-stop, accessible neighborhood services for residents

2. Meets specific needs of neighborhoods

3. Residents and community familiar with the current DSMD

4. Staff members like the convenience of free parking

5. The administrative structure (including reporting systems) is well developed

Cons:

1. Inconsistency of case-management practices

2. Reports of poor customer service

3. Inability to provide adequate staff coverage

4. Problems with staff accountability in meeting state performance measures

5. Inefficient use of staff

Centralized Service Delivery
Pros:

1. Easier to initiate new programs

2. More on-site provider presence

3. Easier to co-locate from staff to different programs

4. Better communications between clients, providers, staff, and the community

5. Better administrative oversight and performance-monitoring to meet state standards

6. Far less expensive to operate

7. Much higher level of supervision

Cons:

1. Less accessibility for clients, since they will have to travel farther from their neighborhoods

2. Community or political fallout from leaving the neighborhoods

3. Staff would have to pay $1,000 in additional parking costs

The task force, which includes both management and program staff, has spent several meetings developing and reviewing these options. In two weeks, the task force needs to make a recommendation for the executive team, which will then make a proposal to the board of directors.

Performance Difficulties in Behavioral Health

The behavioral health program faces different challenges. The program has served residents well for 15 years, but it is now underperforming according to state standards. Their state funding agency is expecting treatment agencies to be more accountable and to develop evidence-based practices. Until about three years ago, grants only required that agencies report their performance statistics to the state. Typically, they would receive the same funding level each year, based upon their previous annual performance reports. But now the state requires reimbursement for services based on current performance, and agencies have to perform services first and then be reimbursed. It is a much more open, competitive environment for our member agencies, who are vying with each other for our limited resources. Agencies that fall short during any given quarter will have their funds cut, and those funds will be given to other agencies that document their ability to increase services. The state has issued the program a warning that they must provide outcomes-based performance data. According to the state, the program's performance is so far below standards that it is in danger of losing 40% of its funding. The loss of so much funding would, of course, require major cutbacks in staff and in clients served, and this could mean the end of the program.

Clinical staff members are very disturbed about this trend in funding. They have asserted that the difficulties facing these inner-city clients with serious mental illnesses are so complicated that requiring such performance standards is unrealistic. They have also said that the program has been providing highly regarded services for 15 years and that should be recognized in the state contract requirements.

In response to the warning, some members of the agency's board of directors have resorted to putting political pressure on the state. Recently, both the ward council member in the ward in which the agency operates and the mayor have communicated with the state, stressing how important this agency is to the people in the neighborhood. The state sees the agency as a good one, serving a population that is in need, but it cannot support continued funding under the current circumstances.

The Executive Team

The agency's program directors have been operating quite independently in recent years. When times have been good, the CEO has been happy to let them operate as they liked, as long as funds continued to come in. With agency survival being threatened by major challenges in each program, the CEO believes that the agency as a whole needs to act aggressively to make significant alterations. This will lead to major changes in each program, and perhaps in the direction of the entire agency.

Discussion Questions

1. What are the most urgent concerns regarding the senior center? What factors should the executive team consider as they make decisions about what programs to keep, discontinue, or change? Which courses of action (e.g., watchful waiting in the hope that things will get better, eliminating one or more programs, reducing services to the bare minimum to keep the center open, making a case to the state that an exception is warranted) would you consider? Explain your rationale.

2. Regarding the reorganization of employment development services, which of the pros and cons would most affect your decision? How would the perspective of different stakeholders (staff, clients, administrators, state officials) influence the decision for centralized or decentralized services? What should the task force recommend?

3. What should the behavioral health program be doing to address the new state performance standards? How should staff perspectives be considered?

4. Are there common themes in the issues facing each of these programs? What should the executive team be doing at an agency-wide level to deal with this crisis and ensure the survival of the agency as a whole?

Suggested Debriefing Framework: 2.5 Strategic Issues Management

CASE 5.7   Hillside Community Center

In the 1930s, Hillside Community Center was founded in a small Southern California community by a local church to serve the many immigrants from the Dust Bowl who moved to California during the Depression. For years, the community had been predominantly working class, but over the past 20 years has shifted to a heterogeneous mix of ethnic groups, now predominantly Latino, and a socioeconomic mix from lower to lower-middle class.

Until two years ago, the agency had been run by a minister who had worked there for 20 years, the last 10 as executive director. He led the agency during a period of moderate but regular program expansion, during which time programs such as a day care center, a counseling program, and a welfare advocacy program were implemented. Program administrative functions had not developed equally rapidly during this time, and when he retired two years ago, the board of directors hired an executive director with an MBA and prior experience as an executive with the Boy Scouts of America. This new director instituted many administrative reforms, particularly in the areas of budgeting and management information systems, but staff resented his hard-driving style and generally did as little as possible to comply with his initiatives. In fact, all the employees in the counseling program had sent a memo to him and the board complaining about his policy change toward short-term counseling only, regardless of need. He had responded that there were unit-cost problems with long-term counseling. Aside from this reply, he did not act on the memo in any other way. He had begun installing computers for data collection and fiscal management; and although they had been installed, they were not being used on a regular basis. When funding source program monitors continued to express concerns about the agency's management and accomplishments (including fiscal controls and progress on objectives), and with staff morale suffering and turnover increasing, the board decided to remove this director and hire a new executive. The board consists primarily of local community representatives and other service providers. They are committed to the agency and the surrounding community, but they have not filled a major role, other than to review reports submitted by the executive.

The new executive, Gloria, had been a program director at another agency in the county and was hired because she had had some administrative experience, as well as direct service experience as an MSW. The management team she joined consisted of four program directors at four facilities and the director of administrative services. In the past, they had met as a management team, every two weeks; but, in general, the programs had been functioning rather autonomously. At her first meeting, the new executive sensed an overall feeling of disorganization. The meeting rambled from topic to topic and there seemed to be no rationality in how decisions were made. She felt that program managers were jockeying for position regarding scarce resources. Over the past two years, clients had been increasingly served by more than one program (for example, many day care clients also receive career counseling and training). The program directors have been used to running their own shows, although the previous executive had made attempts to link the programs through a common computerized information system. He had also been successful in bringing in grants and contracts for four new programs. These had been subsumed under the existing program managers in what seemed a haphazard manner.

Over the past few years, funding has become increasingly tight, and program managers find themselves faced with competition from other agencies and also among themselves. Community needs have been changing, and the new director recognized from her previous job that agencies face increasing expectations to document program success and value to the community. Two major government grants held by the agency are due to expire in eight months, with no clear plan for replacement.

When Gloria began reviewing agency documents, she found that the agency's budget seemed to show a deficit of $15,000. The board had not mentioned this to her, and she wondered if they were aware of it. She also discovered that a recent audit showed that the agency's accounting system was not able to adequately track all funds following the addition of many new programs. She could not get a clear picture of the programs' accomplishments beyond their scopes of services delivered (see Figure 5.1). Staff records did not clearly show which people were working in which programs, and she had a feeling that not all staff members were being scheduled as efficiently as possible. At all the programs, in her initial meetings with staff, Gloria sensed disinterest in agency-wide issues and a lack of positive energy in general. People were mostly interested in working with their own clients and didn't seem to care much about funding, documentation, evaluation, or planning, as long as their own program funding continued.

The board had asked her to take a good look at agency operations, programmatically and administratively, and to report back to them.

Figure 5.1   Sample Goal and Objectives: Counseling Program

Goal:
To provide comprehensive mental health services to individuals, groups and families

Objectives:

1. Conduct 75 family counseling sessions per month
2. Maintain four ongoing peer support groups in the areas of single parenting, drop-out prevention, child-abuse prevention, and self-esteem
3. Assist 200 persons per month with crisis-intervention services
4. Refer 300 persons per month to other agencies for services

Discussion Questions

1. What should Gloria do to build her team and establish a common set of directions and priorities? Next, what should be done to get all staff committed to making necessary changes?

2. What should be done to make the agency's management-information system more useful?

3. How could the program goal and objectives be rewritten to better focus on outcomes?

4. Is the restructuring of programs and facilities appropriate? If so, what new organization design would you suggest to improve service delivery? Provide support using relevant theories of organization design and structure.

5. What financial management issues need attention? What actions would you recommend?

Suggested Debriefing Framework: 2.5 Strategic Issues Management

---

CASE 5.8   Empowering Staff to Advocate for Chicano/Latina Clients

This case describes the efforts of the staff members at the Department of Family and Children's Services (DFCS), Social Services Agency, County of Santa Clara, to develop a five-year strategic plan for delivering culturally sensitive services to the Chicano/Latina population in the county. The ultimate objective of the strategic plan was to reduce the disproportionate number of Chicano/Latina children in out-of-home placements (the term Chicano/Latina serves to describe and empower Mexican-Americans, Chicanos, as well as provide a more inclusive gender description of Latina). The strategic plan was made possible by the high motivation of Chicano/Latina and non-Chicano/Latina staff at the DFCS who volunteered countless hours to develop the strategic plan while continuing to carry out their regular job responsibilities. The staff members were empowered by the support of top management, who were very encouraging and interested in their progress.

The past decade witnessed an alarming increase in the number of child abuse and neglect cases handled by the Department of Family

---

NOTE: Gil Villagran was a social work supervisor, Sylvia Pizzini was director of Family and Children's Services, John Oppenheim was deputy director, and Richard R. O'Neil was Director of Santa Clara County Social Services Agency.

and Children's Services at Santa Clara County as a result of greater poverty, inequities of resources distribution, substance abuse, dysfunctional families, domestic violence, single parenthood, teenage pregnancy, housing problems and immigration issues. The rise in cases of child abuse and neglect was especially alarming for the Chicano/Latina population, as the increase in cases in this community was disproportionately higher compared to other ethnic communities. Chicanos/Latinas represent roughly 18.5% of the adult population and Chicano/Latina children (under 18 years) constitute 29% of the child population of Santa Clara county. However, Chicano/Latina children make up 42% of the children placed in the child welfare foster care system. During the years 1985–86 to 1991–92, the overall number of children in foster care in the county increased by 51%. During the same period the number of Chicano/Latina children in foster care in Santa Clara County increased by 91%.

Staff members at the DFCS felt that greater poverty, social stresses, and isolation among the Chicano/Latina population, plus cultural biases in service delivery, were important contributors to the problems depicted by these disturbing figures. There was growing consensus among Chicano/Latina staff members that the creation of culture- and language-sensitive service programs; research into the specific factors that exposed Latino children to greater risk of abuse and neglect; creative strategies to avoid out-of-home placements; and new social legislation were essential to arrest the spiraling cases of child abuse and neglect among the Chicano/Latina community in Santa Clara County. In many cases, client needs for housing, jobs, and financial support did not coincide with the agency's programs related to income maintenance and child welfare. In April 1991, a formal effort was initiated by Chicano/Latina workers, backed by top management and workers of other ethnic backgrounds, to address these broad issues.

Background

Efforts to provide culturally sensitive services to the Chicano/Latina population date back to 1967 with the creation of El Comite, the agency-wide Committee on Services to the Spanish-speaking population, a group formed by the small number of Chicano/Latina professionals and support staff working in the agency at that time. The years since the late 1960s also saw a metamorphic transformation in the economic and social fabric of Santa Clara County, which evolved from an agrarian valley to a high-tech industrial area known for its computer-related industries throughout the world. These changes obviously had important implications for the

Chicano/Latina population, most of whom were employed as farm workers before the rapid transition. Due to the need to make the change from being employed in agriculture to being employed in the increasingly competitive manufacturing and service sector, the social fabric of the Chicano/Latina community came under increased stress.

Latino staff members were acutely aware of these problems and committed to providing culturally sensitive services to the Latino population to help it deal with the increased flux in their lives. Over the last 25 years, this group persevered and flourished and was able to make important changes in service delivery to the Latino population.

Latino and other ethnic-minority clients were expected to bring their own translators for accessing services at the agency during the early 1960s. Usually, this took the form of school-aged children, often themselves in need of intervention, translating for their parents and the social worker regarding extremely traumatic events such as sexual and physical abuse or other issues. Staff members felt that communication problems and lack of understanding of the Latina culture could result in non-Latino workers perceiving a family situation as more dangerous for the child than it was in reality, resulting in more removal decisions. El Comite members were perturbed at this practice and pushed for ensuring that only Spanish-speaking workers were assigned to Latino clients. Due to advocacy by El Comite members, this policy became formalized, and the agency started a certification procedure to enable workers to provide services to Latino clients on the basis of an oral language-proficiency test. Later on, a writing and reading comprehension test was also added, along with a pay differential for workers providing bilingual services. DFCS now provides services, through bilingual workers or official translators, in almost 30 languages, including American Sign Language. Over the years, the efforts of El Comite workers have also resulted in the DFCS providing official agency forms in Spanish and other languages.

Despite these successes, major problems still existed. For instance, despite the disproportionate number of Latino children in foster homes, there were very few Latino family foster homes. In most cases, Latino children had to be placed with Caucasian families, which often caused negative cultural ramifications. A staff member narrated the case of three children who were removed from the care of a poor, mentally ill mother and placed with an affluent white family. After a few months, the children did not want to go back to their mother, and the eldest child developed negative perceptions about the whole Latino culture, equating being Latino with poverty and mental illness.

Thus El Comite members became increasingly aware that "our successes were largely piecemeal and incremental and there was a need to develop a comprehensive plan to effectively deal with the rapidly deteriorating problem of out-of-home placement for Latino children." In 1990, a sub-committee of El Comite was formed to garner support for a strategic plan. In April 1991, 48 staff members, including El Comite members and DFCS management and administration, gathered for a two-day retreat to formulate an overall vision for reducing the disproportionate number of Latino child placements. Staff members felt that the retreat was extremely helpful as "people got to know each other more intimately and started communicating candidly across levels of divisions." The committee set itself the goal of "reducing the number of Latino children who are placed in out-of-home care by the Juvenile Court to at least the percentage level that the Latino child population represents in Santa Clara County by the year 1997."

To achieve this goal, the participants developed the following nine vision priorities:

1. **Responsive, Accountable, Customized Services** that are neighborhood-based, easily accessed, and combined in a multi-service environment.
2. **Empowering Culturally Competent, Client-Oriented Services** that are customer-focused and sensitive to clients' cultural and language needs.
3. **Advocacy for Family Preservation Policy** to provide services that keep families together.
4. **Advocacy for Family Programs** with an emphasis on prevention.
5. **Collaborative Resources and Strategies** that use partnerships and a team approach.
6. **Professional Development/Cross Cultural Expertise** to enhance employees' skills.
7. **Raza Staff Development** involving recruitment and retention of Latino workers.
8. **Client Resources Development** through legislative action and inter-agency cooperation.
9. **Agency Risk-Taking** to successfully implement the plan.

After the establishment of these vision priorities, nine staff committees were formed involving 84 staff members, guided by a steering committee composed of 22, and supported by 11 office professionals. The goal was to formulate a detailed and specific strategic plan to achieve the vision priorities. Through the reassignment of a staff member, the agency director created a temporary planner position (80%). The Harvard Strategic Planning Model for Non-Profits (Hardy, 1984) was followed in developing the detailed plan since staff members had experience in the implementation of this model and were willing to play the role of "Process Champion" to coordinate the whole activity. This model requires the articulation of a long-term goal for each activity area. Once the particular sub-goal has been accomplished, the long-term goal is then broken up into sub-goals with expected outcomes for each sub-goal. These expected outcomes, in turn, become objectives for further planning for achieving the outcomes, and staff members are required to visualize the relevant collaborating units and organizations for the objective, the measurement of achievement of the outcome and the responsible staff member(s) for the outcome.

Nine working groups were also formed to come up with specific recommendations in each of the following service/activity areas:

1. Emergency Response

2. Dependency Investigation

3. Family Preservation and Support Services

4. Continuing Services

5. Foster Home Recruitment and Licensing

6. Adoptions

7. Professional Development/Cross-Culture Expertise

8. Research

9. Policy, Planning and Legislation

Each group was co-chaired by a member of El Comite and the program manager for each of the above activities and included Latino and non-Latino workers who volunteered for each area according to their own expertise and interests. The working groups met approximately twice a month over an 18-month period and translated the vision statements into specific goals, objectives, and action steps, along with measures of performance for each action step. Based on the required services to implement the vision priorities and actual service delivery system, the working groups identified gaps in service delivery that had to be filled through program addition, expansion, or improvement.

The working groups periodically shared their progress with the steering committee, which met at least once a month and critiqued and approved the working groups' suggestions. Staff members felt, "Initially the group members were hesitant to be open and honest in communication but were later able to develop a great deal of trust and communication, which facilitated the exchange of opinions across agency hierarchy, sub-sections and ethnic boundaries."

In January 1993, the final plan was adopted by the steering committee and the top management group. The plan has subsequently been sent to and approved by the county board of supervisors, some of whom have expressed great interest and the desire to be kept informed every six months about the plan's progress. The strategic plan summary included nine long-term goals for each activity area related to each working group, along with sub-goals for each activity area and expected outcomes for each. (These goals and outcomes are included in Case 6.9, Evaluating a Strategic Plan for Children's Services.)

Conclusions and Future Prospects

The DFCS staff has evolved an ambitious strategic plan to deal with the disproportionate number of Latino children in out-of-home placement. The plan relies on the development of culturally sensitive services at each step of the Family and Children delivery system to ensure better mutual understanding and respect on the part of workers and clients. The plan emphasizes family preservation and the need to focus on preventive aspects of service delivery to reduce public costs and private suffering.

In working on the strategic plan, staff members felt that they and the agency took on a lot of risk, as it was the first major assessment of minority issues within the agency. The staff and the administration risked criticism for participating in such a nontraditional effort focused on a single problem area. Further risks will have to be taken in the political, legislative, and budgetary arena in order to implement the plan.

A high level of trust and dedication was required because, over the years, line workers and program managers rarely met to engage openly in a program planning process. In addition, line staff rarely met, let alone consulted with, top management. Given such limited opportunities to promote collegiality, it was not surprising that it took time to develop trust and shared understanding. In the past, the suggestions made by line staff were rarely acknowledged or accepted by middle and top management. These perceptions were challenged early in the planning process by the openness, receptivity, and encouragement of senior managers. There was a willingness to deal with internal and external obstacles. Internally, the staff's sense of isolation and separateness was dealt with directly when supervisors and managers were strongly encouraged, from the top, to release line staff to attend El Comite meetings. Externally, top management secured the participation of line staff from other county departments to participate (e.g., public health nurse).

Similarly, top management quickly addressed criticism by Anglo staff members who were not involved in this non-traditional planning effort focused on a single problem area. As the planning process neared completion, anonymous letters from staff who felt excluded were sent to the board of supervisors. They were swiftly addressed by the agency director.

The biggest task ahead lies in acquiring the necessary resources (e.g., more funding for family preservation services) and accomplishing the necessary legislative changes (e.g., more prevention, rather than crisis management legislation, extension from the 48 to 72 hours to investigate alternatives to court dependency). These issues will require considerable ingenuity in view of the funding cuts in the state and the bureaucratic nature of the bodies involved. Staff members plan to investigate the possibility of federal and private funding sources through grant writing as a supplement to state and county funding. The staff members also feel that an extensive publicity campaign will be required to reach public officials, representatives, and the general population.

The process of involving staff at all levels in addressing the needs of Latino children was a significant empowering of staff to plan together for the future. As noted by a co-chair of the steering committee, the "El Comite planning process involving 84 staff members has fundamentally changed the culture of the organization for the better." New lines of communication have been opened, and a new level of teamwork is evolving. Staff members also feel that they have a broader view and understanding of the total organization as a result of the interaction with staff members from other units during the planning process. The planning process also helped the staff members to sharpen their thinking by encouraging them to specify goals, outcomes, and measures. Staff members, including top management, also acquired useful experience in conducting strategic planning. The process also helped staff members acquire a greater sense of empowerment by active involvement in an organizational-change process. As one of the important spin-offs, the El Comite structure of staff participation has spawned the development of similar staff groups related to the needs of African American and Asian American families and children. A staff member has been assigned to assist in the development of an African American service project. The Asian American initiatives are still at the beginning stage. The support and encouragement of top management, combined with the energy and

investment of supervisory and line staff, have resulted in staff empowerment and a positive change in the agency's culture.

Reference

Hardy, J. (1984). *Managing for impact in nonprofit organizations: Corporate planning techniques and applications.* Erwin, TX: Essex.

Discussion Questions

1. Does this process appear to have been successful in addressing
    the needs and issues described at the beginning of the case?
    What gaps, if any, need attention?

2. What factors or strategies seem to have been important in com-
    pleting the plan?

3. What will be the key challenges in implementing the plan?
    What should be done to prepare to address these challenges?

Suggested Debriefing Framework: 2.3 Analytical and Interactional
Aspects

❖ PROGRAM DESIGN

CASE 5.9   Banksville Human Services Center

Ned Callery was delighted when Maura Richey, the state's deputy
secretary of public welfare, paid an unexpected but welcome visit to
his agency, the Banksville Human Services Center (BHSC). Richey's
visit gave Callery the opportunity to showcase the work of his agency
and also to do some impromptu lobbying for certain items on the fall
legislative agenda in the state capital. But Richey seemed to have other
things on her mind, and after a brief tour of the agency, she asked if she
could meet alone with Callery on a matter of some urgency.

Callery could hardly believe his ears as Richey wasted little time
getting to her point. She wanted Callery to apply for funds controlled
by the governor's office in order to establish an assessment and referral program for people suffering from physical, emotional, and mental
disorders that might prevent them from finding and keeping decent
jobs under the state's new welfare system. Richey said that BHSC was
the perfect agency to play a critical coordinating role in the emerging

SOURCE: Kearns (2000).

managed care network that the governor wanted to establish, on an experimental basis, as part of the state's welfare-reform program: "I probably shouldn't say this, Ned, but I could almost guarantee that we would fund such a proposal from your agency. You could practically write your own ticket on this project. It's the perfect chance to expand your program of services beyond crisis intervention. If you get this contract, BHSC will be given the central coordinating role in this part of the state, involving a wide network of other social service and health-care organizations." It seemed that Richey could hardly contain her enthusiasm for the idea. She admitted that she had followed the progress that BHSC had made over the past few years and was impressed by its potential: "I've gone out on a limb with the governor by giving all of my support to BHSC on this project," she said. "The governor has a lot riding on this demonstration project, and I just know that BHSC is the agency to pull it off."

Callery was flattered by the attention that BHSC had received from Richey and the governor's office. Until recently, BHSC had struggled in relative anonymity as a small nonprofit social service organization that provided a wide range of services to families in need—individual and family counseling, economic assistance, housing referrals, job training, and other services. BHSC had been conceived as a sort of one-stop shop for social services, an idea hatched among a group of professors in the department of social work at the local university. In its early years, though, BHSC had barely survived and had once come perilously close to bankruptcy. Only an 11th-hour rescue by the United Way saved the day.

Callery had been hired as the executive director two years ago and immediately launched a strategy of aggressive growth. During his interview for the job, he impressed the board by asserting that BHSC had been far too timid in its strategy. He was convinced that BHSC was well positioned to respond to the many needs brought about by the national welfare reform effort. He provided an impromptu environmental scan and portfolio analysis during his interview, showing that BHSC had some comparative advantages that had not been exploited. He said that only an aggressive growth strategy would ensure the future of BHSC.

Callery soon lived up to his promise by securing several major grants, including a national demonstration grant, to integrate several types of family services that had previously been spread among different agencies with little coordination. He also added a sophisticated and highly effective advocacy division, which had played an important role in crafting the state's welfare reform bill. BHSC grew horizontally as well as vertically. It had opened three branch offices in the last six months, providing easier access to families in need. Moreover, new services had been added to the portfolio, including a drug and alcohol assessment and referral program. In the past two years, BHSC had nearly doubled its budget, with proportionate growth in the number of paid and volunteer staff.

As he listened to Richey conclude her pitch, Callery felt justifiably proud of what he and his staff had accomplished. In many respects, Richey's overtures were confirmation that BHSC was an agency on the move. This could be the right opportunity to launch BHSC on a trajectory of continued growth and greater statewide influence for many years to come.

"Your idea is very interesting, Maura," Callery said. "I am inclined to submit a proposal. But I need to give it some serious consideration and talk with my staff about it. Of course, in order to make a major commitment like this, I'll need the endorsement of my board of trustees. Coincidentally, they have a meeting at the end of next week. I'll put this at the top of their agenda and will give you an answer then."

Richey pressed on, "OK, Ned, but don't take too long. The window of opportunity may close very rapidly. The governor's office is very high on BHSC right now, but there are other agencies that have been lobbying for this assignment. The governor would like us to make a decision soon in order to avoid increasing pressure." As he walked her out of the building, Callery assured Richey that this opportunity would be his top priority.

When Callery returned to his office, his mind was racing. There was much to do before sharing the idea with his staff and the board of trustees. He decided to devote the weekend to preparing a preliminary assessment of the impact the program would have on his agency. How many people would be needed to staff the new program? What skills would they need? Would the program have a significant impact on facility space? How would it affect the mission of BHSC? The staff and trustees would have many questions, and he wanted to be as thorough as possible.

Even before beginning his analysis, however, Callery was bothered by a nagging feeling. He should have been euphoric about Richey's proposal. After all, she had practically told him that the program was his if he wanted it. But he was beginning to suspect that BHSC might be biting off more than it could chew. He was even more skeptical after completing his weekend analysis. He estimated that no fewer than 15 new staff, 12 professionals and 3 clerical workers, would be needed to support the program. This would represent a 50% increase in staff size. The coordinating program would likely need its own offices and support infrastructure, including an elaborate information system for tracking clients through the maze of social service and health care providers who would be part of the managed care network. Ned wondered whether the culture of the managed care program would be compatible with the culture of the traditional BHSC services. And he wondered whether BHSC would need to stretch the interpretation of its mission in order to accommodate the new program.

Ned also worried about his clients, the individuals and families who had come to rely on BHSC for a wide variety of services and advice. BHSC had become a kind of community center in a blighted neighborhood—a place where people gathered to gossip and share news, to hold neighborhood meetings, and to pass the time with friends. How would the radical expansion of the portfolio affect this informal mission of BHSC? Would BHSC be able to remain in its current facility? It seemed likely that the organization would need to move to a larger building in order to accommodate everyone under one roof. Or perhaps the various parts of the organization could be housed in different locations around town.

Finally, there was the political uncertainty connected to the program. The governor was facing a tough opponent in next year's election, a candidate who was strongly opposed to the state's welfare reform program, including the managed care component. Most political experts gave the governor no more than a 50% chance of re-election. Some insiders said his chances were even worse.

Beyond all the facts and figures, however, Callery simply had a gut feeling that now was not the appropriate time to be taking on a significant new responsibility. He scheduled a Monday morning breakfast meeting with his board chair, Lorna DeFazio, to discuss the idea with her. "On the one hand, the past twenty-four months have brought dizzying growth to BHSC," he told Lorna. "With the staff stretched to the limit, we have not had time to develop the administrative infrastructure to keep pace with the growing portfolio of programs, not to mention our new branch offices. Most days we just fly by the seat of our pants, making up the rules as we go along. We need time to consolidate the gains we have made over the past two years. Also, this new program would fundamentally alter our relationship with nearly every other social service agency in the region and perhaps with our clients in this neighborhood. We would become the gatekeeper for clients and funds. We have good relations with these agencies now, but I am sure that this program would create some tensions for us that might affect the success of our other programs.

"On the other hand, there are huge risks in not taking on this program. I suspect we will lose favor in the governor's office. A chance like this may never come along again. This could be our one opportunity to really solidify our position. If only Maura had brought us this opportunity next year, or even last year before we undertook all these new responsibilities! Despite its appeal, I'm worried that now is not the right time for us to take on this major new responsibility."

Lorna was surprised by Ned's ambivalence toward the opportunity. Was this the same man who had boldly pushed BHSC to the forefront of the human services marker? Over the past two years, Callery had taken some risks that had made even the most entrepreneurial board members a little nervous. "Can we afford not to take this opportunity?" she thought. "But maybe now is just not the right time."

Ned Callery faces a very difficult decision. His organization is desperately in need of some breathing room and a chance to consolidate its recent gains. A period of stability would help BHSC develop the operating procedures, policies, and administrative infrastructure it needs to support and sustain its expanded role. But what will happen if Callery turns down the opportunity that Maura Richey has practically handed to him on a silver platter? Will BHSC lose credibility in the governor's office? Will it lose momentum? After all, growth opportunities don't always happen just when we are ready for them. What message will Callery send to the employees and the board if he decides to turn down this opportunity? Will they conclude that he has become complacent?

Discussion Questions

1. Besides the questions and concerns raised by Ned Callery, what other factors should he and his staff consider in making this decision?

2. With the information provided, what would be your decision? With the choice you made, what would be the downside factors which would need to be addressed?

Suggested Debriefing Framework: 2.6 Policy Practice

CASE 5.10   Massive Retrenchment

Centerfriends, an agency based at the state prison, has worked for the past 25 years with prisoners and their families providing direct support services, health education for the inmates, and advocacy on behalf of the incarcerated and their families. Centerfriends was founded to provide hospitality for visitors who had to wait outside the gates when coming to visit at the prison. Over time, the hospitality center became a visitor center. It provided food, day care, information regarding the prison, and other support services. Centerfriends then decided to expand the services to other state prisons. After operating visitor centers at many of the state prisons, Centerfriends worked with legislators to create legislation that would require the Department of Corrections to contract with a nonprofit, to run visitor centers at all state and federal prisons throughout the state. The legislation passed and the Department of Corrections contracted with Centerfriends for approximately $2 million to operate the visitor centers at 35 different sites.

As Centerfriends was expanding their visitors program and managing their state contract, they also received a large grant from the local medical school to administer HIV/AIDS education programs at the prison. With this grant money, they developed a Centerfriends health education division, staffed by a division director, program coordinator, case managers and support staff. By 1999, Centerfriends had expanded to become an agency with a $3 million dollar operating budget and approximately 150 staff.

Then, in July 2000, Centerfriends received word that the Department of Corrections did not accept their bid to run the visitor centers and had decided to contract with another nonprofit who had submitted a lower bid. By September 2000, Centerfriends had diminished from 150 employees to approximately 20 and was only operating two programs, health education programs at the prison and one remaining visitor center, which was part of a separate contract with the state youth authority.

With the loss of the state contract, Centerfriends was in the midst of a major organizational crisis, in which management, programming, and agency focus were all in question. During this crisis, the management team was made up of an executive director, health division director, and finance director. Within the health division, there were two program coordinators, and six case managers who worked at the prison and at another correctional facility in the state. In terms of viability, the only active part of the agency was the health division. However, the executive director did not want the agency to become solely a health-focused agency, which caused significant tension between the executive director and the director of the health division. The executive director's rationale for not focusing on health came from his desire to be loyal to the agency's long-standing commitment to families and children of the imprisoned. The executive director felt that there were very few services for this population and that Centerfriends needed to honor its commitment to its founding mission. However, the energy and momentum of the agency was growing consistently on the health side. Recognizing the tension, the board agreed in December to give the executive director three months to demonstrate some progress in funding for programs related to families of the incarcerated.

As the year progressed, the Executive director worked on possible ideas and leads, but, in the end, Centerfriends did not have the funding nor the infrastructure to move these ideas past their conceptual stage. In addition, the management team was not communicating well or meeting regularly. From an outsider's view, it appeared that the health director was acting in isolation and was waiting for the executive director to step down so that he could become the next executive director. Meanwhile, the finance director was caught in the middle. Tension continued to grow as it became more apparent that the agency could not afford to pay for three administrators. Knowing this, the executive director announced that he would retire by the summer of 2001, but he wanted to see Centerfriends in a somewhat stable position before he left. With this announcement, the executive director received full support of the board and was encouraged to stay on as long as he felt was necessary. This left the health director and finance director in an uncertain managerial position.

In May 2001, the board was scheduled to meet to discuss agency leadership and mission. At this point, the agency staff was not informed of the possible changes and there had been no discussion of agency focus or mission with the staff or clients. Only the management team was involved. Leading up to the board meeting, it was clear that the executive director had serious concerns about handing over the agency to the health director. Accordingly, he contacted the chair of the board and asked her to call an executive session within the first half hour of the meeting. Under the rules of an executive session, which can only be called by the chair of the board, the executive director meets in a closed session with the board.

The meeting was brought to order and the agenda was approved. The chair of the board then quickly called the executive session and everyone except the executive director and the board members exited the room. This meant the health director, the finance director, administrative staff, and program coordinators who had come to give an update on their programs stood outside in complete uncertainty. The session lasted approximately 90 minutes, and then the meeting re-convened. The board then asked to meet only with the health director and the executive director. Following that session, the board reconvened once again and announced to everyone present that the executive director was retiring as of July 1, 2001, and that the health director would become the interim executive director until further discussion regarding the agency's leadership. In terms of agency focus, the health director agreed to work with the board on developing programs for children and families of those in prison; however, he made it clear that it was not his area of expertise. The executive director was asked to stay on through December as a consultant on issues relating to children and families. The board arranged to meet in September to further discuss program and funding ideas. However, the issue of leadership and focus was still in question.

Discussion Questions

1. Did the agency ever resolve what their focus would be and what that would look like in terms of programming and funding? If not, what should they do?

2. Are they in any better shape than they were six months ago? If not, what steps should be taken now?

Suggested Debriefing Framework: 2.5 Strategic Issues Management

Case 5.11   Productivity and Performance

The Southside Services Center provides a variety of services to many different clients, serving three counties with a $10-million budget. Programs include:

- Employment Development, which is responsible for finding jobs for low income people,
- Teen Mental Health, which provides counseling for teenagers, and
- Home Care, which provides services including bathing, meal preparation, and limited house cleaning to physically disabled adults and those recuperating at home after being in the hospital.

The agency's CEO, Jan Park, is currently facing significant challenges related to productivity in the Employment Development and Teen Mental Health programs. The third program, Home Care, is operating well; but recently, problems with a particularly difficult client are creating serious public-relations issues.

Performance-Based Contracting in Employment Development

The Employment Development program is divided into two segments. The first segment, called the JOBS Program, is responsible for obtaining jobs for people and making sure that they retain their jobs. The second segment provides support services, including transportation, day care, tools, uniforms, and other supports that help people get to jobs and stay on the job. This segment differs from the JOBS Program in that the staff does not provide counseling services.

Two years ago, Jan Park, as a new chief executive of the agency, concluded that staff members were not as productive as they could be. Having come from the business world, she was used to having people measured for their productivity and given incentives. With the backing of the board, she initiated a productivity incentive system in the Employment Development program. Each job had measurable and specific outcomes against which people's performance could be determined. It took about six months of hard work to come up with the metrics for determining productivity. Because this was a growing program, they were able to put aside money in the budget for rewarding those who performed beyond an agreed-upon threshold.

They tried the program for about six months and then had to abandon it because of growing staff resistance. Staff members complained that it was not possible to measure how much support they were giving to clients, and they were concerned that they were prevented from taking more time to get to know their clients. They said they preferred a gift of a turkey, say at Christmastime, to a financial bonus. In other words, financial incentives around productivity had become more of a hassle than they were worth.

This last month, the CEO decided to re-open productivity standards, because both county and city governments, which provide 90% of agency income, have decided to initiate performance based contracts. Rather than provide funds on a cost-reimbursement basis, they contracted for the agency to provide services with specific outcomes. The agency is reimbursed after review of performance. For example, the county provides the agency with funds after the program places a person on a job and then provides additional funds at the end of the 30 days, 60 days, 90 days, and 120 days that they remain on their jobs. The county has established the threshold that 70% of the people they have contracted for should be on the job for 120 days. If the program falls below that threshold, they will not receive full reimbursement. If they exceed that threshold, then additional money will be made available for the agency. In spite of these developments, the CEO faces considerable resistance from staff members who want to retain their former ways of providing services.

Productivity Incentives in Teen Mental Health

A similar challenge faces the Teen Mental Health program. Until three years ago, the Teen Mental Health program received a cost-reimbursement contract from the local mental health board for services rendered. They only needed to submit an invoice for a standard monthly amount, providing data on services provided. For the past three years, the funding has shifted to productivity-based contracting. This means that the agency can receive funds only after providing designated services. Staff members are required to document results, which are submitted to the mental health board. If they don't produce, then they aren't paid. On the other hand, if they can exceed the pre-established production threshold, then they receive extra money.

Calculating the unit costs is very important in such a system. For example, conducting a diagnostic assessment for chemical abuse is determined to cost $98 per hour. The state assumes that costs for each client will be at this amount. The state further assumes that staff will have 20 hours a week of billable time (50%), the formula used by the agency to construct their budget. The manager of the counseling unit must make sure that staff are being productive and documenting their performance. The program manager is concerned when some staff members spend an inordinate amount of time informally talking during the day, giving outside presentations, coming in late, or leaving early. She also needs to ensure that they are efficient in doing their paper work.

About six months ago, she initiated a program to provide financial incentives for those in the counseling unit who exceeded productivity standards. She did this because she became aware that different staff members have different work-performance styles. Clearly, some are much more competitive and push themselves to make more money by exceeding productivity standards. She thought this could also be a plus for the agency because the more that staff members exceed the standard, the more money the agency would receive. Some staff members are willing to put in extra hours (as many as 50 to 60 hours per week) to earn the extra $15 per hour. On the other hand, those staff members who were satisfied with putting in a regular work-week understood that they were not eligible for the incentive pay. The manager was pleased with this arrangement of rewarding highly productive staff.

A week ago, the human resources department began raising concerns with the agency CEO because people in Teen Counseling were receiving extra pay. Apparently, staff members from other units, such as Home Care, were complaining that the approach in Teen Counseling was unfair. As a result of these attacks, the human resources department agreed that equity should occur across all units of the organization, and the program manager was accused of having "elitist practices." Instead of continuing with an incentives system, they wanted her to provide only normal salary increases for all her staff, in the same manner as for everyone else in the agency.

The HR director was concerned that the other departments are not based on fee reimbursement and therefore do not have funding available to reward people who perform at a high level. The Teen Counseling manager argued that their staff does not put in the extra hours that her staff does. They can leave work early or go to workshops without having to worry about the pressure of meeting productivity standards. All agreed that within the overall organization, there may be a clash of cultures. The Teen Counseling director wants to be a good team player within the organization, but she is very upset at the prospect of abandoning a system that works well for her program.

Discussion Questions

1. What are the pros and cons of inaugurating a pay-for-performance program in this agency? Is it worth the effort to change to this system? Should Employment Development and Teen Mental Health use the same system? Why or why not?

2. In this case, the units receiving productivity reimbursements operate within a larger context of other units receiving their funding from sources that are not productivity oriented. Can a managerial case be made for rewarding different units differently based on their funding streams?

3. How should the director deal with inevitable staff resistance?

Suggested Debriefing Framework: 2.5 Strategic Issues Management

CASE 5.12   Responding to Changing Client and Community Needs

Hope Services, a nonprofit organization whose primary service is the provision of job counseling and training to unemployed automotive factory workers, has been in operation for nearly two decades. The organization is highly regarded both by the automotive industry and in the human services field. The recently named executive director of Hope Services holds a client advisory committee session each month. Typically, about 10 clients come to each meeting to voice their concerns or provide advice concerning the direction of the organization. They are highly relied upon to craft the vision of Hope Services. The executive director is joined by several other staff members, including the director of programs and services. The rest of the staff is briefed on the meeting topics and major issues that were raised by the clients. The client input is highly regarded among all staff members as it is seen as central to providing effective service.

At this month's meeting, a group of 20 clients arrive to raise a common concern. They are displeased with the training they are receiving. They contend that the organization has not advanced the substance of its training courses to effectively prepare the clients to work in today's technologically sophisticated factories. They recommend using more organizational resources to obtain new machinery that matches the equipment found in the automotive factories.

The executive director, in typical fashion, begins a more thorough inquiry into the clients' suggestions. In meetings with staff, he learns that 90% of the clients completing the program are able to successfully find employment in major automotive factories. Most of his staff recommends incremental changes as opposed to the radical changes proposed by the clients. In order to fulfill her due diligence to the clients, the executive director contacts several industry experts. It is evident from discussion with the experts that clients who complete the program are sufficiently trained to secure employment in most major automotive factories. Yet, there is little chance that they will be able to advance into higher paying and more stable employment positions, as they have insufficient knowledge of state-of-the-art automotive manufacturing techniques. Moreover, most of the organization's curriculum will be inapplicable and obsolete within the next 10 years, as more manufacturers invest more resources in hybrid and fuel cell powered engines.

Astonished by these findings, the executive director contemplates the massive organizational changes that would be required to implement a more technologically advanced curriculum. A great deal of capital would have to be raised to afford the new machinery. She will have to convince funders that there is a need for change after reporting the great successes of the program in a recent newsletter. Many funders were convinced of the program's effectiveness by the remarkable employment rate for program participants. Would they feel deceived by those statistics now that major changes are being recommended?

In addition, many reliable and committed staff would have to be laid off in order to bring in more technologically competent staff. This type of mass exodus could change the entire culture of the organization. It would be quite difficult to retain the compassionate atmosphere in the absence of the staff members who have developed and fostered it over the 20-year history of the organization. Would this change jeopardize the effectiveness of the program? What are the consequences of failing to change?

Discussion Questions

1. Given the information provided about present and future needs, should the program make the radical changes that are suggested?

2. If it does make those changes, how can it deal with the antici-pated negative side effects? If it does not change, what is likely to happen when the program model becomes obsolete?

Suggested Debriefing Framework: 2.6 Policy Practice

❖ CHAPTER EXERCISES

Exercise #1

Similar to the classroom exercise in Chapter 3 on comparing organiza-tional charts, students could bring the executive summary of the most recent strategic plan from their fieldwork agency to share in small groups. The implementation plan and the progress reports could be reviewed as well. The purpose would be to compare and contrast the plans and then engage in a class discussion of the comparative strengths and limitations of the plans reviewed. Plans could also be assessed in relation to different models or formats for strategic planning noted in the readings (e.g., Allison & Kaye, 1997; Bryson, 1995).

Exercise #2

A second exercise could simulate the program-design process whereby the class or instructor identifies a program need or opportunity (e.g., an after-school program in a low-income community) and divides the class into work groups to address the different components of the Kettner, Moroney, and Martin (2008) model. If possible, use evidence-based practice guide-lines and research methods to identify program models that are likely to be most successful. After each group completes its work, it can report out and see the full scope of the program-design process.

Design Phase

Defining the problem

Assessing needs

Setting goals and objectives

Selecting intervention strategies

Implementation Phase

Using goals and objectives

Program design elements

Information systems

Budget and planning

Evaluation

6

Financial Management and Information Systems

❖ FUND DEVELOPMENT

CASE 6.1   Should We Accept the Gift?

Five years ago, our founder—and current executive director—developed our organization, Second Chance. We are an agency that provides counseling and skill development for professional women whose substance-abuse problems have caused great upheaval in their lives. As a result of their alcoholism or drug use, they have become alienated from their families and dismissed from their jobs. We provide both in-house treatment for 30 days and intensive follow-up. Our dedicated commitment has resulted in a success rate of 80%.

In fact, we have done so well that we have broadened our target population to include low-income women who need employment-skill development. This was made possible through a government grant of $2 million. We continue to provide services for professional women who have substance abuse problems, but this population now represents only 10% of our total budget. I was hired as the director of development last year to help diversify our funding.

Because of our success and higher visibility, we have attracted the attention of the Altruistic Foundation. It has offered to help us develop an endowment program. We had actually been thinking about this for awhile because we knew we needed to diversify our funding base. It's quite possible that someday our large public grant could either be reduced or discontinued. Although we had considered developing an endowment program, current demands on us have been so great that we decided to put this issue on the back burner. Now, given the Altruistic Foundation offer, we are considering making this a priority.

There is a catch, however, to the offer. They are prepared to give us $400,000—if, in four years, we can match their amount with $400,000, privately raised. Specifically, what they propose is that in each of the next four years, if we can raise a minimum of $100,000 each year, Altruistic will match the amount with $100,000 each year.

So the question for us is: Do we want to take advantage of this golden opportunity? Our board of trustees' resource committee has been meeting with me for the past two months trying to determine how we should proceed. They've asked me to explore whether we could raise the money through private foundations, but my computer search reveals that this cannot be a significant source of matching funds—almost all foundations prefer that their funding be used for actual operating projects and not for an endowment. We've also looked into whether we could expand our current fundraising efforts, which includes an annual campaign and three fundraising events. The funds raised from these efforts are needed for our current operations; there just is no way that we could significantly expand current fundraising to meet the matching requirements.

We're in the process of exploring whether our previous donors could be considered to make an endowment pledge. About five families have indicated some interest in making commitments in their wills to pledge to our endowment campaign. But these commitments would total only about $50,000, falling far short of what we will need in the next few years.

We find ourselves in an impossible bind. Yes, an endowment of $800,000 would be wonderful because we could draw upon the interest of 5% in perpetuity. This translates into having an additional $40,000 operating funds every year for as long as the organization exists. It would certainly enhance the long-term viability of the organization. On the other hand, we're not sure if this endeavor is a prudent risk worth taking or whether it would divert our energies from concentrating on less ambitious but more viable funding efforts. The questions we face are: (1) Should we embark on this effort, knowing that the odds are not in our favor, in the hope that somehow we'll be able to pull it off? or (2) Should we set our sights on more realistic fundraising endeavors that would require passing up this opportunity to create a significant endowment?

Discussion Questions

1. If you were the administrator and development director of this agency, could you identify other possible funding that might qualify as a match to the Altruistic Foundation challenge grant?

2. What kind of due diligence should Second Chance undertake to determine if this project is worth undertaking?

3. If you didn't think that you could raise the money, what kind of persuasive case might you make to the Altruistic Foundation to get them to alter their requirements?

4. If, in response to your inquiry, the Altruistic Foundation insists on its original requirement, what would your decision be?

Suggested Debriefing Framework: 2.6 Policy Practice

CASE 6.2   Changing the Ground Rules

For the past five years, I have been the director of the Coyago Neighborhood Center (CNC). Our funds are derived partly from United Way allocations, some funding from our county government, but mostly from foundation grants. The problem with grant funding is that foundations constantly require innovative projects that can then become self-sustaining. My staff and I have been able to generate new ideas, but typically our foundation grants are limited to a three-year period, after which time we either abandon the project or have to look for sources of funds from our current budget to keep the programs going. So far we've been fortunate in being able to sustain our programs with foundation grants, an important part of our funding mix, but we are nearing the end of our financial rope. We've pleaded with the foundations to fund us for more than the usual three-year period—but to no avail. They say we have to keep coming up with new ideas. At the present time, we're running out of truly innovative projects, and we have to consider diversifying our funding base.

Several months ago, I began talking with our board president about the need for our board to become more active in fundraising. In principle he agreed with the idea, though he noted that this would be a major change for our trustees. Yes, they've had a little experience with the annual fund-raising drive and they have sponsored one special event, a dinner, but they don't have corporate connections or access to people who could make significant contributions. He agreed that we should establish a retreat for the board so that we could introduce the idea of greater board involvement in fundraising. I'm faced with trying to change the board's culture from being a fairly passive group that meets quarterly to a much more engaged group of trustees that will take greater responsibility for increasing our funding base. I realize that a major funding shift may take some time, but I think we've got to start now or else the agency, though doing well presently, could face severe cutbacks or even go out of existence.

Discussion Questions

1. If you were this director, how would you go about altering the culture of the board to enhance its fundraising capability?

2. What specific steps might need to be taken prior to the board's undertaking a fundraising campaign?

3. How do you help board members, who have had little experience in fundraising, become comfortable with asking people to contribute to your agency?

4. How would you deal with trustee complaints that the ground rules are being changed by adding major fundraising to their responsibilities?

5. Assuming that foundations want to see that your board is contributing 100% to any fundraising efforts, what kind of board policy should be developed?

6. How would you assist the board in identifying corporate and individual donors?

Suggested Debriefing Framework: 2.2 Managerial Problem Solving

❖ BUDGETING

Case 6.3   Showdown

Until this year, I had paid little heed to the directive, "Run the organization like a business." But now I am very much involved with precisely this issue.

Five years ago, I founded The New Life Alliance. Because I had been on the board of a battered-women's organization, I became keenly aware that women who lived in transition housing, such as a battered-women's shelter, were having a difficult time getting started in new housing. Frequently, these women, who were able to find low-paying jobs, did not have the start-up money to purchase furniture and appliances. At a time in their lives when they were experiencing so much turbulence, they needed concrete support to turn their lives around. I decided to create The New Life Alliance so that we could provide household goods free of charge to these women.

In the first few years, I worked hard at locating funds, mainly through foundation grants and a few wealthy benefactors. Within three years we developed a 15,000-square-foot warehouse, hired 10 employees, and drove two vans. Fortunately, companies that wanted to upgrade their furniture could donate to us, and many individuals supplied us with well functioning appliances. In addition, I went to the county administration and arranged for them to purchase appliances and furniture for clients who are on public assistance or moving into the job market.

Until this year, the operations have moved smoothly, but now some of the foundation grants are drying up and the county's purchases can only support about 70% of our operating budget. My board president has been insisting that we run the organization like a business and says we must generate revenue to balance expenses. She has told me that I must charge a delivery fee for those who receive our goods, or charge the battered-women's agencies and other organizations that refer clients to us. I have explored this possibility and have concluded that this is not realistic because the resources are just not there. Besides, charging a fee would violate the very reason for our existence. A showdown is in the offing because we have a fundamental disagreement about how we should operate our program. Either she goes, or I will leave.

Discussion Questions

1. Would you agree with the director that charging a fee is counter to the essence of this organization, or could you see a way of fulfilling the organization's mission while charging a fee?

2. What fundraising options might be considered?

3. If the board president does not change her position, should the executive work to have her resign? Or, conversely, should the board president call an executive session of the board for the purpose of firing the director?

Suggested Debriefing Framework: 2.2 Managerial Problem Solving

CASE 6.4   Improving Cash Flow

My cash-flow problem is killing me, and it could potentially cause my School for the Disabled to go under. I've got 90 students in my non-profit special school, drawn from various school systems throughout the tri-county area. Although the school operates from September to June, I'm obligated to pay my teaching staff on a 12-month basis. It is now the month of April and I'm projecting a shortfall of $120,000 by the end of my fiscal year, August 31. This is a result of a decline in student enrollment that we had not anticipated. Unfortunately, I was not receiving enrollment data in a timely manner, so I could not make mid-course corrections in reducing expenses.

I know from past experience that I should receive contracts from the school systems beginning in September, but that is not going to help me with this year's fiscal problem. I'm desperately exploring various options:

1. I could lay off non-teaching staff, but that would really crimp our operation. For example, I could terminate our development director, but that would affect our longer term ability to obtain needed outside funds to subsidize our operations.

2. I could ask our board of trustees to try to raise money, but I've never done this before. They may resent being in the position of making contributions or raising money when this was not originally communicated as a board responsibility.

3. I could ask staff to delay their receiving income, but I know they would resent this since for the most part they are not able to manage without a biweekly check.

4. I could consider a line of credit from a bank to tide me over, but I've checked this out and I've been told that I don't have sufficient collateral to cover a loan.

5. I could cut certain items from the budget—such as computers, supplies, and travel—but this would likely save only pennies when we need dollars.

6. I could increase our income by raising per-pupil fees on the premise that schools similar to ours in the tri-county area charge $10 more a day than we do. We could raise the fees by $5 and still be competitive. This would produce $45,000 in additional income. Alternatively, we could expand to take in 20 more students, which could help cover

our expenses. Unfortunately, neither of these ideas will be a solution to our current projected short-term cash flow problem because they could not be implemented until the next fiscal year. I'm not sure if a bank would allow me to apply this as collateral against a bank loan.

7. Finally, I'm considering whether to offer school systems a reduction in their per-pupil costs if they were to enter into a contract and commit funding to our school in June rather than wait until September. This would solve my immediate cash-flow problem.

Discussion Questions

1. What is your reaction to the first five options? If any of them appeals to you, what further explorations would be required before you were to move on them?

2. What should the director have done to prevent this cash-flow problem from getting out of hand?

3. Assuming option #7 is a viable possibility, what would you need to find out to determine whether this was realistic?

4. Supposing that you determined that option #7 is a realistic possibility, and it does provide a solution to your cash-flow problem, what are possible long-term consequences of going down this path?

5. On further reflection, if option #7 is not workable, what would you do to deal with the impending shortfall?

Suggested Debriefing Framework: 2.2 Managerial Problem Solving

CASE 6.5   Desperate for Program Funding

As the director of the Multi-Service Children's Agency (MSCA), I'm responsible for overseeing three major programs: (1) a children's counseling program, (2) a foster family care program, and (3) a day care program. The first two programs are self-sufficient, in that the fees and grants we receive cover our direct and indirect costs. It is the day care program that concerns me the most, because it's a cost center that is not able to generate its own funding. In fact, it is draining money from our agency. I am in full support of our board's strategic position that day care is a priority service for low-income families. My dilemma is whether to give it up or find ways to prevent its continuously hemorrhaging funds.

As I analyze the situation and compare our agency with other day-care programs in our community, I realize that our expenses are much higher because we are committed to hiring quality (and therefore more expensive) staff. There are a number of religious organizations that offer smaller programs at lower expenses. Of the 100 children in our program, approximately 20–30 each year receive special subsidy vouchers so their low-income parents can work or obtain training. Our problem is that we end up annually subsidizing each of these 20–30 children for about $1,000 each. We can't ask the other parents to make up the shortfall because this would make us truly uncompetitive. Last year our shortfall was $20,000, which we covered by denying staff raises and pushing our board to solicit outside donors. The fallout was that the staff members were very upset and the trustees complained at having this added pressure put on them to raise money. As I look at the first-quarter budget figures, I anticipate that by the end of the year we will be $30,000 in the red, and I don't see any clear answers to my dilemma.

I suppose the easy answer to my budget problem is to severely reduce the day care program by not accepting children whose families have to rely on a subsidy. However, discontinuing these children would not necessarily solve our financial problem. Even if we were to deny them service, we would still have fixed costs to pay our cooks and incur building-maintenance expenses. Nor would seeking internal or outside subsidies offer an easy solution. Given the reaction from the board last year, I don't think I can go back to them for subsidy money; they feel strongly that each of our cost centers should be self-sustaining. My staff certainly will not want to go another year without raises.

Discussion Questions

1. Given that the board has determined that day care for low-income families is a high priority and given the reality of the financial situation, if you were the executive, what kind of presentation would you make to the board? What kind of dialogue would you carry on with your board members?

2. Suppose you could find ways to reduce both your fixed and variable costs by discontinuing acceptance of families with vouchers. This would significantly balance the budget. What do you tell irate parents who come clamoring at your door desperately needing day care?

3. Can the issue be reframed in order to stimulate the possibility of other remedies?

Suggested Debriefing Framework: 2.3 Analytical and Interactional Aspects

CASE 6.6   Painful Choices

Florida's Recovery Resources Inc. is a large nonprofit mental health and substance abuse agency serving approximately 3,000 individuals in Kwimper County. We provide a wide range of services that include case management, residential treatment, medication, drug and alcohol services, supportive-living services, and vocational training. Our mission is to provide a network of mental health and recovery services that help every individual grow to his or her fullest potential.

The problem we face is that we must reduce our budget by 20%, or $200,000, for this coming budget year. This was caused by a huge decrease in funding from our two major funders: The Mental Health Board and The Substance Abuse Board. Because we did not have any money in reserve, we have had to make difficult decisions about which programs and support services to keep and which ones to terminate. This is probably one of the most painful dilemmas we've ever faced. It was like having to decide which of our children to give away.

Contributing to our dilemma is that our agency had merged only two years ago, and we were still operating as if we had two separate agencies under one roof. Although the merger was supposed to have provided for a more efficient operation, little, if any, efficiencies have occurred. No positions were eliminated during the merger. We still retain the same quality assurance, fiscal management, and human resources departments as the two separate agencies previously had. We also have a technology staff to help with our information system, and the development staff for both agencies continues. Both agencies continue to offer the same program services as before, with one focused more on housing and vocational services, and the other on case management. People have a vested interest in maintaining their own programs. In addition, as a unionized agency, we could not eliminate full-time positions and replace them with part-time positions, even if the staff agreed to this. Salaries and benefits are locked into a three-year contract, which has two more years to go. Support staff, however, is not included in the union. The organization's management team has now been called into a meeting. Our co-directors have said to us that we've got to come up with ideas to cut $200,000 from our budget and that they would welcome our suggestions. We have to consider which administrative programs we could pare down, which programs we might eliminate, and which staff we would have to let go.

Clearly, we have some painful decisions ahead of us. There is no way of avoiding them.

Discussion Questions

1. Knowing that you face a major funding cut, what criteria would you consider for determining which staff to cut?

2. What criteria would you use in considering which program to cut or reduce?

3. How would you go about processing your decision? Which stakeholders would you involve and why?

4. What planning should have been done earlier in anticipation of dealing with this kind of situation?

Suggested Debriefing Framework: 2.3 Analytical and Interactional Aspects

❖ INFORMATION SYSTEMS

Case 6.7   Measuring Performance

Child welfare, specifically the provision of child protective services, is just one of many fields of practice in which there are increasing demands from funders and policy makers to identify service outcomes. Your agency wants to increase its capacity to assess outcomes. You have just attended a training session on the development and use of management information systems.

The training session was useful in defining the kinds of measures that are used to document human services activities and results. You learned that program goals are broad statements regarding what a program intends to accomplish, such as ensuring that all children in a community are safe and leading fulfilling lives. You also learned that objectives need to be developed to show how goals will be accomplished, and that objectives should be SMART: specific, measurable, achievable, realistic, and timely (i.e., have a time frame for completion). *Process objectives* measure activities that need to occur to reach outcomes, such as how many clients are served and with what type of services. *Outcome objectives* measure actual end results or accomplishments, such as a youth getting a living-wage job. Finally, you learned that objectives can measure *inputs* such as client demographic characteristics, *throughputs* describing the types and amounts of services provided, and *outcomes,* which are the end results achieved.

You now know that every program should have a system to measure all these factors. Such a system starts with identifying the data needed to measure inputs, throughputs, and outcomes, and then developing forms and reports to document and summarize all the data. In assessing your agency's current information system, you now realize that it does not provide all the information needed to track program outcomes, let alone convey these results effectively to staff and policy makers. Now you have an opportunity to apply some of your new knowledge.

Part A: Performance Measures

About two years ago the county social service agency opened family resource centers in various parts of the county that offer services to the community as well as specialized services like child care, case management, parent education, and information/referral. The agency needs to set performance measurement to insure that 75% of the children adjudicated to the family reunification program in our Child Welfare Division will be referred to the Family Resource Centers and that in 50% of these cases they will be reunited with their families within 18 months. The managers of each resource center needs to determine the nature of the data reports needed to measure and assess the outcome of this new goal.

Discussion Questions

1. What data on the characteristics of the client population, services provided, and outcome should be collected?

2. What format could be used for monthly reports?

Part B: Data-Based Funding Proposal

You are the manager of a children's shelter. You notice that many of the children recently admitted are coming from the homes of relatives (kinship foster care). You mention this observation to your director. She encourages you to work with other managers to develop services to relatives to prevent admissions to the shelter and to preserve the foster-care placement. You know that money may be available to help with day care if this is the problem, but you are not sure what would help or what services are actually needed. The director promises to make the services of an experienced grant writer available to you if you can define your needs clearly.

Discussion Questions

1. What data should be collected to document and analyze this need?

2. How would you format the data in a report to a potential funder?

Part C: Monitoring Client Outcomes

In your county, an article was recently published in the daily newspaper about an eight-year-old child who had been waiting for two years for his foster parents to adopt him. The article stated that the rights of the biological parents have been terminated and the only obstacle to adoption is the completion of the legal process by the county adoptions unit. Community response to the article has been critical of the agency. The administration has responded by making a commitment that within three months, 60% of the children who are in adoptive homes and whose parental rights have been terminated will complete the adoption process within six months and their cases will be closed. An agency committee, of which you are a member, is formed to lead and monitor the efforts to accomplish this goal.

The committee has also been requested to design a series of reports to facilitate the monitoring of the unit's progress toward completing the adoption process and closing cases within six months after parental rights have been terminated. The reports should provide information that is relevant to line workers, supervisors, and the unit manager. The reports should be clear and easy to read. Most important, the reports should provide information that helps staff at each level of the agency to work toward accomplishing the goal of completing the adoption process and closing cases within six months for 60% of the adoption unit's cases.

Discussion Questions

1. What information should be collected for each report? Examples might include aggregate data, individual case data, and average length of time that cases are open.

2. How should the information be displayed in each report and how should it be labeled? Sample formats include lists, graphs, and tables.

Suggested Debriefing Framework: 2.4 Executive Coaching

Case 6.8   Information Services Overload

The agency is the Division of Psychosocial Medicine, a division of the Department of Psychiatry at Urban General Hospital. The division was established in 1994 to provide services to individuals whose psychosocial problems affect their medical problems. A motivating factor in the division's creation was the advent of managed care. Under managed care, the division is required to document staff productivity, patient outcomes, and cost effectiveness.

The clinic consists of three programs: the Cognitive Behavioral Depression program, the Trauma Treatment program, and the Brief Psychodynamic Psychotherapy program. The programs are overseen by six clinical staff: two licensed clinical social workers, two MDs, one PhD, and a PsyD. They are staffed by 12 interns this year—pre- and post-doctoral, as well as social work interns. Intern training consists of a three-day orientation that reviews division mission and structure, the training program, safety issues, and documentation. Interns attend a weekly seminar in the focus program where they have chosen to work. Additionally, interns meet weekly with supervisors to review cases and have progress notes signed. A weekly staff meeting serves as a forum for interns to raise concerns and questions and for staff to communicate about guidelines, clinical issues, etc.

The clinic sees a very high volume of patients: In the past fiscal year, it received almost 900 referrals. In order to document outcomes and staff productivity, the clinic management information system requires that the interns and clinical staff complete extensive paperwork. There are 17 forms to be completed by the clinician who performs the intake, 11 forms to be filled out by the primary therapist during the course of assessment and treatment, and an additional 3 forms to be completed at closing of the case. These include forms to record diagnosis, initial and ongoing assessment, treatment plan, progress, patient status (e.g., case open, closed, or assigned to wait list), consent forms, and billing.

The billing forms and progress notes are required by the hospital administration. The initial assessment and treatment planning forms are required by the Department of Mental Health Services. The diagnostic, ongoing assessment, consent, and patient status forms have been developed and implemented within the division. The clinical staff reviews progress notes for content, and signs them. The support staff is responsible for reviewing billing forms and progress notes to ensure they are complete, before sending them to the hospital records and billing departments. The research director is responsible for overseeing the diagnostic, assessment, treatment planning, and patient status forms.

The research director has observed that the clinical staff and interns are not providing all the data requested with regards to ongoing assessment measures and patient status. She has asked for an analysis of what data are missing on these forms and for an assessment of the reason(s) why the data are not being collected.

Discussion Questions

1. Now that the analysis has been completed, what do you think might have been some of the causes for the missing data?

2. If your speculation is correct, what additional steps should be taken to ensure complete and accurate data entry?

3. What steps would you recommend regarding having a task force formed to improve the information system?

Suggested Debriefing Framework: 2.4 Executive Coaching

CASE 6.9   Evaluating a Strategic Plan for Children's Services

A County Department of Children and Family Services engaged in a two-year process to develop a plan for delivering culturally sensitive services to the Chicano/Latina population in the county (See Case 5.8 for background and detail on the planning process). Following are the goals and outcomes developed by nine staff work groups.

❖ EMERGENCY RESPONSE

Long-Term Goals

By 1997, the Emergency Response program will divert the Chicano/Latina referrals from dependency investigations through early identification of problems and collaboration with community resources for the provision of services that will strengthen the family and promote a healthy environment for children.

Specific Goals

1. Develop an Emergency Response program tailored to the needs of Chicano/Latina clients.

Expected Outcomes

IA.   There is an Emergency Response unit composed of staff with skills, knowledge, and experience in working with Chicano/Latina clients.

NOTE: These goals and outcomes were developed through the process described in Case 5.8, Empowering Staff to Advocate for Chicano/Latina Clients, by Gil Villagran, Sylvia Pizzini, John Oppenheim, and Richard R. O'Neil.

IB. Effective services are developed and evaluated that involve the extended family and strengthen the client's ability to function in the community.

IC. An improved, supportive, and collaborative relationship is established between social workers and other professionals who work with children.

2. Identify service needs necessary to divert Chicano/Latina children from the child welfare system.

Expected Outcomes

2A. Social and economic problems that place targeted children at risk are identified.

3. Develop DFCS resources to address service needs.

Expected Outcomes

3A. Social worker supportive tools and resources are in place that expand knowledge and meet clients' needs.

❖ DEPENDENCY INVESTIGATION

Long-Term Goals

The goal of Dependency Investigation is to provide protection for Chicano/Latina children within the least restrictive legal environment possible. By 1997, special emphasis will be placed on reducing out-of-home placements of Chicano/Latina children and provide for an equitable assessment investigation and diversion process in D.I. that is culturally sensitive and language competent.

Specific Goals

1. Identify ethnic composition and language relative to Dependency Investigation cases.

Expected Outcomes

IA. A complete survey, ethnic breakdown, and demographic listing for Dependency Investigation is developed and available for planning purposes.

2. Develop appropriate resources to reduce out-of-home placement of Chicano/Latina children.

Expected Outcomes

2A. A plan which allows one additional Dependency Investigation day (total of 72 hours) of family assessment is implemented.

2B. A Dependency Investigation transportation support program is designed, developed, funded, and implemented.

2C. Make Family Preservation services resources available to families served in Dependency Investigation to assist them with financial crises, regardless of eligibility or immigration status.

2D. An agency-wide recruitment plan for D.I. Backup Program is established to ensure ongoing sufficient Chicano/Latina staff to cover the cultural and Spanish-language needs of clients.

3. Develop appropriate coordinated legislation to increase the number of children placed or maintained with their extended family.

Expected Outcomes

3A. Legislation is developed and implemented to expand and clarify the definition of "family" in law and regulations related to eligibility, foster care, licensing court, probate, family, and juvenile so that children will be diverted from non-relative foster care.

3B. Legislation is developed and implemented that provides for a child to be held in temporary custody for a maximum of five days without filing a petition when the parent is absent from the county.

4. Develop a process which will provide for the ongoing translation of legal documents which are acceptable to the juvenile court, the judicial council, and the local rules of the juvenile court.

Expected Outcomes

4A. A language-competent paralegal is available to D.I. for translating relevant legal documents to the respective standards of the judicial council and local rule of county to handle all administrative detail associated with court approval, so that these documents will be available to D.I. staff.

5. Develop an appropriate culturally sensitive interdisciplinary alternative process for juvenile court intervention with Chicano/ Latina families.

Expected Outcomes

5A. A culturally sensitive, community-oriented Latino family-mediation project will be established.

❖ FAMILY PRESERVATION AND SUPPORT SERVICES

Long-Term Goal

Family Preservation principles are based on the conviction and long-term experience that children are best reared within their own families. By 1997, with client/intra-agency/community collaboration, DCFS will have empowered Chicano/Latina families by identifying and developing a full range of customized services and resources. These services and resources will be increasingly responsive, culturally sensitive and competent, which will enhance, strengthen, and maintain the family unit and reduce the number of Chicano/Latina children in out-of-home placement.

Specific Goals

1. Identify the full range of needed services and resources to preserve families.

Expected Outcomes

IA. A comprehensive, computerized resources directory targeted for Chicano/Latina families is designed, funded, and implemented.

IB. A collaborative and periodic human services needs-assessment process is designed, developed, funded, and implemented.

2. Develop a full range of services and programs in order to strengthen Chicano/Latina families.

Expected Outcomes

2A. Areas with a high density Chicano/Latina population will have family resource centers that are designed, developed, funded, and fully operational.

3. Increase knowledge of SSA services to staff, community agencies, and Chicano/Latina families.

Expected Outcomes

3A. An intra-agency, multi-media Latino community-response information and educational project is established and functioning, which focuses on SSA services and positive outcomes of those services.

4. Ensure an ongoing, culturally responsive/sensitive in-service awareness program to reaffirm treating Chicano/Latina clients in a respectful, courteous, humane, and dignified manner.

Expected Outcomes

> 4A.   An ongoing evaluation process will be designed, developed, funded, and implemented.

5.   Support legislation that provides funding for family preservation programs.

Expected Outcomes

> 5A.   DFCS supports an Assembly Bill.

❖ CONTINUING SERVICES

Long-Term Goals

By 1997, DFCS will have strengthened and empowered Chicano/Latina families and children through its culturally competent, responsive, and sensitive social services staff, and its comprehensively designed continuing services. This will effectively reduce the disproportionate number of Chicano/Latina children in out-of-home placement

Specific Goals

1.   Developing a full range of services designed to meet the needs of the Chicano/Latina families and children in continuing services.

Expected Outcomes

> IA.   Explore feasibility of a case aide program to provide child/family visitation, supervision, transportation, and other ancillary services to assist case managers and social workers.

> 1B.   A procedure is developed for orientation of social workers who work with Chicano/Latina families to prepare families to accept and obtain mental health counseling.

> 1C.   Services are designed, funded, and implemented with a variety of community-based public and private agencies that can demonstrate ability to meet the needs of Chicano/Latina families.

> ID.   Determine the need for an additional Spanish-speaking continuing unit and insure expertise in dealing with sexual abuse. Provide social workers with the necessary support, training, and supervision.

2.   Identify potential culturally sensitive mental health providers who are available to and affordable for families and children.

Expected Outcomes

  2A. DFCS psychological evaluator services will be available and will provide culturally and linguistically competent psychological evaluators.

  2B. A listing of mental health providers is developed and available to case managers and families.

❖ ADOPTIONS

Long-Term Goal

By 1997, El Comite DFCS will have culturally relevant family preservation services for Chicano/Latina children who are in adoptive, guardianship, or long-term foster homes. Post-adoptive services will be provided in order to preserve adoptive families and prevent adoptive disruption. Adoptions will introduce and support legislation to open new sources of revenue to fund these services.

Specific Goals

  1. Identify and assess for use all existing post-adoptive services in Santa Clara county.

Expected Outcomes

  1A. A computerized tracking system for post-adoptive services requests and services provided is operational.

  1B. The results of a comprehensive compilation of all pertinent data relevant to post-adoptive services in Santa Clara county and on a national level is completed and analyzed, and recommendations for appropriate services for Chicano/Latina children are submitted.

  2. Improve and develop post-adoptive services to better preserve families.

Expected Outcomes

  2A. A culturally responsive, adequately staffed post-adoptive services program is operational.

  3. Develop federal and state legislation that address the fiscal and policy changes necessary to facilitate and adequately fund a comprehensive post-adoptive services program.

Expected Outcomes

3A.   Federal legislation and state regulations reflect the adoptive homes.

3B.   Enabling legislation is enacted that permits counties to fiscally claim the time spent in post-adoption services for adopted children.

❖ FOSTER HOME RECRUITMENT AND LICENSING

Long-Term Goal

By 1997, the El Comite DFCS will have enhanced the out-of-home placement program for Chicano/Latina children through the "professionalizing" of foster parents and the increased collaboration between foster parents and social workers. This will be achieved through the recruitment and retention of an adequate number of homes to allow placement choices, while meeting the ethnic and cultural needs of the Chicano/Latina children in care. Foster parents will be empowered to work with social workers as members of the service teams.

Specific Goals

1. Increase the number of Chicano/Latina foster families recruited and retained in order to meet the ethnic and cultural needs of Chicano/Latina children.

Expected Outcomes

I A.   The percentage of Chicano/Latina foster-care families available is equal to the percentage of Chicano/Latina children requiring out-of-home care.

2. Develop training for placement social workers regarding vacancy match to enhance utilization and ensure a Chicano/Latina match.

Expected Outcomes

2A.   Social workers are aware of their part in updating and using the vacancy match system, which helps social workers locate ethnically matched foster homes.

3. Develop programs to increase the professionalization of foster parents and the collaboration between them and social workers to work as a service team.

Expected Outcomes

    3A. Social workers' and foster parents' roles are clarified within the service team.

    3B. Social worker/foster parent training is collaboratively designed and developed.

    4. Develop practices to remove barriers to the certification and licensing of Chicano/Latina foster homes.

Expected Outcomes

    4A. A compilation list is completed of existing licensing regulations that currently have a negative impact on Chicano/Latina applicants.

    4B. A specialized educational program, including English as a Second Language (ESL) for monolingual Spanish-language foster parent applicants and licensed foster parents is designed and implemented.

❖ PROFESSIONAL DEVELOPMENT/CROSS CULTURAL EXPERTISE

Long-Term Goal

By 1997, DFCS will have competent, culturally responsive, sensitive, Spanish-speaking staff who will effectively serve to reduce the disproportionate number of Chicano/Latina children in out-of-home placement. Professional Development/ Cross-Cultural Expertise will develop training programs, improve recruitment/ retention programs, and create career-path programs that will enhance the professional and ethnic expertise of all DFCS staff.

Specific Goals

    1. Develop and implement a comprehensive Chicano/Latina cultural training package to enhance professional and ethnic expertise. Incentives are given to ensure a maximum level of participation.

Expected Outcomes

    1A. A comprehensive Chicano/Latina cultural-training package is designed, developed, funded, and implemented. All DFCS staff must complete a minimum of one day per year cultural-sensitivity training.

    1B. A social work cultural competency certification program designed to encourage staff to increase their knowledge and skills to more effectively serve Chicano/Latina families and children is designed, developed, and implemented, and incentives are in place to attract participants. The social worker's professional as well as life experience will be acknowledged within the certification process.

2. Improve, develop, and expand an aggressive recruitment program based on identified needs.

Expected Outcomes

2A. An ongoing outreach program at the high school and college levels will target bilingual and bicultural students to interest them in social-work careers.

2B. An ongoing formal recruitment program will be conducted at all schools of social work identified as having bilingual and bicultural students.

3. Improve, develop, and expand proactive social work retention programs.

Expected Outcomes

3A. Develop a DCFS orientation program.

3B. Develop a comprehensive Chicano/Latina care path program.

❖ RESEARCH

Long-Term Goal

By 1997, DFCS will have a comprehensive data-collection system and an active research unit that will continuously study ways to improve services. Programs based on research data will reduce the need for child protection and out-of-home placement, initially for the Chicano/Latina families, and, ultimately, for all children.

Specific Goals

1. Implement a system for tracking all data items relevant to child-welfare system families and children.

Expected Outcomes

IA. An automated data system is in place.

2. Improve and expand existing internal and external data sources and collection mechanisms in order to maximize our ability to evaluate.

Expected Outcomes

    2A. List of data needs and sources is compiled.

    2B. All collection mechanisms are identified, and the means to access them are known.

    2C. Gaps between needs and data available are compiled, and strategies to obtain needed data are determined.

3. Develop and test hypotheses based on current available data to identify barriers that may be contributing to the disproportionately high number of Chicano/Latina children in out-of-home care.

Expected Outcomes

    3A. A preliminary survey of current data indicators, trends, and patterns of child-welfare system services to Chicano/Latina families is completed.

    3B. A formal research project is designed and carried out involving (1) hypotheses formulation; (2) design of research instruments; (3) data collection; and (4) analysis of data.

    3C. Conclusions are drawn, and recommendations are made regarding what is needed to reduce the incidence of out-of-home placement of Chicano/Latina children.

4. Oversee research projects to better understand the child-welfare system population and to serve it appropriately.

Expected Outcomes

    4A. A fully functioning research unit is designed, funded, and implemented.

❖ POLICY, PLANNING, AND LEGISLATION

Long-Term Goals

By 1997, DFCS/El Comite will have developed and implemented a legislative platform with short- and long-range guiding principles that serve to reform, restructure, and prioritize a social service delivery system which supports the collaboration of child welfare, income maintenance, and employment services to better assist Chicano/Latina families.

Specific Goals

1. Expand the annual legislative priority planning. Process to formally involve all interested groups, including El Comite.

Expected Outcomes

IA. Establish and maintain an annual legislative platform from El Comite guiding principles and mission statement.

1B. Establish a formal/informal communication process between El Comite and governmental relations and planning to monitor progress and make modifications to the legislative platform and priorities.

1C. Establish a process to receive recommended legislative initiatives from the work group, and to incorporate those recommendations into the annual legislative platform.

2. Focused ability from the social services agency executive team to build collaborative partnerships that address case planning needs and frustrations through a community organization and planning approach (preventative, proactive) versus a service needs approach by becoming an integral collaborative part of the community.

Expected Outcomes

2A. Create in-house staffing capabilities that are culturally sensitive and competent that encourage an organizational culture of community input, collaboration, and sensitivity, engaging the community at large in public policy objectives affecting children and families.

2B. Create a process that will foster innovative approaches that combine community relations and governmental relations with the public and private sectors and nonprofit entities in establishing collaborative services to families and children.

3. Focused ability from the social services agency executive team to build collaborative partnerships within the social services delivery system that reduce dependence of Chicano/Latina children with integration of child welfare, income maintenance, and employment services.

Expected Outcomes

3A. Establish intra-agency collaboration that would provide supportive services leading to the reduction of child dependency.

3B. Develop intra-agency memorandums of understanding between income maintenance, child welfare, and employment and training services to provide more unified services to clients. (The members of the committees were acutely aware of the need to provide accessible services to the targeted population so that service utilization would be high. Thus, the plan built by the committee members emphasized the availability of a range of neighborhood-based services, including three family resource centers and continuous parent education in a community setting.)

Discussion Questions

1. In each program area, are the long-term goals, specific goals, and expected outcomes aligned? In other words, if the outcomes are met, will the specific and ultimately long-term goals be achieved? Do you see any gaps? If so, what additions or changes would you recommend?

2. How would you assess each outcome in terms of its capacity to be measured? How would you reword any of the outcomes to improve their measurability?

3. What specific measures or data elements would you recommend to document each expected outcome?

Suggested Debriefing Framework: 2.6 Policy Practice

❖ CHAPTER EXERCISES

Exercise #1

Drawing upon the student's experience in a fieldwork agency or place of employment, he or she can be encouraged to review the agency's annual report and make copies of the pie charts or other figures that reflect the multiple revenue sources and the multiple expenditure categories that are often shown as percentages (raw numbers are fine here, too) of the annual budget. In small groups, students can share their charts with each other and explore the similarities and differences between their respective agencies. A class discussion can follow that involves the sharing of each group's findings.

Exercise #2

In a similar way, students can gather information about their agency's annual budget development and monitoring process and share the findings in small groups, followed by a class discussion of each group's findings.

Exercise #3

With regard to information systems, bringing a copy of a quarterly report from the agency's client-information system can provide an opportunity for sharing and comparative analysis. Since logic models can provide the underlying structure for an information system, students can work together to build a logic model for a program (e.g., an outreach program to reach the frail homebound elderly). Most models include goals, objectives, processes, outputs, outcomes, and evidence to inform practice.

McDavid, J. C., & Hawthorn, L. R. (2006). Understanding and applying program logic models. In J. C. McDavid & L. R. Hawthorn, *Program evaluation and performance measurement: An introduction to practice* (pp. 39–78). Thousand Oaks, CA: Sage.

7

Human Resource Management and Supervision

❖ HUMAN RESOURCE MANAGEMENT

Case 7.1   The Case of the Missing Staff

Jane Dole, Integrated Services program coordinator, worked for a nonprofit agency providing vocational, day rehabilitation, and residential services to adults with developmental and psychiatric disabilities. The agency's location, marked by a relatively high cost of living and small labor pool, contributed to its history of financial difficulties and high turnover of staff at all levels. Jane's "promotion" to her current position was a symptom of this tumultuous past.

After her former supervisor and a few other supervisory staff left the agency, a grand organizational restructuring took place, almost solely under the direction of a somewhat new C.O.O. This restructuring meant that Jane would continue to supervise the supported employment program that she had taken on two months prior, and she would be coordinating two new day programs. In addition, she continued to act as job developer (her original position). It was not clear when that position would be filled. Task and personnel management, formerly an exciting challenge to her, became almost unbearable. Individuals in upper management also expressed feeling similar stress due to confusion about new roles and job duties. Consequently, they were not able to provide her with much needed support.

One crisp March morning, approximately eight months into Jane's new position, she received a very troubling phone call. Two staff members working in one of the agency's day programs did not show up to work on this morning. Tardiness and attendance issues were not new for these staff members; however, as time went by it became clear that they would not be showing up to work at all that day or any other day after. Fortunately, the two staff members turned in resignation notices and no formal termination of the individuals was required. While Jane got through that day by chaotically shuffling staff from program to program and performing a fair amount of direct service, she knew that the imminent future would be nothing less than a staffing crisis.

Through her own analysis and discussions with her supervisors, Jane assessed the situation. Her program strengths included employees that were cross-trained in a variety of programs. The staff from both day programs were often called upon to work in either program due to current vacancies in both programs. In addition, staff might perform duties in both programs to fill positions on days when workers either called in sick or had been granted time off for other reasons (e.g., doctor appointments, vacation). Other assets included a few key staff Jane knew she could depend upon, due to their excellent attendance records and willingness to perform "other duties as necessary," often without complaint. Another asset was Jane's flexibility, organizational skills, and commitment to the job. She often worked many more than 40 hours per week. With thought and planning she had been able to fill required direct service between herself and a careful arrangement of the staff she supervised.

Jane also considered the continuing challenges she would be facing in dealing with this overwhelming problem. The primary difficulty was the problematic issue of recruiting appropriately skilled employees. The job coaches that she supervised were hired at a salary between $8.00/hour and $9.00/hour. She knew recruitment for these positions would be challenging due to the difficulties of recruiting in the local labor market, where the median price for a four-bedroom home was close to $400,000. The one human resources employee responsible for recruitment and all other human resources issues also needed support because she was a new employee herself.

Since her old supervisor left the agency, Jane and her new supervisor both often felt confused and unsupported. Jane understood her supervisor's challenges and empathized with her, as she was often feeling the same way. However, when Jane did seek out support and direction from her supervisor, she often felt worse after their meetings. Her supervisor often projected an image of gloom and doom. When Jane would present a problem, her supervisor would concur, telling her, she "just didn't know" what was going to happen, or what they were going to do. Jane would leave a meeting with her supervisor feeling very alone, her problem unsolved.

Discussion Questions

1. How can Jane raise these human resources system issues with her supervisor in a way that the issues can be proactively addressed?

2. How can Jane and the agency use their existing assets and at the same time develop a viable plan for recruiting, hiring, and retaining qualified staff?

Suggested Debriefing Framework: 2.2 Managerial Problem Solving

CASE 7.2   Client-Centered Administration or Organization-Centered Administration?

I was a program director in an agency that provided vocational services to adults with developmental disabilities. Clients were paid for the hand-assembly work they performed, such as collating documents and putting together packets for companies that contracted with the agency. I had a situation where the mother of a client contacted me and stated that her son was upset because he was not paid correctly for the work he produced. She stated that she was concerned about the organization's wage practices and wanted to discuss this further. After I got off the phone with the client's mother, I spoke with him directly. He let me know what types of tasks he performed and relayed to me that he thought he was being cheated by the agency.

As a result, a meeting was scheduled to discuss the concern in detail with the client and his mother. I also invited a staff person from the accounting department to the meeting in order to explain how wages were calculated because I did not supervise the production side of the program. During the meeting, we looked at paperwork documenting the client's work hours and noticed several discrepancies between the in-house production sheets and his official wage statements (pay stubs). The staff person and I were unable to explain the difference in the numbers; therefore, I spoke with my supervisor, the deputy director, to ask for further guidance and to request her presence at the meeting. Unfortunately, I had another obligation and could not stay for the entire the meeting. Afterwards, my supervisor briefed me about what was discussed and informed me that the caregiver was looking for trouble. I asked my supervisor about the discrepancy in the numbers. She informed me that it was probably an entry error by staff. She also stated that it was not a programmatic issue; therefore, it did not concern me, and I should not worry about it.

Later in the day, my client told me that he felt nothing was solved during the meeting and filled me in on what took place after I left. His mother also called and relayed to me that she was still unsatisfied because the numbers were not adding up. She shared with me that she was unhappy that the situation was not resolved, and she did not like the way the deputy director spoke to her. She asked my opinion on how to pursue the matter. I informed my client and his mother that I would relay their comments back to the deputy director and set up another meeting to clarify any issues or concerns they had. The mother stated that she did not want to speak to "that woman" again and wanted to speak with someone who could give her answers. My client also asked me if I could sit in on the next meeting because he felt I listened to him and helped him more than my supervisor did.

At that point, I apologized to my client and his mother for the unresolved issue. I let them know that since they were unsatisfied after speaking with me, as well as with the deputy director, the executive director was the next person to speak with. I proceeded to inform my client and his mother of the agency's grievance procedure. I also explained that according to the grievance procedure, if my client and his mother still felt the situation was unresolved after meeting the executive director, they could take the next step and speak with the board of directors, as well as contact the Department of Labor and the state agency on developmental disabilities for further information and assistance.

I relayed the conversation back to my supervisor, who informed me that I should not have spoken to the caregiver and shared the agency's grievance procedure with her. My supervisor also stated that my client's mother was manipulating her son to say what she wanted him to; therefore, I should not have listened to either of them. I explained to the deputy director that it was my understanding that as part of state regulations, my client and his mother had a right to know about the grievance procedure. Furthermore, they had a right to take a concern—which I thought was legitimate—to the highest level possible, until they felt it was resolved. I also stated that the grievance procedure was posted on all the walls for anyone to see. It was also reviewed with the clients on a quarterly basis. I mentioned to my supervisor that I did not understand how the numbers were documented for my client's production sheets and asked her to explain them to me in case a situation similar to this happened again. I was then instructed by the executive director to let go of the issue and not bring it up again. Both the deputy director and executive director notified me that I had an obligation to protect the organization at all costs, which meant nondisclosure of certain information.

Discussion Questions

1. What agency human resources policies and procedures should be in place to deal with a situation such as this?

2. Should the program director "let go" of the issue? What should the program director do to ensure that due-process rights are ensured and the situation gets resolved?

Suggested Debriefing Framework: 2.3 Analytical and Interactional Aspects

---

Case 7.3   Union Headache

I work for a government agency that assesses families for child abuse or neglect, removes children from their homes, places at-risk children in foster homes, and attempts to reunite families after determining their need for support services. I supervise 25 overburdened case managers and have to deal with a powerful union that represents them. My budget is regularly trimmed despite growing caseloads. The clerical staff and support services are minimal. I have been told in no uncertain terms to make things work and not complain, in spite of the challenges that I face.

My dilemma stems from having to deal with Labana Smith, a case manager who has been with the agency for 11 years. For the past three years, I have received a series of complaints from clients, families of clients, and social workers about her way of threatening clients and abusing her power with them. Last year, for example, the agency agreed to a $200,000 out-of-court settlement over her alleged mishandling of a child-endangerment case. A six-year-old girl on Labana Smith's caseload was killed in a foster home, allegedly after the child's father phoned Ms. Smith repeatedly warning that his child was in danger there.

Even though we lost a large amount of money in that settlement, the director of children's services decided not to discipline Ms. Smith for fear that she could incite the agency's workers to conduct a "sick-out" or work slow-down. Ms. Smith is a union steward and has tremendous influence in union negotiations. Apparently, the director was concerned that a possible slowdown could affect the agency's billable hours and reduce services to needy clients. Moreover, a union strike would make the agency look bad.

I should note that Ms. Smith's work record reflects a mixture of strengths and limitations. She is able to settle many cases, and her numbers are fantastic. As a result of her high quantity numbers, I have given her positive evaluations. But she does not always do what she is supposed to, and her evaluations occasionally show my questioning of her methods.

Now we are faced with a new situation that may require a more drastic response: Ms. Smith may have abused her authority in taking away the daughter of one of her clients, Ms. A. I have just been informed by Judge McPherson that Ms. A. has sent him a letter stating that Ms. Smith forced her to give up permanent custody of her infant son to the boy's father in exchange for assurance that her drug conviction would disappear so that she could apply to have her other two children returned to her. Ms. Alexander also states that Ms. Smith has been spending a great deal of time during office hours and afterwards with the boy's father. She suspects that Ms. Smith is sexually involved with her ex-husband.

Because of the seriousness of the charge, I confronted Ms. Smith with her client's accusations, but she vehemently denied them and maintained that she went to the father's house to check up on the living conditions. When I asked her about the documentation for the home visits she had made, she replied, "I haven't gotten around to it because I'm behind in my paper work."

My discussion with Ms. Smith took place yesterday. In this morning's paper a big article is splashed across page one in which the reporter describes Ms. A's accusations and lists five other complaints of abuse from former clients of Ms. Smith. The article also states that the union leadership is lined up squarely behind Ms. Smith and is calling this a racial attack on a successful African American female who has been active in union organizing for over a decade. No mention is made that Ms. A. is also African American. Union officials have made it clear that any attempt to sanction Ms. Smith would lead to a work stoppage.

Discussion Questions

1. Suppose you were the supervisor in this situation. The director of Children's Services asks you to meet with her in 10 minutes. What position do you take on a course of action regarding Ms. Smith?

2. What facts have to be ascertained and how would you go about determining them?

3. If you recommend that Ms. Smith be fired, how would you respond to:
   a. the lack of a proper paper trail of mishandled situations?
   b. the lack of evidence, other than the client's word, of Ms. Smith's alleged behavior?
   c. repercussions that might occur from union retaliation?

4. Suppose later the assistant county prosecutor arranges to meet with you and the director in separate rooms. What do you tell the prosecutor?

5. Suppose that this afternoon a reporter calls you saying that she intends to do a follow-up story to appear in the next morning's paper in which she will be identifying other clients' stories about Ms. Smith's alleged abusive behavior. The reporter asks what your reaction is to these accusations since you are Ms. Smith's supervisor. How do you respond?

Suggested Debriefing Framework: 2.3 Analytical and Interactional Aspects

CASE 7.4   The Influence of Religious Beliefs

I work for a faith-based nonprofit agency that delivers services to homeless, drug dependent men, as well as to needy families suffering from unemployment and domestic violence. The agency provides counseling, a homeless shelter, community meals, job training, and employment.

I was hired to work in fundraising and major gifts, and my primary job is to locate and cultivate corporate donors as well as affluent individuals. Most of my donors support conservative causes. When I was hired, I was given a personnel policy manual that contained the following religious moral provision: "We expect Christian morals in the workplace and in the home. Any overtly immoral behavior will be subject to disciplinary action up to and including firing." This year my agency required all staff to fill out a form that requested our religious affiliation and asked how often we attend worship services.

I have just learned that Frank, who acted informally as my mentor the past 12 months when I was working with potential donors, is being promoted to director of major gifts. When the current director becomes vice-president of giving, Frank will be my new supervisor. I am delighted to learn this because Frank has been so supportive of me professionally and was also tremendously helpful in getting my mother into assisted living. He deserves the promotion because he has worked so hard to develop the agency's donor base. He's literally raised hundreds of thousands of dollars for the agency in the past seven years.

Here's my dilemma: At lunch last week, Frank confided to me that he is gay. He said he could trust me and respected my views. Frank said he is thinking of getting married in Canada to a man he has been with for 12 years. I didn't know what to say except to wish him and his partner well. I've been thinking about the matter all week, and I'm about to meet with the CEO who said he wanted to discuss something confidential with me. I suspect the CEO has heard rumors about Frank, and I'm worried that he may ask me to confirm if I know anything about Frank. I know that the agency is homophobic and that, if word got out, our conservative donors would direct their philanthropic dollars elsewhere. Services to our clients could seriously be jeopardized. I'm in a real quandary about how I should handle this upcoming meeting with the CEO.

Discussion Questions

1. If you truly have the best interests of the agency at heart, what would your position be regarding Frank?

2. Suppose you consider yourself a good Christian. You personally do not consider homosexuality as being immoral, but you recognize that this is the stance of your CEO and of certain major donors. How do you reconcile your own beliefs with those of your agency?

3. What factors would you consider in responding to the CEO's inquiry about Frank?

4. What if you tell the CEO that you will not answer his inquiry about Frank because this is a private matter, and he responds that your own job is on the line if you are not forthright in what you know?

5. What if the CEO hints that if Frank were to leave for any reason you would be considered for a promotion?

6. Should any changes be made in agency policy? What would your answer be if the organization received government funding?

Suggested Debriefing Framework: 2.4 Executive Coaching

CASE 7.5   Growing Pains

A large nonprofit health organization has recently experienced significant growth. The agency is a national call center staffed by approximately 200 line staff whose primary role is to provide cancer information and patient resources to callers. Line staff members are required to possess a college degree and complete three weeks of training prior to starting their positions. Line staff members are continuously being hired and trained in order to respond to high call volume. Line staff members receive a competitive salary, although not sizable, and generous benefits, including three weeks of paid time off in the first year. Line staff members are grouped into teams of approximately 15 and are assigned to a team supervisor. Despite being organized in teams, little interaction occurs between team members, as they are generally not seated near one another and do not have a need to work together. There are between 12 and 15 team supervisors; three to four supervisors report to one team manager, who is overseen by the center manager.

Morale among line staff is very low. The primary indicators of low morale are the high turnover rate and the fervently voiced frustrations and boredom of line staff. The frustrations of line staff stem from a lack of autonomy and a lack of opportunities for advancement. First, the activities of the line staff are dictated by numerous strict procedures. Appropriate responses to calls are outlined in a database, and calls are strictly monitored to insure adherence to these procedures. Line staff members are prohibited from providing information that was not available in one of their databases and are monitored, up to eight times monthly, both remotely and face-to-face by a member of the quality team and a team supervisor. Calls are awarded scores ranging from zero to 100. These scores, along with attendance and productivity—number of calls taken—form the basis of performance evaluations. As a result of the rigid procedures and monitoring schedule, line staff members feel discouraged from developing any independent knowledge or from responding uniquely to callers. In addition to being frustrated by the lack of flexibility in call handling, front line staff members object to the inflexibility in scheduling. Front line staff members are required to begin and end work at the same times every day and to take scheduled breaks and lunches. Only a pre-determined number of line staff members are allowed time off on a given day, depending upon expected call volumes, seniority, and order of request. Thus, line staff members are often frustrated by their inability to get holidays and other needed days off.

The lack of opportunities for advancement is a second source of frustration among line staff. Many line staff mastered the skills necessary for their position within the first few months, but faced a limited career track within the agency. Although all of the team supervisors were once line staff, most line staff members left the agency before being promoted, and the demand for supervisory positions far exceeded the availability. A small number of positions are also made available to the line staff in the quality management and training departments. Promotions are not typically awarded until one and a half to two years of employment. All interested front line staff are allowed interviews for available positions at six months of employment. Thus, most front line staff interview multiple times before or without ever being promoted.

Although the number of promotions is limited, line staff members are offered opportunities to assist in the training of new staff, to work on task forces and committees, and to join pilot projects. Pilot projects include a car donation queue, smoking-cessation line, and more specialized teams that handle calls for a specific region. In addition, many opportunities exist to acknowledge the work of line staff, including gift certificates, additional paid time off, and public displays of appreciation. Similarly, procedures and groups exist for line staff to voice frustrations. Brown-bag lunches with center management; task forces; focus groups; and comment boxes were instituted to hear and address the complaints of line staff. Despite these activities, many of the most active line staff left the agency due to frustrations over boredom and the lack of opportunity for advancement.

The frustration of line staff was partly the result of the rapid growth experienced by the agency. Senior staff members often speak of the old days when a handful of line staff answered the phones by simply picking up the telephone receiver and providing referrals from lists of resources. However, the rapid growth of the call center led to the need for standardized procedures and evaluation measures. Management stresses the importance of the procedures as a means to insure professionalism. Conversely, the line-staff members are confident in their own abilities to act professionally and only resent the attempts to control their behavior.

Discussion Questions

1. What theories of motivation could be used here to inform your analysis? How would you apply them?

2. How could these jobs be redesigned and motivation and rewards systems be changed to minimize staff turnover?

3. What could management do to ensure both quality of services and a satisfied work force?

Suggested Debriefing Framework: 2.3 Analytical and Interactional Aspects

CASE 7.6   Challenges on the Line

Southeast Behavioral Health (SBH) is a community-based not-for-profit organization specializing in services to teens and young adults. The agency CEO is Elizabeth Miles. Elizabeth oversees the central administration office, including finance and human resources, and the directors of two programs: clinical services and prevention services. Although SBH has been a valued and thriving organization, the state has cut back funding for the agency by 6% for the past three years and more cuts are expected. At a recent meeting, the CEO learned that state priorities are shifting, and while the program will continue to provide counseling services, more and more of the resources will be expected to be devoted to education.

The director of clinical services, George Larvick, employs five supervisors who oversee various units of clinical services. This morning, George was confronted with several pressing issues from his supervisors. All of these situations involved ethical dilemmas with no easy answers.

• One of his supervisors, John Bartle, who oversees a substance-abuse group for young adults, has been asked by a television reporter to allow filming of the group for a national television show, an idea that seems attractive to his boss, the agency's CEO.

• In another unit, supervisor Minnie McCoy has a highly regarded counselor who, she has just learned, did not disclose at his hiring three years ago that he had been convicted of a felony 15 years ago, a violation of agency policy.

• Yet another supervisor, Rachel Yank, has just been told by one of her workers that the staff car checked out to her was in an accident caused by her 17-year-old son. The agency has a policy that staff mis-use of agency property is grounds for dismissal, and in fact, another employee was recently fired under this policy.

In each case, George must make a recommendation for action to the CEO. Each situation involves highly regarded programs and staff, possible negative impacts on clients, and, in two cases, clear violations of agency policies.

The Substance Abuse Group on Television?

John Bartle, the supervisor of a unit serving young adults with sub-stance abuse issues, told George that yesterday, one of the counselors, Walter Davis, was contacted by a national television network planning a show on substance abuse and young adults. The national reporter had read about the program in an article in the local paper. John is torn about whether to pursue this high visibility opportunity for the program. The young adult support group that he oversees has only been meeting for two months, and Walter believes that the group members are in a fragile state of sobriety. He is concerned that any spe-cial stress could push the members into relapse. But he also recognizes that, as young adults (18–20 years old), they have a right to make up their own minds. The television producer said the show would be tele-vised live and that interaction between group members would be important. Although she said that she would block out their faces and disguise their voices, John fears that other students at the college would recognize them by their gestures and their clothing, and that the exposure could have a negative impact on their future employment.

The CEO is highly enthusiastic about the interview because it could be a way to attract the interest of potential donors. She has even met with some of the group members without first checking with John or Walter. She thought that this would be a great opportunity to educate the public about the agency's value. This heightened visibility, in turn, could help the agency gain additional funding for the clinical services program.

Last year, one of Walter's 18-year-old clients spoke to a parent group about recovery. Because of the anxiety of appearing before the group, he relapsed the day after the meeting. Walter fears this could happen to several members of the group. His professional judgment is not to subject them to this high level of publicity because they are so fragile. Walter knows that if he takes this strong position, and the group agrees with him, the CEO will be extremely annoyed. He has asked John and George whether he should go against the CEO by alerting the students of the potential problem, acquiesce to the CEO's wishes and encourage the students, or remain silent and let the students make their own decisions without his advice.

Staff Disclosure of Prior Felonies

Another dilemma is facing George. Elizabeth, the CEO, has called a special meeting of George and his five supervisors to discuss a special issue that has just surfaced regarding Fred McGee, a five-year employee. Because the agency provides mental health and substance abuse counseling services to adolescents, a policy was initiated eight years ago requiring all employees to disclose at the time of their hire whether they have been convicted of a felony or misdemeanor. The policy specifically states that having committed a felony or misdemeanor would not preclude hiring. However, not disclosing this information in the application would be grounds for terminating employment.

Minnie McCoy has been Fred's immediate supervisor since he was hired three years ago. She has come to appreciate his dedication and his commitment to kids. He's regarded as an excellent diagnostician with a real knack for helping youngsters turn their lives around. The CEO just informed George and Minnie that the fingerprint and background check that has been initiated for all current employees reveals that Fred was sentenced to three years in prison for forging checks when he was 22 years old. That happened 15 years ago, and he hasn't been in trouble since.

Elizabeth has asked George and the supervisors for their input on whether or not they should automatically fire Fred. Minnie argued that the agency has made a tremendous investment in developing him, and that he, in turn, has made an outstanding contribution to the agency's mission. Furthermore, she said that the program wanted to convey to clients that people who make a mistake in life should have the opportunity to redeem themselves. One of the other supervisors stated, "A policy is a policy and unless we uphold it, we will all want to make exceptions. As good as Fred is, he didn't follow the rules and now has to pay the consequences."

Another supervisor said, "If he had admitted to his offense, we probably wouldn't even be arguing this point now. After all, we have several other staff who admitted committing misdemeanors or felonies and we hired them because they had rehabilitated themselves."

A third supervisor, whom Minnie considers to be extremely legalistic, observed, "If we don't stick to the letter of our policies, we will open ourselves up to lawsuits in the future when we have to discipline or terminate staff for not following policies. As good as Fred is, keeping him on, in violation of our policy, will cause us to have lawsuits and expensive payouts in the future."

The CEO then asked Minnie for her opinion. She responded, "Letting Fred go will convey to our clients that we care more about our policies than we do about keeping somebody who can make a genuine impact. I'm uncomfortable saying this, but I think we should get out in the open the fact that you, our director, are the only African American in this room. Eighty percent of our clients are African American, and Fred is African American. What kind of message do we want to send to the community if we let Fred go because of a mistake he made 15 years ago?"

"Since we're being frank," the "legalistic" supervisor said, "let me tell you that I worry that if the director decides to make the exception for Fred, she will be perceived by some members of our staff as making a decision based on favoritism to one group. Also, what happens the next time we learn that someone has not admitted to a misdemeanor or a felony and we like his work? Are we prepared to make one exception after another? Then why have a policy?" Elizabeth thanked the supervisors for their input and said she wanted to sleep on it before making a decision.

Use of a Staff Car

Over the past weekend, another of the supervisors, Rachel Yank, received a call at home that a staff car loaned out to one of the staff members, Mrs. Wainewright, was involved in an accident. Her son had driven the car without her knowledge or authorization. Rachel was upset that agency property was used improperly, and she recognized that this was grounds for firing Mrs. Wainewright. In fact, when she told the director of the human resources department, Rachel was told that while the decision was hers to make, she thought it would be in the best interest of the agency to fire Mrs. Wainewright.

When Rachel met with Mrs. Wainewright the next day, she was very contrite and visibly upset about what had happened. She explained, "I placed the keys on a table and my 17-year-old son found them. He's a good kid, but he decided that he wanted to drive around for a little while. We can't afford to have our own car, and he always has to rely on his friends for transportation—so he wanted to show them that he could drive. I'm really sorry about what happened, and I've grounded him for a month. I'm prepared to replace the fender."

Rachel has worked with Mrs. Wainewright as her supervisor for the past six years and knows what a good, caring person she is. She is also seen as just the right kind of person to have working with the agency's

African American clients. And because she is such a good staff recruiter for our agency, she really doesn't want to lose her. However, the human resource department director told Rachel that they must treat all staff equally. Recently the agency terminated a staff member caught stealing $50 worth of supplies. Agency policies clearly state that staff's misuse of agency property is grounds for dismissal. The human resources director asserted, "It can't appear that we're treating our employees differently. Staff will lose respect for you if they see that you are not even-handed in the way you deal with violations of agency policies."

Rachel has a personal reason for wanting to keep Mrs. Wainewright. She provides real strength to the department, and if it were not for her, they would not be as well staffed as they are. Her dilemma is whether to respond to the human resource director's request to be consistent or to retain a valued employee.

Discussion Questions

1. Which of these situations is most urgent in demanding George's action? Why? What would be the implications of not acting quickly?

2. Regarding the television show, what are the trade offs in managing the needs of the agency (as interpreted by the CEO) and the needs of the clients (as interpreted by the counselor). What recommendation should George make to the CEO, using what rationale?

3. In the case of Fred not disclosing his prior felony, how should the CEO account for the different stakeholder perspectives presented here? Should individual considerations outweigh the general policy? What should the CEO do about Fred?

4. Regarding the damaged staff car, what are the possible repercussions if management were to adhere to the policy and make no exceptions? Conversely, what are possible consequences if management made exceptions to the policy? What should be done about Mrs. Wainewright?

5. What changes, if any, should be made to agency policies or practices to prevent such problematic situations in the future?

Suggested Debriefing Framework: 2.3 Analytical and Interactional Aspects

CASE 7.7   Selecting a Clinical Director for Friendly House

After five years of relative staff stability, John Lyons, director of Friendly House, a community alcohol rehabilitation center, was faced with a series of conflicting interests in replacing his clinical director, Ed Green, who had recently resigned. John had been able to maintain within the organization a delicate balance between those groups who believed the treatment program should be dominated by recovering alcoholics and those groups who favored placing the program direction in the hands of social workers. Ed's departure had upset this balance, and political pressure from the two groups was being exerted on John. For the first time since he had become director, he was faced with a decision in which he had to balance his professional judgment and what he thought was in the best interests of the patients against political pressure from his board and from funders, all the while maintaining consistency and equity in personnel practices.

In thinking about the past five years, John was proud of how he had managed internal and external pressure and conflict and had created an effective organization. Friendly House was established in 1982 as a private nonprofit organization through grants from United Way and a local foundation. Its budget had increased dramatically through insurance payments for cost of care and grants from the federal and state governments which were channeled through the state's regional agency on alcoholism. The program had an active outpatient department and 12 residential beds for acute cases.

Pressure to establish the agency had come from recovering alcoholics, Alcoholics Anonymous, and the social-work community. The board represented these various interests. John had been an ideal choice for director, since he was a recovering alcoholic and had returned to school, where he obtained a master's degree in social work with a specialization in alcoholism. But he could still remember the phone calls he received immediately after being appointed director, telling him, "You have to hire a social worker. You have to hire an alcoholism counselor and member of AA. You have to hire an African American. And you have to hire a female."

Recognizing the competing interests, John had built his management team carefully. He defined the director's role as administrative and developmental. He created the position of clinical director to include responsibility for the treatment program. John had seen the

SOURCE: Arthur Blum, Grace Longwell Coyle Emeritus Professor, School of Applied Social Sciences, Case Western Reserve University.

need to include among the staff both social workers and alcoholism counselors who had received certificates and were recovering alcoholics. It was John's strong belief that some patients could benefit from the type of counseling provided by the alcoholism counselors and inclusion in AA groups, while others needed the type of help provided by social workers. The key to a good program was differential treatment planning and the recognition of the value of different approaches.

With this in mind, John hired Ed as clinical director. Ed was a social worker who had beliefs about treatment that were similar to John's. Ed was given responsibility for treatment planning, as well as supervision of the social workers. To balance this appointment, John hired Howard Clark, a recovering alcoholic and certified alcoholism counselor, as supervisor of the alcoholism counselors but responsible to Ed. For the inpatient program, John knew he needed an excellent administrator. He was able to hire Helen Jones, an African American nurse, as supervisor of the residential program. Not only was Helen competent, but this appointment relieved some of the pressure to have an African American and a female in an administrative position.

The board and funders were pleased with this balance. John knew that staff balance would also be important in obtaining government funding, since the director of the regional alcoholism agency, which had to approve all projects, was a social worker, while the chairperson of the State Legislative Committee on Alcoholism was an African American legislator and recovering alcoholic. As one board member remarked, "It's amazing how John has been able to keep his focus on what's best for the clients and still play all the political games required of the director."

After two years, the program had expanded to the point where Ed could not adequately fulfill his dual role. Accordingly, John hired a social worker, Jack Scott, as supervisor of treatment planning and social work on a level equal to Howard and Helen. Although Howard had not always been pleased with the treatment-planning decisions made by Ed, he felt alcoholism counselors should get all the cases. He respected Ed and did not openly challenge his decisions. Under the new arrangement, Ed was even more able to operate freely as a clinical director, since he could mediate treatment differences between Howard and Jack without being directly responsible for supervising the social work staff.

For three years, this had been an ideal arrangement. John had been free to put all his energy into administration, management, and development. Within the agency, he had developed excellent personnel policies, including internal career ladders, yearly evaluations of staff, respect for seniority, and a sound affirmative-action program. Ed's resignation to become director of another agency, however, created a real dilemma about how to fill this position and still maintain balance between competing interests.

John's board president, Jane Ames, was sensitive to the situation. She had been a major mediating force among the various interest groups. Although board policy was very clear that the board hired the director, while the director had full responsibility for hiring all staff, John had already received calls from various board members "suggesting" who he should appoint. Calls had also come from the United Way executive and the director of the regional alcoholism agency. Speculation was rampant among the staff. John knew this was only the beginning of the buildup of pressure. He had to make an early decision. He decided he would call his board president to discuss the situation and use her as a sounding board.

As John outlined the situation for Jane, her immediate reaction was, "Let's avoid the whole potential for conflict and go outside the organization and look for a clinical director who is both a recovering alcoholic and a professional social worker."

The idea was intriguing, but John wondered if the solution was really so easy to implement. John asked Jane, "If we go in that direction, assuming we can find such a person, how do we explain the decision to the board, staff, and community? For five years we have been raving about how great our administrative staff is, how great our program is because of our competent staff, and now we say that none of them are good enough to be promoted. I've also been selling like crazy the whole idea of career ladders within the agency, and staff members have really been motivated by the potential to move up in the organization. Now there is a top position available. If we go outside, what happens to staff morale? If I could justify this decision on the basis of needing a new person to initiate a program change, I would feel more comfortable, but I just can't."

"OK! OK!" Jane responded. "Let's explore the pros and cons of your other options. Who would you like to appoint?"

John thought a minute, then said, "Jack, the treatment and social work supervisor, thinks most like myself and has consistently operated in the best interest of the patients. But he is the youngest of the administrative staff, has the least seniority, and the latent differences between Howard and Jack could explode into open conflict. Appointing Jack could polarize board, community, and staff, and destroy current team relations."

Jane responded, "Other than creating the same kinds of polarization, are there other issues in considering Howard?"

"I've got some real problems with considering Howard," John said. "First, I would have to become involved in the clinical aspects of the program, or Howard would assign all the cases to alcoholism counselors. Even if I decided that a change in my role was in the best interest of the agency, Howard is not a very good administrator or team leader. He's a good team player and cooperative even when he doesn't fully agree, but I'm not sure he can lead."

Jane jumped on these statements. "We could use your evaluation of Howard's poor administrative skills to make a case for Jack with the board."

John reacted to this with considerable embarrassment. "It's not that easy. In order to keep the peace among staff, I've avoided in my annual reviews of Howard any mention of those administrative weaknesses or differences in treatment ideology. I've emphasized his cooperation, fine work with patients, and good direct supervision of the alcoholism counselors. If I now bring up his weaknesses, I don't have a word in the annual reviews to support my case.

"The other big problem is that the director of the regional alcoholism agency would be upset, since he is so committed to social workers. That might give us trouble getting approval for grants. On the other hand, the chairperson of the state legislative alcoholism committee would favor Howard's appointment."

"Wow, do I have an idea!" Jane said. "Let's avoid that whole ideological conflict and give the job to Helen. She's done an excellent job as supervisor of residential services, she's neutral on treatment ideology, she's a great administrator, and we can justify it further in relation to our affirmative action plan. Who could publicly attack the appointment of a competent African American female?"

Another intriguing idea, but John had his reservations. "The attack may not be public, but my professional social-work and alcohol-counseling staff would be upset. Helen really doesn't have the credentials or the therapeutic expertise to be a clinical director. Her public image as clinical director would be questionable, as would the public image of the agency."

Jane looked puzzled. "You have a real dilemma," she said. "Trying to keep our focus on the best interests of the clients and the agency in the middle of a political minefield is no easy job."

All John could do was to thank Jane for listening. He told her that he had better sleep on it. As Jane left, she said, "Sweet dreams, or, at least, not too dreadful nightmares."

Discussion Questions

1. What ethical issues do you see in the case?

2. What are the issues (in rank order of importance) in selecting the clinical director, and how would you justify the rank ordering?

3. Should the best interest of the patient supersede all other considerations, short of actual agency survival?

4. How far should an executive go in the attempt to maintain good morale and staff relations in omitting negatives in annual reviews that do not bear on the immediate responsibilities of the staff member?

5. To what degree should outside pressure impact personnel decisions?

Suggested Debriefing Framework: 2.3 Analytical and Interactional Aspects

CASE 7.8   Fire a Competent CFO?

For 10 years, John, my chief financial officer, has competently managed our finances. As the executive director for the last eight years, he has been a loyal employee who is committed to our organization. Our faith-based nursing home is responsible for the care of 120 patients, and it is important that we maintain financial stability and credibility. A great deal of the credit goes to John. Our board, too, has been pleased that we have always achieved high marks for our audits. In light of his positives, it is a big surprise to me that I should now be considering firing him.

This is the situation that is leading me to ponder this dreadful idea: Two months ago, when John was on vacation, I decided to examine the budget on my own. I noticed that the patients who are supposed to pay for their own care because of their high income were not in fact paying for it. These are patients whose families have insurance, or who can afford to pay for their care. When our CFO returned from vacation last month I confronted him with the fact that these private-pay patients were not being actively pursued, and, as a result, our agency was falling behind in our income expectations. John and I both acknowledged that for the past five years he had an assistant accountant who handled these receivables, but when she retired six months ago, we had decided not to replace her, and he had agreed to take on her assignment. As a result of this discussion, I assumed that the accounts receivable would be handled properly.

Two weeks ago, when I checked back with John, I learned that he had not actively pursued these paying clients. His only explanation was, "This is not a job I'm comfortable with." His response was entirely unacceptable to me, but I controlled my anger and said I would give him two weeks to move on this. Today, when I approached him, he meekly responded that he had been under too much pressure to get around to the problem of the private-pay clients.

Complicating this situation is that I am planning to leave for another position in six months. If I were to fire John, the search for a new CFO to replace him would need to begin immediately. On the other hand, in light of his long history of competence, I'm wondering whether I should just let this ride and let the next director determine a course of action. Probably the least stressful approach I could take would be to not fire this loyal CFO. I am aware, however, that such a legacy might leave the organization facing a potential financial crisis.

Discussion Questions

1. Does the executive director have cause to let the CFO go?

2. If he were to fire the CFO, should he strive to have his replacement before leaving the organization?

3. If he decides not to let the CFO go, what should he be communicating to the board and his successor?

Suggested Debriefing Framework: 2.4 Executive Coaching

❖ SUPERVISION

Case 7.9   SOS in DHS: A Problem of Motivation

About 18 months ago, Jess Johnson was appointed to direct a newly authorized and funded unit in the state's Department of Human Services (DHS). Shortly thereafter, she interviewed and hired six new employees to staff the unit. The name of the unit is Service Outreach for Seniors (SOS). Its purpose is to coordinate services for the vulnerable elderly. This is Jess's first supervisory position.

Susan Jones and Bob Martin were two of the new employees hired by Jess. Initially, both were very productive, enthusiastic, and industrious. Bob had taken the initiative to work closely with several prominent private service providers to ensure their cooperation and involvement in the new program. Susan had done a terrific job of producing publications and other materials describing the goals of the unit and explaining SOS services to the elderly. But after this initial spurt of activity and enthusiasm, both Susan and Bob have become less-than-ideal employees, in Jess's estimation.

SOURCE: Denhardt, Denhardt, and Aristigueta (2002).

Within six months of his hiring, Bob developed what Jess considers to be poor work habits (e.g., very long lunches and coffee breaks, tardiness, absenteeism). Bob demonstrates little interest in or enthusiasm for his work. Although he generally accomplishes, at least in a minimal manner, those tasks that are directly assigned to him, he rarely volunteers ideas or takes initiative. From Jess's perspective, employees who take initiative and demonstrate creativity are critical in helping the unit to establish itself politically and to create a service where none had existed before.

Susan, on the other hand, has become quite "creative," in the sense that she has ceased to check with Jess (or anyone) on important policy matters before speaking to external groups and individuals. On several occasions, she has promised things to representatives of organizations and to elected officials that the SOS program simply could not deliver. On other occasions, she has misrepresented her role as a staff member, instead leaving the impression that she was directing the unit. This has embarrassed Jess and her supervisors more than once. Despite Susan's apparent desire to be in the limelight in the political and community arena, she has developed an open disdain for the regular workload in her area. She routinely misses deadlines and fails to complete important paperwork.

Jess has met with Bob and Susan separately to discuss her dissatisfaction with their performances. Being a matter-of-fact person, Jess simply told them that their work was not up to par and that she expected them to improve. For a week or so, things seemed to get better. But the same problems quickly resurfaced.

The other four employees Jess hired are doing well. They have what she considers good work habits; they usually are on time and are willing to work hard to help the new unit succeed. They seem to be eager to do well. She can count on them to complete assigned tasks and meet deadlines. Each of them, in his or her own way, also has demonstrated a willingness to go above and beyond and to make positive suggestions for improving the operations and services of the unit.

But the problems with Susan and Bob are beginning to drag down the morale of the other employees and certainly are causing Jess's attitude toward their work to suffer. Jess has not talked to either of them about these problems for several weeks because she has not been able to figure out what to do or say. But at different times this morning, both Susan and Bob came to Jess's office asking her to recommend them for promotion to a position that opened up recently in the Child Welfare unit similar to SOS. Jess does not know how to handle these requests. More troubling, she does not know how to address the longer-term problems of motivating all of her employees to do well.

Discussion Questions

1. How would you define the problem(s) in this case, especially in relationship to relevant theories of motivation?

2. Using a contingency theory of leadership (e.g., Situational Leadership), how would you assess each of these workers? Based on the theory and your assessment, what leader behaviors by Jess would you recommend?

3. How should Jess address the larger morale issues of the other employees?

Suggested Debriefing Framework: 2.2 Managerial Problem Solving

CASE 7.10   Deteriorating Performance of a Supervisee

Mary Ann was a very energetic employee and wanted to do the best she possibly could. However, shortly after the beginning of her employment she experienced serious physical and emotional setbacks as a result of a car crash in which she was involved. She missed four months of work and seemed to have a difficult recovery period that was further exacerbated by interactions with the insurance company during the related legal proceedings. Upon her return to work she demonstrated a rather flat affect and remained closed off to most of the other team members, whom she had trained with for six weeks and formed positive relationships with during her orientation period.

Throughout the initial months of her return, the program director worked closely with the human resources department, the executive director, and Mary Ann to ensure that labor and safety codes were upheld during her transition back to work. Modifying her tasks as per a doctor's request, the program director arranged for an abbreviated schedule and access to a single-floor office building where she could complete paperwork and attend staff meetings. Mary Ann had a reduced caseload and was only working 30 hours a week during this time. She attended staff meetings and training sessions to ensure that her skill set was still current and received one to two hours of regular weekly supervision from the program director and other clinical staff as needed. Two months had passed and medical documentation indicated that Mary Ann could return to work without any accommodations. It is at this point that significant gaps in Mary Ann's performance became more apparent.

Mary Ann became quite guarded and conveyed a sense of anger towards certain staff members. Supervision became a progressively uncomfortable exercise for her. She often expressed being agitated by other staff members and professionals involved in her cases. More importantly, she noted feelings of overt distrust towards others and recurring moments of emotional outbursts. Within guidelines of HR policy, she was reminded that behavioral health care was part of full-time employee benefits. A review of her clinical notes and service-activity recording found it replete with mistakes and inconsistencies. Mary Ann was provided with detailed feedback on the areas of weakness she was demonstrating and offered assistance to strengthen them. Shortly after this time allegations were made suggesting Mary Ann's improper use of both language and behavior when providing services to clients. In detailed discussion with family members, supervising clinical staff, and Mary Ann, it was confirmed that she had, in fact, used inappropriate physical force with a client.

Four months had passed at this point, and the family that she had provided services for withdrew from the program due to the complications with Mary Ann. A new case would need to be assigned to Mary Ann if she continued working. Two weeks after this she became ill and missed three days of work. Furthermore, she arrived late to group supervision the following week. Mary Ann had seemed to reach a point of burnout. Other staff members were beginning to bring concerns to the program director about her poor performance, low morale, and rude behavior.

Discussion Questions

1. What principles or requirements of human resource management, including providing reasonable accommodations, need to be attended to in this case to ensure that laws are followed and staff rights are protected while agency quality of services is ensured?

2. What steps should Mary Ann's supervisor take to help Mary Ann become a well-functioning employee?

Suggested Debriefing Framework: 2.4 Executive Coaching

CASE 7.11   Helping Supervisors Manage Their Staff

As the deputy director of our agency's substance abuse counseling program, I oversee the work of four supervisors who oversee 30 staff members. I have two direct reports (office manager and communications coordinator). We provide drug abuse counseling to teenagers and adults referred to us by the court, and we find it of great value to hire some staff who themselves have been substance abusers and who have been rehabilitated. These staff members have a real knack for helping their professional colleagues empathize with our clientele. They are also effective in working with clients because they can convey to them that they truly understand what they are going through and the challenges they face. Though they are rough around the edges, they are street-smart and add considerable credibility to what we do.

My supervisors, however, are beginning to complain that we are on a collision course with several of our staff because they are not responsive to our job-performance expectations. One of our major problems is that some of our staff members are not completing paperwork properly. In order for us to be reimbursed, state regulations require us to keep accurate and timely records and submit proper billing that complies with state standards. Progress notes must be written up according to set protocols so that we can comply with audit reviews. Our streetwise staff members continually complain about bureaucratic demands.

Joan and Her Non-Compliant Staff Member

Peter is one person, among several, who reflects this problem. His supervisor, Joan, reports that she thinks Peter is not actually conducting home visits. She trusted him until she learned from a school contact that he had not been there to meet with his clients for two months. Moreover, one of his client's parents called to say Peter wasn't returning her phone calls. The supervisor asserts that Peter needs to be terminated. My concern is that if we are justified in firing Peter, we probably would have to fire one third of our staff who, like Peter, are not performing up to professional standards. If we do this, we're going to be very limited in our ability to work with our client population. So I am faced with the dilemma of balancing staff members who work well with our client target group versus the need to find ways to make them more professionally responsible. My inclination is to encourage supervisors to be direct with their staff members and to work with them to become more responsible. Of course, they must set standards and explain fully why we must follow through. We must also take the time to find out what may be causing some of the problems affecting them. We have to be mindful that in requiring accountability for their actions we do not treat them in a demeaning manner.

Alex—My Supervisor of Volunteers

As a new supervisor of our scouting unit, Alex is confronted with a huge problem. He has 30 volunteers under his supervision and from what I can see almost all of them are doing a great job of working with our clients. One of them, Jack, stands out among all of the volunteers under my supervision. On the one hand, he has done a tremendous job of recruiting his friends and being instrumental in growing our volunteer core for the past 20 years. As a master leader, he has been responsible for working with volunteers from eight neighborhoods, and he has been permitted a great deal of independence. Jack has also been terrific about getting a few of his contacts to make significant financial donations.

On the other hand, Jack's long tenure has resulted in his thinking he can always do his own thing, and this is causing me great consternation. When Alex took over the job six months ago, he learned that Jack had not been to a monthly meeting in over two years. This was of some concern to Alex, but he rationalized that after 20 years of service he could take the liberty of not attending meetings. Of greater concern was his not turning in the proper documentation that we request of all of our volunteers. Also, some of the volunteer leaders in his eight neighborhoods were threatening to quit because of his heavy-handed style. Frankly, I think the previous supervisor may have been lax in not setting up rules and procedures, so Jack may have felt he had complete autonomy to do things his own way. The most significant issue occurred when Jack finally showed up at a meeting this week and passed out flyers for a fundraising campaign of a competing organization. This fundraiser was happening at the same time we were conducting our own fundraising event. He ignored my request to discontinue passing out the flyers at the meeting. I am struggling with whether or not to fire him.

Erica—Supervisor of Our Day Treatment Program

One of my supervisors, Erica, recently took the reins of our day-treatment program. Many of her staff members were working two jobs, absenteeism was as high as 20% on any given day, and there was a complete lack of discipline. She suspected people were abusing alcohol and drugs but I had no verification. Then she found out about Mary Jones, one of our assistants, who has been working for us for 10 years.

Yesterday, one of our clients called, saying that she had seen Mary using crack. This was not the first time that questions had been raised about Mary's behavior. Three months ago, Erica suspended Mary for five days for being absent for a doctor's visit without being able to provide proof that she had really seen a doctor. Two months ago Erica gave Mary a verbal warning for her excessive absences. A month later, she gave Mary a written warning, in compliance with agency and union rules. When Erica heard seven weeks ago from the rumor mill that Mary had a drug problem, she considered firing her at that point, but

Mary is a single mother with two children. Erica had no firm proof, and, besides, she believes in nurturing her staff members and giving them a chance to change. That Mary admitted to the crack addiction and that she was willing to go into rehab for six weeks made Erica feel more confident about the situation.

Now that Mary has been out of rehab for a week, Erica is still concerned with whether we should keep her. Erica heard via the grapevine that Mary refers to her as "that bitch," and she walks around with "an attitude." Mary does not appear to appreciate the support that she has received, and Erica is concerned that she could easily relapse. Erica knows that other staff members are watching to see what she will do.

My Long-Time Administrative Assistant, Longonia

My problem is with my administrative assistant, who has been with the agency for 20 years and has worked with three previous program managers. She drives me nuts. Every time I ask her to do something, she tells me, "That isn't the way we did it before." Most of the time, Longonia either ignores what I say, or she manages to modify my approach. To give one of many examples, she has been doing the newsletter for the past decade. The graphic design is terrific—if it were still the 1980s. She is not able to incorporate the layout provided by new technologies, such as Adobe® Illustrator. Moreover, mailing the newsletter is costly and labor intensive, especially since we could post it on our Web site. When I suggested that we outsource some of her work, Longonia complained that I was trying to take her job away. I tried to convey that her record-keeping skills are very important but that we need to modernize.

Things have gotten so bad that it is draining my energy to try to placate her. In fact, I was so angry with her the other day over an argument about her pitching in to help clean the office that I sent her home. Here is my problem: As a long time employee, Longonia has access to information about the organization that I need; without her knowledge of the past, I would be in deep difficulty. For example, she has information about past programs that I need to draw upon. Moreover, she uses her close relationship with the board to bolster her position that the board will back her in any confrontation.

Things came to a head yesterday. I had wanted to arrange for a meeting at a hotel that was willing to give us a good price. I gave Longonia instructions to make arrangements at this hotel. Instead, she informed me that she made arrangements at the hotel she has been using for the past eight years, which I considered to be second rate. Here is my dilemma: Should I fire Longonia immediately for insubordination and move on, or should I continue to put up with her? I am concerned that in firing her I run the risk of a lawsuit (she is over 50 years old), she has information in her computer that I know I will need, and she has good relationships with some of my influential board members. I do have a paper trail of all the problems I have experienced with her. The question is, should I make a decision now or wait?

Supervising a Loose Cannon

I was recently assigned to supervise the communications coordinator who is responsible for agency publicity and information inside and outside of the organization. Michelle is a loose cannon and I'd like to fire her, but I'm not sure I can.

Since the day she was reassigned to me two years ago, I have been involving her in unit meetings with other supervisors and encouraging them working together. For example, I thought that items in our newsletter could strengthen our fundraising efforts by highlighting the contributions of our donors to a greater degree than we have in the past. Michelle appeared to be in agreement, but in our latest newsletter, she continued to focus on staff activities rather than on our volunteers and donors. The resource development director complains that since she's been with the organization this past year, Michelle has been quite negative about working together and insisting on doing her own thing.

In my discussions with Michelle, I've become aware that she has been in her job for 30 years. She takes credit for playing a significant role in heightening community awareness of our agency—and my supervisor backs her up in this conviction. As a result of publicity that she has generated, board members and donors have been attracted to the organization. She works 50–60 hours a week, produces spectacular brochures, and has responded exceedingly well to politicians' inquiries.

I've been hired specifically by the director to improve coordination between development and communications. Toward that end, I've requested work plans from my two directors. The resource development director complied with some excellent ideas; Michelle absolutely refused, saying, "I haven't done a work plan for 30 years and I'm not about to start now." She now says that she doesn't agree with the idea of featuring donors. "We're not a popularity rag."

I'm very upset with her negative attitude and would like to replace her with someone who is more of a team player, has fresh ideas, and with whom I can work more easily. I'm hindered from doing so because Michelle is very close to my supervisor. Almost every night she takes the subway home with him, since he only lives two blocks away from her. Their families occasionally connect with each other socially on the weekends. Also, she has excellent connections and has been competent in her job. Moreover, I'm concerned that she might file a lawsuit on the basis of age discrimination.

Discussion Questions

1. It is common for managers to experience simultaneous problems with their supervisors and direct reports and need to find a way to prioritize. Given these five staff members under your supervision (Joan and her non-compliant staff, Alex and his volunteers, Erica and her substance abusing Mary, the administrative assistant Longonia, and Michelle the communications coordinator), which situation would you address first and why? What would be your second priority and why?

2. In Joan's case, if you know your turnover has been excessively high and the people you bring in as replacements will have some of the same issues as the ones you let go, what new approaches can you consider to meet the challenge?

3. If you were a new supervisor like Alex, what are some examples of rules and policies you would develop to deal with staff like Jack?

4. What might be some of the consequences for Erica and others of keeping someone like Mary on the staff? What are the consequences of terminating?

5. What would a candid dialogue sound like between the executive and his administrative assistant, Longonia? Could you foresee any kind of resolution where she might stay?

6. Knowing that Michelle has a long-standing personal relationship with the director, and given the mandate to improve coordination, how should the manager approach the director with his dilemma?

Suggested Debriefing Framework: 2.2 Managerial Problem Solving

CASE 7.12   Supervising Five Case Managers

My responsibility is to supervise five case managers in our large nonprofit child welfare agency. In the past two years, our method of operating has had to change considerably. Staff members have been required to provide 50% of their time to clients and properly document their productivity for quality assurance purposes. That's how our agency gets reimbursed. The demands on our staff are tremendous. In reality, staff cannot meet the productivity standards and document them properly within a 40-hour work week. To keep up with their duties, they have to put in 45, sometimes even 50, hours. I constantly have to keep after them to complete their paperwork, and they, in turn, incessantly protest at the unfairness of the demands made on them. I can understand how they feel because so much of what they have to do does not qualify for billable hours, such as driving time to clients' homes, making needed telephone calls, and writing their progress notes. Nevertheless, this is the system we have to operate under, and my job as supervisor is to make it work. Three of my five case managers are keeping me up at night worrying how to handle each one of them.

Dealing With a Non-Productive Employee

Of my five staff, one of them, 55-year-old Ms. Rodriguez, has consistently been functioning at far below our productivity standards. Although she is American-born, she does not communicate well in English. As a result, she finds it difficult to complete her reports on time. She is terrific as a case manager working with Spanish-speaking clients, who constitute about 40% of her caseload, because she is the only one of the five staff members who speaks Spanish and knows the culture. She tends to spend more time interacting with her clients than our billing process allows. I've talked with her about this, but she replies that in her culture it is important to carry on informal conversations. It is our agency's practice to provide supervision so that staff can achieve productivity standards. It is also our practice to then let staff go who continue to fall below standards.

I've just received word that I must cut one of my staff, due to a reduction in funding. Because of her below-level performance and her inability to improve (even after several warnings), Ms. Rodriguez has to be the one. While the other staff members have complained about productivity standards, they have been able to meet and even exceed them. I'm really pleased by how energetic and resourceful they have been. Unfortunately, compared to my other staff, Ms. Rodriguez stands out as being way below par. My other staff members have been grumbling that she is not carrying her weight with the clients we must serve.

I face two major problems in letting Ms. Rodriguez go: First, none of my remaining staff speaks Spanish, and we will lose the ability to communicate effectively with an important population we serve. Second, my remaining staff members are not members of a minority group, and they are all under age 40. I worry that she could have grounds for suing the agency on the basis of age and minority discrimination.

Dealing With Impaired Staff

Since one of my case managers (Roberta Saunders, a 15-year veteran) supervises volunteers, I recently agreed to meet with a potential volunteer, Mr. James, a recently retired teacher, who wanted to discuss his experience with Roberta. This is what he told me:

"About two months ago I offered to serve as a volunteer child companion. Roberta seemed pleased at my interest and said she would get back to me. A month went by, and I still hadn't heard from her so I called. She said she was glad to hear from me because the program was hurting from not having enough volunteers and would have to cancel the Saturday outings. I told her that I had volunteered a month ago but Roberta didn't seem to remember meeting with me, so I asked her for another interview.

When I met with her the second time she brought a notepad with her. She said she was sorry for not getting back to me. She had just found the note about our meeting, but her note said nothing about my wanting to volunteer on Saturdays. I saw her write down the information on the pad. We talked for about an hour, and she gave me lots of tips about being a child companion. She said she teaches a class for companions every month, and I wanted to sign up right away.

Just to make sure that Roberta was aware of my schedule, before I left the meeting with her I asked if she had recorded my availability. She couldn't remember my telling her my schedule. I was really annoyed that she hadn't remembered or recorded my availability."

I apologized for Roberta's lack of response and expressed appreciation that Mr. James thought enough about the program to register his concerns. Afterwards I reviewed Roberta's general behavior and demeanor. She seemed more irritable lately, and was falling behind in her administrative responsibilities. She had missed the last three weekly departmental meetings, saying that they had "slipped her mind." Her departmental budget was due two weeks ago, and she was behind in her volunteer reports by six months. With this new information from a potential volunteer, I was concerned that Roberta might be discouraging others. I've got to have a good administrator in this position, and up until the last six months or so, Roberta has been doing a great job. But now I am concerned that her memory is becoming too impaired for her to function in her current position.

My dilemma is that if I were to let Roberta go, it is unlikely that I could recruit a replacement quickly. With federal cutbacks, no one is being replaced. Also, I know that Roberta is 60 years old, and I am afraid that she might file a lawsuit against the agency for age discrimination. I recognize that Roberta has strengths that she could build upon, including making presentations to volunteers and sharing practice wisdom about tutoring. I also considered whether another staff member who is good at schedules and numbers could be released from some of her responsibilities to be reassigned to handle Roberta's administrative tasks.

Deteriorating Performance

One of my case managers, Marcia, has been with us for three years. She came to us after having been laid off from another agency, the consequence of financial cutbacks. Her reference checks were positive, reflecting a history of professionalism with no reported job performance problems. For the past two years, she has performed quite well, demonstrating herself to be a reliable and enthusiastic member of our team. She has received high marks for her productivity and proficiency in completing paperwork. She's exceeded service expectations and has taken the initiative for obtaining resources for our families. In summary, Marcia displayed a high degree of professional dedication to her work.

About six months ago, however, I began noticing deterioration in her work. Her record keeping was falling behind. She reported on making home visits for billing purposes but documentation had not been completed. This is a serious matter because her inability to keep up with the records could have a negative impact on our quality assurance procedures and could put our program and even our agency at risk.

After a number of conferences with Marcia we worked out a corrective action plan detailing expectations and a timeline for completing her paperwork. In an effort to explain her behavior, Marcia revealed that she was experiencing tremendous difficulty in getting organized and focused. She was unable to concentrate, having trouble sleeping at night, and coming to work late looking disheveled and exhausted. Apparently she was experiencing serious marital difficulties and told me her marriage was falling apart. I encouraged her to seek counseling and referred her to our Employee Assistance Program (EAP) that is operated by another organization under contract from us. For the past two months we arranged a slower timetable in recognition of her personal problems. Marcia initially consulted the EAP, but then discontinued because of her discomfort about being in counseling. Our staff began to talk about her appearance and demeanor, and they wondered whether she could carry out her responsibilities with her clients. Staff morale was clearly becoming an issue because of her behavior. As

Marcia's supervisor, I had concerns about her productivity and record keeping, which could conceivably threaten the continuation of the program. These are among the options that I needed to consider:

1. Terminate her based on lack of timely compliance with the corrective plan. We could then replace her with a more productive employee. On the negative side we could be perceived as a dehumanized organization and possibly face a lawsuit. This decision would put Marcia at financial and medical risk.

2. Continue her employment and put her on medical leave, following which she would be provided with intensive supervision. The positive consequence is that she can retain her income and full medical coverage. The agency might be able to salvage a formerly productive employee. The negative consequence is that we would have to take the time to find and train a temporary replacement and deal with the lack of documentation required for compliance.

3. Transfer her to another position requiring less autonomy. The benefit to Marcia is that she could continue to receive income, although it would be reduced to reflect her reduced responsibilities. The negative consequence is that she might continue to have problems in the new unit.

Our dilemma is that our agency is built on a culture of caring for both clients and staff. Marcia is a formerly productive employee who is now unable to fulfill her professional responsibilities because of her personal situation.

Discussion Questions

1. It is common for managers to experience simultaneous problems with their subordinates and need to prioritize. Given these three staff members under your supervision (Ms. Rodriguez, Roberta, and Marcia), which situation would you address first and why? What would be your second priority and why?

2. In the first situation, 40% of Ms. Rodriguez's clients are Spanish-speaking and none of the other staff are fluent in Spanish. If the supervisor were to let Ms. Rodriguez go, what should she do regarding the Hispanic clients?

3. As Roberta's supervisor, what responsibility, if any, should you take to get help for Roberta's apparent impairment? How would you broach the subject with Roberta?

4. If you were Marcia's supervisor, which of the options would you select, why, and what kind of discussion might you have to carry on with Marcia?

Suggested Debriefing Framework: 2.3 Analytical and Interactional Aspects

CASE 7.13   Supervisory Leadership

Kevin Traube is the executive director of an institution for emotionally disabled children, overseeing the work of six supervisors. After 20 years in the field, he is still energized by his work because of his commitment to improving the quality of life of youth with special needs. Currently he supervises six first-line supervisors. Problems with three of them have recently come to a head:

- Leanne Jones has been using increasing amounts of sick leave, and this is now seriously impacting her work.
- Tim Coleman, well-liked as a counselor, was recently promoted and has been throwing his weight around as a new supervisor.
- Another supervisor, Doris Alexander, is also micro-managing, but at least her concerns are legitimate ones, related to productivity.

To complicate things further, line staff morale has been in decline, and the union has just made salary-increase demands which Kevin believes are not affordable. Kevin presents the situation as follows.

Leanne Jones: Excessive Absences

Three years ago, I promoted Leanne Jones to supervisor. She had been employed as a case manager for 15 years. She obtained this position because over time she demonstrated her commitment to the work of the organization and its clients. One year after her promotion, I became concerned about Ms. Jones's performance as supervisor. I wanted to give her the benefit of the doubt, however, so I didn't make a big deal of her use of sick time and occasional absences. Now, though, it appears to me that her performance is deteriorating, and I am worried.

The issue of her absences became a special concern a year ago when the agency instituted a policy of allowing staff to convert the regular five-day, eight-hour work week to a four-day, ten-hour work week. Ms. Jones would call in sick one or two days each week and would miss the equivalent of two weeks worth of work in a month. The consequence is that her staff members were often left without supervision and were required to go to other supervisors when a crisis occurred. The other supervisors have begun to complain to me about this extra load on them. An additional problem is that when Ms. Jones does not attend monthly meetings, she is unable to disseminate important information to her staff members, who are thus not updated on current policies. Finally, I am concerned that her staff members are not completing their job responsibilities in her absence.

To date, Ms. Jones has exhausted all of her sick leave and vacation time, and she is now on family medical leave because she needs to take care of her sick husband. I can appreciate that she has a special problem at home because occasionally I, too, have to take time off to care for a sick child, but I'm afraid that her family responsibilities are greatly interfering with her ability to do her work. She is basically a good person and was once a terrific worker, so I would like to find a way to deal with this current dilemma.

Tim Coleman: Tough Facade

Three months ago, I promoted another staff member, Tim Coleman, to replace his supervisor who left for another job. The supervisor who left, Margery, had 16 years with the agency and was an outstanding leader. Many staff members were upset at her leaving and wondered whether her shoes could be filled. Tim had shown high promise as a staff member and was truly committed to working in the agency, so we thought he could do a good job as a supervisor, even though we had some reservations about his leadership ability.

Within a few weeks, serious concerns emerged regarding Tim's handling of the supervisory role. Staff began complaining to me about his openly reprimanding staff, resorting to hostile and demanding e-mails, discounting people's ideas during meetings and case reviews, and threatening to write up those who did not agree with his leadership style.

After hearing these complaints from individual staff members, I decided to respond to a request to meet with Tim's staff without his being present. The meeting almost broke into a riot of vituperations as each complaint stirred up more complaints culminating in the staff demanding Tim's resignation. Several said that they were shocked at the way Tim had changed. As a staff member, he was well mannered, supportive, and genuinely involved with his clients. As a supervisor, he now seemed to maintain a tough façade to demonstrate his leadership competency. The general sense of the group is that Tim was on an ego trip, using his position to demonstrate his newfound power.

I responded to the staff by saying that I needed to take time to talk to Tim directly. I wanted to determine whether this was the right role for Tim. I said that I thought he had leadership potential and that in the next four weeks I would take responsibility for improving the situation.

Doris Alexander: Micro-Management

Coincidentally, another case manager, Doris Alexander, was recently promoted from case manager to supervisor after four years of exemplary work. In giving her the promotion, I told her that the agency had to tighten its belt and gain greater control over expenditures because of reduced departmental funds. Ms. Alexander realizes that part of her evaluation will be influenced by how well she keeps costs down.

Dave, who was formally Ms. Alexander's colleague, now reports to her. He is puzzled by what he considers her "nitpicking" approach to him and other members of the staff. In inclement weather, for example, Ms. Alexander watches carefully as Dave and other workers enter the office, upbraiding them if they don't wipe their feet. She says that the carpeting will wear out if it becomes soiled and that floor coverings are expensive to replace.

Ms. Alexander shares practice wisdom liberally and generously supports line workers, often making helpful suggestions on working with clients. However, she tends to be quite frugal, carefully rationing office supplies and requiring staff to surrender worn pencils and used pens in order to obtain replacements. She expects staff to explain in writing their reasons for requesting personal days. She insists on a doctor's certificate following an absence due to illness. When Dave occasionally arrives late to work or returns late from lunch, Ms. Alexander is waiting at the entrance and informs him how many minutes he is late.

To her credit, under Ms. Alexander's supervision, staff productivity has increased as more clients are being served. In addition, she has written several grants and implemented innovative ways of providing client services. This morning, Ms. Alexander took an envelope out of the mail box, weighed it, and determined the postage was 60 cents higher than needed. She confronted Dave about his mistake, berating him in front of other staff for "senselessly wasting agency assets."

Dave was very upset with how his supervisor was treating him and was considering quitting. "I don't have to put up with this belittling attitude."

That afternoon, I gave Ms. Alexander her six-month performance assessment. I told her that I was delighted on the one hand that our productivity was up and that we were getting costs under control. On the other hand, I expressed concern with the high staff turnover, which is costing us money to train new staff and bring them up to speed. She acted flustered, saying that she thought she was doing exactly what I had requested, suggesting that staff turnover could not be blamed on her. We ended the meeting without clear agreements for next steps, and I said I would schedule a meeting to finish our discussion by the end of the week.

Unionization

Staff morale has become an issue throughout much of the agency. I have always been highly committed to the well being of our professional and support staff. In fact, five years ago when our support staff requested that they be unionized, I agreed to this initiative and did not try to persuade our employees to vote against unionization. As a young adult, I had worked in another agency where there was a union and saw that there could be important benefits for people being properly represented. I was comfortable with the union in my own agency because I felt we treated our employees fairly. Their wages and benefits were probably the highest in our community. Of course, as the one ultimately responsible for our budget, I had to constantly be watchful that our expenses, including wages and benefits, were kept in balance with our income.

Two weeks ago, I was taken aback by a union demand to raise the wages of support staff (child-care workers; laundry workers; and kitchen staff) by 10% each year for the next three years. Yes, part of me was sympathetic to the desire to raise wages of our lowest-paid staff, but, as I indicated previously, they were being paid at the highest wage levels in our community. I knew that our budget could only manage a 3% increase, based on our budget review. Unfortunately, certain leaders of the union are unwilling to compromise and are threatening to strike if we don't acquiesce to their demands. As much as I would hate to see this happen, I feel I may have to gird myself for this possibility.

All of these problems—Leanne's excessive absences, complaints about Tim's and Doris's management styles, and the union demands—seem a bit overwhelming right now.

Discussion Questions

1. What should Kevin do to resolve the problem of Leanne's excessive absences and ensure necessary coverage of her duties? Should her excessive absences now be included in her evaluations? Under what conditions might she be fired?

2. In retrospect, what would have been a way of preparing Tim for his new supervisory responsibilities? What should Kevin suggest that Tim do from now on? Is a corrective action plan necessary?

3. How could Doris Alexander respond differently to her dilemma of dealing with reducing costs while not being overbearing with staff? What can Kevin do to help her in this regard?

4. How can Kevin respond to the union's demands in a way that satisfies their members and also maintains the financial health of the agency? How can he deal with a possible budget shortfall or a strike?

5. What systemic changes in human resources policies and procedures, staff training, or leadership might prevent problems like these in the future?

Suggested Debriefing Framework: 2.3 Analytical and Interactional Aspects

❖ CHAPTER EXERCISES

Exercise #1

With respect to one of the most difficult aspects of human-resource management, this exercise is built upon the principles and process for supervising staff with performance problems. The exercise involves the use of a continuum of supervisory interventions described in Hopkins and Austin (2004). In this exercise, participants are asked to reflect on the poor performance of a former colleague or supervisee, then identify the potential actions that could have been taken using the following items in the continuum of coaching interventions: (1) creating a supportive environment that encourages workers to ask for help, (2) listening and talking through problems, (3) making suggestions or giving advice, (4) documenting performance problems, (5) coaching workers to improve performance, (6) making referral to helping resources (e.g., Employee Assistance Program), (7) taking disciplinary action based on full documentation of prior efforts, and (8) designing a termination process.

Exercise #2

Dealing with one's immediate superior/boss is another challenge often found in human service organizations. This exercise is based on the process of "managing up," which involves helping your boss with her/his job so that she/he can help you do yours (Austin, 1988). Participants can begin in small groups to identify their experiences with difficult bosses. Then they can select one example and assess the situation using the following dimensions of managing up:

1. Help the boss advocate for the needs of subordinates in relationship to career development; meritorious performance; environmental needs, such as space to work; and social needs in terms of work climate.

2. Seek to influence agency policy by proposing changes in the way in which the organization functions (e.g., travel policies, intake policies, or personnel policies).

3. Seek to influence agency program development by proposing new program directions and identifying implementation strategies.

4. Seek to influence agency leadership and provide constructive feedback by analyzing:
   a. the organizational climate with respect to improving inter-unit communications and team building;
   b. the impact of the superior's management style and actions on staff;
   c. the need for recognition of outstanding staff work;
   d. the changing nature of work life in order to foster maximum creativity and participation.

5. Enhance the superior's capacity to receive and use input from staff who seek to manage up and staffs' capacity to view the managing up process as enhancing their career development (e.g., working to improve relationships rather than simply seeking other employment).

8

Organizational
Dynamics and Change

Maryhill Agency is one of Oakville's oldest, largest, and most comprehensive social service organizations. Founded as a relief organization following the 1906 earthquake, it now provides a constellation of services to address every aspect of human survival, from offering shelter and free meals, to employment training and education, to substance abuse counseling and physical- and mental health care. In pursuing its mission "to support people in fulfilling immediate needs and achieving long-term sufficiency," Maryhill serves over half a million people each year.

To effectively and efficiently achieve its mission and reach its stated goals, Maryhill is broken down into six program areas. These include: health services, food services, shelter services, senior services, child and family services, and employment and training services. Historically, the executive director, chief operating officer, and chief financial officer comprised the executive team and provided only general oversight and guidance to the agency, leaving day-to-day program management and operation to each individual service manager. However, due to the lack of coordination and uniformity between services, the administrative team recently decided to take a more active, hands-on approach to managing the various programs. With the help of outside consultants, senior administrators developed tighter program budgets and new staff performance-appraisal systems; they established process and performance outcomes for each program and revised basic intake and referral forms. They made these changes quietly, with only minimal staff input.

In the midst of these changes, Maryhill's child and family services' veteran program manager, Pamela Harrison, retired. She had experienced mixed feelings about leaving her tight-knit staff. This staff of 20, including some who had been there as long as she, saw themselves as a family. They shared lunch on Fridays, rides to work, and a deep commitment to serving youth. More than any other Maryhill program staff, Ms. Harrison's staff diligently put the needs of their clients before all else. But after 30 years of service to the organization, Ms. Harrison felt entitled to take more time to enjoy her grandchildren, her garden, and her cooking.

To head the child and family service program, the administrative team hired Helen Flagg, a young social worker with over five years of experience in nonprofit management. Though Ms. Flagg did not possess a strong clinical background, she did possess strong technical and organizational skills and an understanding of the needs of children and their families. New to Oakville, but familiar with Maryhill's good works, Ms. Flagg was extremely excited about the job. Immediately after the administrative team hired her into the position, she began meeting with her supervisor, Maryhill's chief operating officer, to learn about the agency's recent changes and to develop an updated vision for her program, one that incorporated the organization's new practices.

Ms. Flagg received a lukewarm reception from her staff during her first week of work. To build a more positive atmosphere, she brought doughnuts to her first child and family service staff meeting and formally introduced herself to the different employees. She then expressed her hopes for the program's future and outlined her aspirations for its short-term service goals. Staff responded with icy silence, followed by biting side comments: "Who does she think she is?" Veteran employees asked her pointed questions about her clinical background, her experience in working with difficult populations, and her reasons behind the changes to their program. Although Ms. Flagg answered honestly about Maryhill's agency-wide changes, the staff greeted these responses with skepticism.

In the next few weeks, Ms. Flagg felt increasingly like an unwelcome stranger in her new department. And as she began implementing the new agency reforms, her staff became increasingly hostile towards her. Many stopped attending weekly staff meetings; those who were present interrogated her about the program's changes. As a result, staff meetings lost their productive functions, and program morale plummeted. The vast majority of employees resisted her requests to use the new intake and referral forms and did not collect data to monitor performance outcomes. Staff continued to follow their previous year's budget, despite the program's significant financial cutbacks. When Ms. Flagg would remind them about the current spending plan, they would, in turn, remind her about their budgetary allotments under their previous supervisor.

As she battled to implement agency policy in her department, Ms. Flagg also began to face pressure from an impatient management team. They could not understand why her department was resistant to change and expressed dissatisfaction with her inability to enact the new policies in a timely manner. Struggling with problems from above and below, Ms. Flagg's dream job now resembled a nightmare.

Discussion Questions

1. Were the management team's new procedures and processes to improve coordination and uniformity appropriate? What other, or additional, processes could be used to ensure necessary coordination while also allowing appropriate autonomy at the program level?

2. As a new leader, what should Helen Flagg do to build effective relationships with staff and also manage the apparently conflicting expectations of the agency as a whole and her own program?

Suggested Debriefing Framework: 2.2 Managerial Problem Solving

CASE 8.2   Diagnosing Managerial Practice in a Budget Crisis

In June of 2003, over 300 state employees received letters from the state's Department of Social Services (DSS), informing them that their positions had been classified as "surplus" by the Department of Finance. The letters explained that the proposed budget effectively called for an 11% downsizing of the DSS operating budget, and that the Department of Finance required each DSS unit to carefully review all operating costs and programs. The letter's intent was to prepare the receivers for the possibility that their position may no longer exist in the near future.

In September 2003, more bad news was issued in a department-wide memo from the office of the Deputy Director of DSS. The finalized budget called for even more downsizing than had been expected. In addition to the 11% projected earlier, an additional 16% of the DSS budget would have to be cut over the next fiscal year. In the end, the DSS expected to be operating on less than 75% of the budget it had the year before.

The letters and memos prompted more questions than certainty. Over 300 upset employees reported to work filled with questions. When would they know if their positions would be cut? What would be the decision process? How had their position come to be considered "surplus"? Where would seniority, experience, and military-veteran status all fit into the new equation of surpluses and cuts? In this atmosphere of uncertainty, even those employees who had not received letters were anxious. Many wondered, "If my colleague, who has been with the state for 20 years, received a letter, and I have only been here for 5 years, can I feel secure about my job?" Many others, reading that their positions were classified as surplus, felt that they themselves were now considered surplus. Program managers were put in a difficult position by this situation.

Most managers at the DSS have worked their way into those positions after many years in the field, and they had personal knowledge of the providers and the consumers of services, of both the dedication of staff and the needs of consumers. Wedged between the directors and the line staff, most managers were told little more than those who had received the letter were told. At the same time, many managers were asked by their directors to review their programs and submit justifications in the concise, fiscally driven terms that the analysts at the Department of Finance required. While the managers were frantically compiling justifications, they were continuously approached by anxious staff members who demanded answers to their questions.

In this tense atmosphere, rumors rapidly began circulating throughout the DSS. Many staff expressed the conviction that the managers and directors knew a lot more than they were revealing, and were withholding this information from the people who needed it most. For example, why the delay in posting seniority rankings? Surely they must be completed by now. Such information would help people get an idea of where they stood and inform their decisions about their future. Feeling threatened, employees wanted to know if they would have a job in a month, and they desperately needed to know so they could begin to look for new jobs as soon as possible if necessary. Rumors grew into questions of whether so many managerial and administrative positions were really necessary: If cuts had to happen, why not more from the top?

The tensions often trickled down into personal interactions. Employees frequently gathered in one another's cubicles talking in low tones and being conspicuously silent when managers passed. In one unit, when the receptionist went on maternity leave, an office assistant was asked to complete one of her duties in the interim. The office assistant lost her temper, and loudly stated that the duty was not in her job description and the management had no right to ask her to do it. She stated that she was protected from unfair labor practices by her union and threatened to file a grievance. Her reaction to the situation rippled through the unit and had a divisive effect as other employees took sides among themselves. The differing views of the situation reflected the growing divide between management and staff, as well as among staff in different job categories.

Meanwhile, many employees were taking retirement options or accepting positions elsewhere to extricate themselves from the impending crisis while they could still do so voluntarily. More and more offices were emptied, and some units were starting to look like ghost towns. The DSS began offering voluntary resume building and interviewing workshops as services for staff.

Discussion Questions

1. How can responsibilities to the administration be balanced with those to the supervisees?

2. How can the real and justifiable anxiety of colleagues be diffused in the face of significant downsizing without invalidating them?

3. How can a manager ensure that programs continue to operate with decreasing resources and increasing interpersonal and professional tension and uncertainty?

4. What leadership styles and behaviors would be appropriate in this situation?

Suggested Debriefing Framework: 2.5 Strategic Issues Management

CASE 8.3   How Are We Doing?

In June 1992, the newly appointed human service director (senior author), began the process of building a strategic plan for the recently

NOTE: Maureen Borland, MA, is the former director of the San Mateo County Human Services Agency; Julie Kelley, MSW, MPH is a manager in the Contra Costa County Health Department.

reorganized agency. The agency had been re-structured by combining programs from other county agencies for the purpose of addressing the growing human service needs in San Mateo County. In recognition that reorganizing the agency alone would not bring about the needed changes, the strategic planning process was launched to establish a shared identity and directions for the delivery of human services in the county. Staff, community members, and service consumers were engaged in the process of planning for a more effective service delivery system (see Figure 8.1).

Early in this effort, three areas were identified as key to the major system change: (1) a focus on prevention and early intervention, (2) developing comprehensive family-focused services, and (3) promoting self-sufficiency. In each of these areas, a task force was assembled to identify issues and areas for change through focus groups, meetings, and various forums. Task force members included representatives from county and city agencies; community-based organizations; businesses; education, health, labor organizations; and customer-receiving services.

The strategic planning process provided a new direction. In order to create a new agency identity, a logo was created by selecting a set of themes embodied in the strategic directions. Two new comprehensive, client-centered pilot programs were created to help staff implement the program changes: (1) a collaborative model of school-based services using a family-focused, interdisciplinary team approach called The Futures Project in Daly City, and (2) two self-sufficiency centers that provide the opportunity for clients on Temporary Assistance to Needy Families (TANF) to develop skills and self-esteem in order to become immediately employed.

Although each staff person received a copy of the strategic plan and was involved in discussions about it, it was difficult to assess the extent to which they had bought into the proposed service delivery changes. An agency-wide newsletter designed to keep staff abreast of important changes was distributed on a regular basis. However, there was no formal feedback mechanism for staff, especially frontline staff, to share their experience and reactions to implementing these significant organizational changes.

The Agency Assessment Survey

To better understand staff perceptions, a nationally recognized corporate consultant was recruited to conduct a service assessment survey to learn more about the impact of changes on staff. The reorganization of the San Mateo County Human Services Agency (HSA) was seen as

Figure 8.1   San Mateo County Human Service Agency Strategic Plan: Themes and Strategic Directions

Theme I: Implement a Proactive, Outcomes-Oriented, High-Impact Service Philosophy

Strategic Direction 1:

We will promote a proactive, outcome-oriented approach to meeting consumer needs through continuous training and support for HSA staff and other service providers as well as providing assistance to consumers in advocating for their own needs.

Strategic Direction 2:

Policy-makers, program managers, and individual service providers at all levels (private, public, volunteer) will make decisions on the most effective utilization of resources by considering a common set of values:

a) We will achieve the most long-term, wide-spread impact at the lowest cost, as determined by the best available, consumer defined outcome measures.
b) We will focus on prevention and the earliest possible intervention, promote self-sufficiency, and strengthen families and individuals within their familial and support environments.
c) We will treat all consumers with respect.
d) We will assure, at a minimum, that all consumers receive assistance in identifying their needs, and be provided information and referral on available options for food, clothing, shelter and health care.

Theme II: Extend the Boundaries of the Human Services System

Strategic Direction 3:

We will create a seamless system of public/private service by fostering cooperation and partnership among government, non-profit and private sector organizations and individuals through the development of a shared vision and values, common interests and objectives and coordinated implementation strategies.

Strategic Direction 4:

We will build public support for addressing human service needs through separate and joint public education efforts. These efforts will stress public involvement in human service issues as well as education for human services consumers.

Early in this effort, three areas were identified as key to the major system change: 1) a focus on prevention and early intervention, 2) developing comprehensive family focused services, and 3) promoting self-sufficiency. In each of these areas, a task force was assembled to identify issues and areas for change through focus groups, meetings, and various forums. Task force members included representatives from county and city agencies, community-based organizations, businesses, education, health, labor organizations, and customers receiving services.

Strategic Direction 5:

We will seek waivers and legislation that remove disincentives to prevention and early intervention services, in order to promote consumer self-sufficiency and strengthen families and support environments.

(Continued)

Figure 8.1 (Continued)

Theme III: Deliver Services That
Respond to the Self-Identified Needs of Consumers

Strategic Direction 6:

We will develop a single intake system from multiple points of contact that provides consumers access to all available resources, both public and private, as well as a system of needs assessment, information and referral which supports a coordinated delivery of service and offers consumers choice in both definition of needs, and selection and design of solution.

Strategic Direction 7:

We will make accessibility to services easier for all consumers.

Strategic Direction 8:

We will use consumer data collected to plan, operate and evaluate human services programs and activities.

Strategic Direction 9:

We will make changes needed to expand service delivery of child care, affordable housing and job training to consumers identified as the "working poor."

similar to many private-sector businesses experiencing the re-engineering of their infrastructures and missions.

The purpose of the Service Assessment Survey was threefold: (1) to measure the effectiveness and quality of the work environment, (2) to identify the staff's perceptions of customer service, and (3) to identify opportunities for improving decision making in HSA. The ultimate goal was to create a pre-eminent public sector organization. The survey was used to create a snapshot of the current organization in order to better understand how the staff perceived the changes and to use the data to assess change on a regular basis.

The Service Assessment Survey process included interviews by trained agency staff (nominated by their peers) and two members of the consultant's staff. Open-ended questions were used in 45-minute interviews of 143 staff members out of a selected 175 staff members. The interviewers were trained as a team to conduct the assessment interviews and collate the data. The interview team helped to develop the interview with special attention to those questions designed to motivate participants to be candid and forthcoming. Confidentiality was stressed at the start of each interview in order to reassure those being interviewed and to establish credibility. The interview team met at the end of each day to summarize and categorize comments.

Survey Results

The staff comments were collected by the interviewers, then clustered and content-analyzed to identify key themes. Many of the comments reflected dissatisfaction with the direction of the agency, especially in areas that were viewed as innovative or radical. The following five broad issues emerged from the data:

1. Lack of understanding of the strategic plan

2. Inadequate feedback from leadership on how we are doing

3. The organization's need for more commitment to be open and honest about current realities

4. Serious concerns about customer service and productivity

5. Insufficient attention to job performance and workplace stress

Each of the five themes included an array of issues that the consultant team used to frame the following themes and recommendations:

1. Understanding the Strategic Plan

Key Findings:

- Initial communication regarding the plan was effective; however, follow-up has been unclear.
- Concern about workload shifts not addressed specifically by the plan
- Little understanding of the plan on the frontline level.
- Lack of understanding about what is happening currently.

Recommendation of Consultant Team:

- Develop a strategy for re-introducing the strategic plan with goals and objectives and establish a step-by-step action plan for implementing changes.

Illustrative Staff Comments:

- The strategic plan is going all over the place. The workers are confused and in a muddle. Our supervisor is off in meetings and running around. We barely see her anymore. This causes low morale.
- I believe in the strategic plan. We've had too many old ideas. But people are afraid of change. What management needs to do is do a better job of communicating these plans to everyone so they won't be afraid.

2. Leadership Feedback on How We Are Doing

Key Findings:

- Need for example setting—"walking the talk"—needs to happen from the top down.
- Support from top management is critical—workers need to know that management understands what they do.
- Staff unclear about whether management understands the complexity of the day-to-day operation of the departments and the daily work functions of employees.
- Lines of communication are unclear, leading to the perception of an abuse of power.
- Risks need to be encouraged so that innovation can occur.

Recommendations of the Consultant Team:

- Agency leadership needs to set an example of supporting staff during times of significant change, especially by creating an environment where questions are valued.
- Leadership needs to be more visible, supportive, and attentive to the needs of the employees.
- Leaders need to develop an awareness of operational realities in their departments.
- Leaders need to recognize that a learning organization encourages risk-taking and innovation.

Illustrative Staff Comments:

- The new vision of service delivery allows me to be more visionary/creative in my work. I look for the positive side—how can I provide better service to the client?
- Management is not realistic about workloads.
- Line workers know how to do their jobs and need more independence and responsibility in making decisions.

3. Commitment to Being Open and Honest

Key Findings:

- Most people are committed to the agency's goals (to the extent they understand them) and consider the work valuable.
- Poor communication is the single most significant impediment to creating a shared and accurate reality.

- Shared reality can be created through open communication at all levels of the organization.
- Competition among division leaders creates a barrier to open communication.

Recommendations of the Consultant Team:

- Revise agency communications system to ensure the free flow of information from the top down as well as from the bottom up.
- Maintain an effort to lessen inter-division competition, particularly at top management levels.

Illustrative Staff Comments:

- Too much information comes from newsletters, memos, and reports. We want to hear from our management directly so that we can ask questions.
- Intervention in the community is a great first step in prevention. I think it is working for us.

4. Customer Service and Productivity

Key Findings:

- One of the great strengths of the organization is its desire to do the best for clients.
- Staff members want increased skills, such as language and cultural competency training, to better meet the needs of clients.
- There is a perception that employee training and professional development are not encouraged by management.
- There is concern about the level of skills and cross training needed to implement generic intake.
- Staff expressed a concern about accountability and performance issues in terms of creating a credible work environment.
- In order to be more productive, additional technology, such as e-mail, needs to be incorporated.
- Arcane rules and impractical regulations are major stumbling blocks to better service, greater productivity, and the successful implementation of the strategic plan.

Recommendations of the Consultant Team:

- Provide frontline workers with more control, responsibility, and independence, giving them the autonomy to make decisions and provide input on their work.
- As a learning organization, make training central to all work activities.

- Develop a shared definition and plan for generic intake.
- Ensure personal and group accountability for performance standards.

Illustrative Staff Comments:

- Productivity needs to be properly measured.
- If there were training, we could keep up with the changes.
- Need more technology and computer use.
- No one has been trained to refer clients to a single intake system.
- Too much training and cannot absorb all of the changes.

5. Job Performance and Workplace Stress

Key Findings:

- Performance evaluations do not mirror the emphasis on service delivery.
- Staff members seek recognition and appreciation for their performance.
- Clerical staff is undervalued within the organization.
- Increasing workload and high expectations of managers increases the stress level.
- Promotion practices are perceived as unfair and not based on merit.

Recommendations of the Consultant Team:

- Decrease the dichotomy between management and line staff by increasing communication and decreasing intimidation.
- Re-design the performance evaluation system to measure employees' effectiveness in delivering internal and external customer service.
- Increase employee recognition.
- Participation of clerical staff needs to be encouraged and recognized.
- Re-examine and re-adjust work/caseloads to prevent unreasonable demands and cut down on stress.

Illustrative Staff Comments:

- Reward for doing more work is getting more work.
- I'm not valued as an employee. I would like a "thank you" for a job well done, but this courtesy is not done enough. Maybe our supervisors and managers are too busy. Is it something in their training?
- Supervisors have been and are supportive.

The survey provided an unprecedented opportunity to hear from staff about the changes in the organization. While the executive team did not expect an abundance of positive responses, they were somewhat surprised by the breadth of negative responses. In response, the executive team looked carefully at the staff comments and recommendations to determine what kinds of changes could be made immediately to address staff concerns. The survey findings provided a new shared sense of reality that needed to be taken into account so that staff could work together toward a set of agreed-upon goals.

The survey results were distributed to the entire human service agency staff with an accompanying report indicating that the executive team was in the process of crafting a plan of action to deal with the survey recommendations. The executive team stressed that it was critical to keep the lines of communication open and identified five immediate conclusions regarding the survey findings:

- We hear what you have to say. We commit ourselves to an ongoing improvement process.
- We will provide the kind of leadership that will move us forward.
- We ask for further help in creating a work environment that inspires trust, creativity, and integrity.
- Together we will create a common set of values to guide how we will work together.

The executive team's action plan was distributed eight weeks after staff received the survey report. It featured a new organizational credo in the form of a written set of values to guide actions for all employees as follows:

- We will attribute goodwill to people's actions and foster a high level of honesty, openness, free dialogue, integrity, ethics, and trust.
- We value individuals and their diversity and treat each other with respect and dignity.
- We will promote partnerships and expect a maximum contribution from employees, customers, and communities.
- We commit ourselves to promoting the highest level of customer service. We will be knowledgeable, proactive, and continuously improving our services.
- We promote innovative and effective leadership, which is guided by fact, encourages rewards based upon merits, and holds us accountable for our actions.

These core values have been disseminated throughout the agency through the use of desk plaques and posters. In addition to establishing core values, the executive team identified the following nine issues that address areas of concern cited in the survey report:

1. Develop agency values (see above).

2. Develop and implement training on organizational change.
   This has been implemented in the managers' and supervisors' training.

3. Promote and implement Suggestion/Recognition Program.
   This has been implemented and a Suggestions/Recognitions Committee meets once per month.

4. Revise performance standards and evaluation to include values, training career development and accountability.
   A work group of staff at all levels, including a Division Director, has been formed.

5. Revisit and revise Communication Plan.
   A work group chaired by a Division Director has been formed.

6. Develop a plan and curriculum for in-depth cultural diversity training.
   A curriculum has been identified and a plan is being developed.

7. Develop career opportunities to include lateral job rotation, career mobility opportunities, and clerical career ladders.
   A work group has been formed, chaired by a Division Director, to develop a plan.

8. Develop and implement a generic intake system.
   Development is completed and a generic intake system is being piloted.

9. Provide budget basics/caseload size training.
   To be implemented in September 1995.

10. Begin "Task Elimination."
    A "Task Elimination Update" is published monthly in employee newsletter.

In addition, the executive team asked for staff input and participation in developing a plan to further deal with the recommendations.

The survey provided baseline data about how the agency was doing at a point in time. In order to gauge progress in addressing the recommendations, the executive team agreed to repeat the assessment survey on an annual basis. Each issue was assigned to an executive team member who agreed to lead the effort and set timelines for developing an implementation plan. Progress is highlighted bimonthly in the agency newsletter.

Reactions Outside the Agency

News of the Assessment/Service Survey results generated a variety of reactions from other county offices. The Health Services Agency was intrigued with the idea of measuring progress through staff perception. Agreeing that the concept was innovative, they are working on a modified version to use in their agency. Another county agency executive noted that the survey seemed to be too risky in a large organization and could lead to more staff dissatisfaction in the long term.

Early in the dissemination process, a copy of the survey results was sent anonymously to a member of the board of supervisors without the accompanying explanation or follow-up plan. The member was deeply concerned. However, after an explanation and an overview of the actions to be taken, he was impressed with the level of self-examination the agency needed in order to understand the direction and progress of organizational changes.

Lessons Learned

The primary lesson learned as a result of the service assessment survey was that assessing organizational change through staff input is a lengthy, all-encompassing process for the entire agency. The depth of effort to implement the survey and establish an action plan was not anticipated. By assessing all aspects of the work environment, every level of the agency came under scrutiny. This exposed both strengths and areas for improvement at many levels of the organization.

The agency self-assessment process provided data for understanding the array of additional changes needed within the organization, especially a higher level of inclusion for staff and clients. The survey also highlighted the impact of organizational change on all levels of agency personnel. The following is a summary of some of the lessons learned:

Organizational changes take time. Changes were demanded of staff at every level over a short period of time, raising staff concern. This contributed to an uncertainty about how the changes would affect individual staff performance. While change is a fact of life in all work-places, it is threatening and often requires extra effort during transitions, especially for those who are enmeshed in a rigid bureaucratic system where expectations have been relatively stable for long periods of time. In some ways, staff felt victimized by the changes that were designed to make service delivery more effective. They had difficulty functioning with uncertainty and less specific directions.

Develop a communication plan. With all new changes, dissemination of general information in an organized, consistent manner provides a foundation for more specialized information sharing. Staff members learn and absorb information differently. Some staff were able to see the big picture clearly and describe their part in it, while others saw the change only as a diminishing of their function in the agency. Staff members conceptualize systems change in different ways and at different times. It was difficult to identify specific issues or levels of dissatisfaction solely on the basis of staff comments because it is not always easy to assess the individual understanding of the organizational change. Direct, timely, and consistent communication from management and supervisors through a variety of methods, including staff meetings, face-to-face meetings, newsletters, and memos, are critical to creating a common understanding.

The change process can be made easier by dividing the process into four or five specific tasks. Information regarding large system change can be overwhelming. It is easy to underestimate the resistance of staff to change. Organizational structure influences staff behavior. When that structure is modified, behavior change and resistance become more prominent. Comprehensive changes can be described, but at times it is difficult for staff to understand how these changes will affect their jobs.

A strategic plan is a living document. The plan and vision of the future are not static. As a living document, it becomes more usable and powerful as staff members learn to interpret it in relation to their jobs. Discussing the plan on an individual program and systems level helps to develop the shared sense of reality. Continuing group discussions are helpful in refining the details of change processes noted in the plan.

Ongoing learning is an important part of staff development and change. Staff development is an essential part of the learning organization. It helps to nurture the concepts and innovations that the agency strives to create. Individuals are strengthened and encouraged to try new and innovative ways of delivering client service and achieving desired outcomes.

Managers need to provide leadership in a way that coaches and encourages staff. Leaders are the messengers for communicating the vision over time and providing staff with an understanding of the manageable components of the vision. Staff expects managers to help interpret the directions and provide guidance on how jobs can be modified to achieve the vision.

One respondent to the survey noted that the process of agency self-assessment was the first time she had talked to a member of the executive team in six years about how she felt about her work and the changes that would affect her ability to do that work. Understanding the concerns of staff and addressing those issues are fundamental in implementing a strategic plan. Until staff perceptions are understood and valued, true progress toward providing caring, quality client service will be impeded.

Discussion Questions

1. Do the action steps developed by the Executive Team adequately address the recommendations? If not, what additional steps are needed?

2. What specific challenges would you anticipate in the implementation of the strategic plan? What actions would you recommend to address these challenges?

Suggested Debriefing Framework: 2.6 Policy Practice

CASE 8.4   Jefferson Hospital

Jefferson Hospital (JH) is a comprehensive psychiatric facility consisting of adult and child/adolescent inpatient units, an adult day treatment program, and an outpatient clinic, all located on a campus of three buildings. There are currently about 300 employees. The hospital's mission and goals are noted in Figure 8.2. Jefferson Hospital is owned by a national conglomerate of psychiatric hospitals that does not provide day-to-day monitoring of the hospital as long as financial goals and accreditation standards are being met. The hospital is in a metropolitan area of two million residents, and in a local community that has predominantly middle- and lower-middle class residents. There is a large number of Navy personnel, primarily from the enlisted ranks and civilian employees, and a substantial Latino population living nearby.

The hospital is in a market-driven industry and competes heavily with other similar hospitals in the area. The insurance companies that provide most of the hospital's funding consistently deny coverage to

Figure 8.2   Jefferson Hospital Mission and Goals

The mission of Jefferson Hospital is to provide comprehensive, cost-effective mental health services of the highest quality and standards that respond to current and future community needs and generate a reasonable return on financial investment.
In support of this mission, we are committed to:

The provision of quality psychiatric services through a continuum of care, with the goal of integrating the patient/client into the community in an improved state

Promoting better mental health and well being through community education, prevention, and therapeutic services

Developing models of service delivery which are compatible with current socioeconomic trends and relevant patient/client needs

Serving all mental health service providers, mental health service agencies, schools, judicial systems, clergy, and related businesses within the county as the principal market area

Delivering quality mental health services in an era of heightened need and in a climate of ever-increasing cost restrictiveness in the health-care field

Maintaining an optimal work environment that promotes employee growth, development, and satisfaction

Being responsive and performing in accordance with the needs and expectations of our various stakeholders

patients and/or attempt to shorten inpatient stays. The hospital takes an aggressive stance in face of these pressures, working to ensure the survival, growth, and profitability of the hospital. All staff must make and document three marketing contacts each week. Program directors must devise and implement treatment for currently "popular" psychiatric difficulties (e.g., eating disorders) to bring more patients into the hospital. Hospital physicians give in-service training sessions for hospital staff and seminars for community members on subjects pertaining to diagnosis and treatment of disorders that JH specializes in treating. Physicians with privileges at the hospital must refer their patients to JH for inpatient or outpatient care. Programs and services are tailored to the patients and treatments that private insurance companies will pay for. In the recent past, Medicaid and Medicare patients made up a significant proportion of JH patients, but intake staff members are now discouraged from taking such patients.

In the past, decision-making authority was largely delegated to the departments, but this changed abruptly three years ago when a new administrator, Bill Koontz (M.B.A.) was hired by the corporate staff as chief executive. He centralized power in his office, sharing some decision making with his assistant administrator, the chief operating officer. The CEO now hires and fires all personnel and routinely transfers staff among programs, leaving program managers little autonomy to design the details of their treatment programs. Until three years ago, the hospital used a department structure, with heads of nursing, social work, psychology, occupational therapy, and medical staff supervising all their own personnel in the various programs. Currently, a program structure is used, with all staff in a program (e.g., adult inpatient, day treatment) accountable to the director of that program.

In the past six months, there has been a large increase in staff turnover. Most leave JH for similar work at other hospitals. All program director positions have turned over during the past three years; a physician, a charge nurse, and two program therapists resigned recently. In one recent case, a nursing supervisor resigned under threat of a severe demotion after making criticisms and suggestions about the management of her unit that were not welcomed by administration. Many vacated positions have not been filled in order to cut costs. The pay scale for all types of staff is below that common in the surrounding area, in spite of a recent raise in some professional categories. Morale is low, particularly among case managers, nurses, mental health counselors, social workers, and family counselors. Due to staffing cutbacks, patients on the units are increasingly anxious, and acting-out behaviors are increasing. Staff hours are regularly cut according to the patient census. The staff population is becoming increasingly younger and less experienced. Recently, JH removed 40 licensed inpatient beds and moved the day treatment program into the vacated area to save money. In spite of morale problems, there are clusters of treatment staff who try to maintain a positive attitude; a prevailing attitude is: "The hell with administration; let's just do our jobs."

A recent large-scale review by the Joint Commission on Accreditation of Hospitals resulted in that regulatory body's considerable dissatisfaction with some of JH's procedures, particularly treatment team planning guidelines. Furthermore, JH's reputation is beginning to slip as its heavy focus on marketing and profit is seen as compromising professional standards.

The chief operating officer recently resigned for a position in another state. JH's corporate office recommended that the CEO hire Steve Grams, an M.S.W. with prior administrative experience at a county-run mental health facility, to become the new chief operating officer. This was to a large extent in response to the aforementioned problems: It was felt that a mental health professional could improve morale and help get programs (and, consequently, income) stabilized. Bill Koontz has begun to feel under the gun to make some significant changes in order to maintain his position. Koontz and Grams have been directed to develop an action plan to address the identified problems.

Discussion Questions

1. How would you analyze the leadership style of Bill Koontz? Does his style seem appropriate for this agency? What changes would make him more effective? What suggestions would you make to Koontz and Grams regarding the most appropriate leadership behaviors for the current situation?

2. What should be done about the turnover and morale problems?

3. Analyze the external forces facing this agency. What strategies would you recommend to address these?

4. How should the hospital address the financial problems?

5. What should Koontz and Grams do to lead the organizational changes needed at this time?

Suggested Debriefing Framework: 2.5 Strategic Issues Management

CASE 8.5   Thurston High School

Thurston High School served an American urban area blighted by drugs, crime, and poverty. The surrounding neighborhoods were marked by boarded up row houses, empty storefronts, and loitering men. Of the 2,000 students in the school, 80% were on some form of public assistance. They represented a mixed population of the urban poor, heavily dominated by racial minorities and immigrants, with a minority of white students. Bars covered the windows of the school. Guards armed with guns and walkie-talkies patrolled the halls, alert for the violence that occasionally erupted between students representing neighborhood gangs. Students and teachers alike attempted to work amidst a climate of fear and hopelessness.

Students organized themselves into warring cliques. Their teachers changed every year and rarely formed ongoing relationships with individual students. Many students were anonymous within Thurston, the exceptions being those who managed to stand out through behavioral problems, or more rarely, academic excellence. This paralleled teachers' relations with one another. Thurston's teachers had a great deal of autonomy within their classrooms, which in practice translated into isolation from one another.

SOURCE: Adapted from Kahn (2005, pp. 147–159).

Community Groups

In response to growing discipline problems, fragmentation of programs, and isolation between students, staff, and administration, a small group of Thurston administrators and teachers created a program called "Community Groups." Education research suggested that small educational communities enhance teachers' professional development, parents' levels of involvement, and the students' academic and social outcomes. The program involved assigning teachers to cohorts of students who meet weekly to talk about issues that students wished to address. Such issues ranged widely, from school policies and teacher-student relations to situations involving peer pressure, drugs, teenage pregnancy and other trials of urban adolescence. Community Groups were designed to form meaningful, long-lasting attachments between adolescents and adults, on the premise that such relationships enable students to express and work through obstacles to academic and social achievement. The Community Groups program represented an intervention in teachers' relations with one another and with school administrators. Working in pairs with their assigned student cohorts, they needed to engage with one another rather than remain isolated. The program required them to plan, reflect, and build curriculum together through mutual decision making.

The Launch

Teachers had varying reactions to the Community Groups program. A number of senior teachers were uninterested, believing that the program would inevitably follow the same path of other failed programs. These senior teachers were jaded and cynical. Some of them had allowed themselves to hope during previous interventions and had been sorely disappointed. They were determined not to allow themselves to be hurt in such ways again.

Other teachers newer to the school or simply more willing to risk disappointment liked the promise of the Community Groups program. These teachers perceived Community Groups as a way to do something small yet significant in the face of the crushing urban blight affecting their students. They were eager to relate more deeply to students. A third group of teachers were unsure about the program and their involvement. They occupied a large middle ground: aware that the school needed some significant change, hoping this program might be that change, but waiting to invest their own energies until it seemed clear that it would work.

Thurston's vice principal brought together a diverse (seniority, race, ethnicity, gender, commitment to program) committee of teachers to design the program. The committee was to develop the process by which Community Groups was to be introduced to teachers, administrators, and students and implemented across the school. The committee met weekly throughout a school year in anticipation of introducing the program to teachers and administrators at the end of the year, providing training over the summer, and implementing the program at the beginning of the following year.

It became clear during those weekly meetings that the Community Groups program threatened to disturb a set of entrenched teacher interests. Some teachers were determined not to lose their autonomy, believing that the program would encroach on their abilities to decide what, when, and how to raise issues with students. Another coalition of teachers on the committee made it clear that they did not wish to work with students who were not in the more advanced tracks. These teachers had always had seniority within the school, enabling them to teach only advanced-track students. The Community Groups program involved creating heterogeneous groups that cut across various tracks, eliminating the multiple-track system and essentially no longer guaranteeing assignment of teachers to specific levels.

The committee grew paralyzed by its accumulated differences. Members ranged from remaining to leveling accusations at each other that did little to encourage empathy and awareness. The committee remained thus, veering between fight and flight, for several weeks. Finally, many committee members were able to hear and work effectively with the consultant to understand the underlying dynamics at play. They were able to better understand the situation and design a process whereby the school's wider community of teachers, administrators, and ultimately students were able to learn about and implement the new program. With some difficulty, members stayed with the task of designing the Community Groups program, figuring out logistics, training, and curricula. They launched the program the following fall, after conducting introductory training workshops for faculty and students.

Success and Failure

The Community Groups program was greeted by the Thurston community of teachers and students with a mixture of interest, cynicism, and caution. The initial training workshops helped staff and students understand the purposes, design, and intended process of the Community Groups. A school assembly heralded the beginning, with supportive remarks by the principal and several students and teachers from another school that had implemented a similar program. The school broke into the new groupings, teachers and students warily entering new rooms and new roles with one another.

The first month of Community Groups meetings was marked by both uncertainty and valid attempts by both teachers and students. Each group engaged in a certain amount of testing: The students were testing to see how safe it was to speak openly without censure or ridicule, while the teachers struggled to respond in ways that demonstrated their acceptance of the students and the process. All were searching for ways to be participants and facilitators while remaining aware of their ongoing roles outside Community Groups.

The initial success or failure of particular Community Groups was largely related to individual teachers' ability to manage boundaries: beginning and ending on time, enforcing stable membership, keeping conversation on track, managing conflict among students, encouraging respectful discourse. When the teachers were able to manage such boundaries, their students felt safe enough to become increasingly open and authentic. The less successful Community Groups were characterized by various disruptions of students who wandered in and out, treated one another and the teachers disrespectfully, were superficial and dismissive, or simply withdrew. These teachers were unable to fully assume an effective facilitator role.

The more difficult proposition was dealing with the parents of some of the advance-track students. They resisted the idea of heterogeneous community groups and complained to the principal. They argued that their children had little to learn from other students who had little academic interest or aptitude, were into drugs or gangs, or who disengaged from the activities and attitudes of the "normal, high achiever" students. The principal listened closely to them. While he supported, in theory, the Community Groups program, he also felt pressure to maintain separate elite tracks to attract "good" students. Academically high-achieving students produced high standardized test scores, which constituted one of the measures by which the school and its administrators were evaluated. The principal did not wish to alienate the administrators, teachers, and students who were beginning to value the Community Groups program.

The principal remained torn between these competing interests until the district superintendent forced his hand near the end of the first year of the program. Several parents of Thurston students had complained to the superintendent's office about what they were hearing from their children about Community Groups. The parents were offended by student discussions of teenage sex, peer pressure, and drugs. The superintendent passed the complaints along to the principal, advising him to halt the program or curtail it sharply. The principal held a series of meetings with his staff and the teachers over the summer to discuss the program. The vice principal argued that they needed to see the program's effects on outcome measures before any decisions about its future were made. The principal said that, as far as he and the superintendent were concerned, the results were in. With much dissension and difficulty, the principal decided to discontinue the program. The vice principal soon after tendered his resignation and took a job in another school district.

Discussion Questions

1. What could the principal, committee, and consultant have done to more effectively create a sense of urgency for change and get buy-in from teachers?

2. What should the principal have done to anticipate and manage reactions from the community and the parents of advance-track students?

3. Analyze the conflicts among the various stakeholder groups. How was conflict addressed? Could the principal have played a stronger role in more proactively managing the conflicts? What could he have done?

4. What could the principal do in the coming year to move beyond this incident and get all the stakeholders committed to a shared vision for the school?

Suggested Debriefing Framework: 2.3 Analytical and Interactional Aspects

CASE 8.6   The Leadership Challenges in Transforming a Public Human Services Agency

Introduction

When I first arrived in San Mateo in 1992 to assume the director position of the county human service agency, one of the members of the board of supervisors shared her concern with me about the number of families who had complained to her that there didn't seem to be a single point of contact for somebody who had any kind of a social service need. She wanted to see the system changed so that it would be easier

SOURCE: Maureen Borland, Former Director, San Mateo County (CA) Department of Human Services, 1992–2005.

for clients and the community to understand. The goal was to reduce the need to shop around or call multiple locations to address the needs of residents. She felt that clients should not have to deal with multiple, separate services and agencies and tell their story over and over to multiple people in order to receive the services they need. The system was not customer-friendly. This board member was convinced that there needed to be a better way to serve clients in the community with a single point of entry or contact. Creating such a systems change would require strategic planning.

We began our planning by assessing all the programs administered by the Human Services Agency (HSA). Most of the programs were mandated by the federal and state government and included different populations, policies, forms, and eligibility requirements. We looked for ways that we could serve clients across multiple problem areas. We began to look at the issues from the client or customer service perspective. Our philosophy was that client needs should drive the organizational processes, not the other way around. I had learned a good deal from my experience in Florida. There, they had created an integrated organizational structure but were never really able to translate the service integration concepts down to the service delivery level. In San Mateo county we undertook a review of the many different processes used in the different programs to determine how much of it was federally or state imposed versus locally designed and how much flexibility there was to change those processes within the confines of federal and state laws or regulations.

Strategic Planning

The Human Services Agency (HSA) was a new agency created by merging programs from five different county agencies. These components had been combined in order to locate most of the critical services for children and families together in one organization to promote integrated service delivery. In order to create a common understanding of community needs, prioritize those needs, and create a common direction, a community strategic planning process was undertaken. Given my background in community service, I felt very strongly that you do not just focus on a strategic plan for a public agency, but rather on a strategic plan for the larger community. The main focus of the strategic plan was to improve outcomes for children and families. Prior to 1992, services for children and families in San Mateo county had deteriorated. My charge was to change the declining social indicators in the county by creating an organization that focused on serving people through the use of comprehensive and less bureaucratic services. There were also many human services being offered in the community by community-based organizations (CBOs) under contract with the public programs. In order to deliver comprehensive services, HAS would need to work together with the community to form a network that provided a continuum of services that improved the lives of children and families. Our first strategic-planning process involved one and a half years of intense discussion amongst 600 people representing different segments of the community (e.g., staff from community-based organizations, consumers and former consumers, staff from our agency, business and others) in 12 different work groups.

One of the things that emerged early in the process was the recognition that people did not really have information about how clients were doing or not doing. While community-based organizations had individual client information, they had no aggregate information that reflected trends in their community. A new set of priorities emerged by looking at data, sharing it, and working with it together to decide what needed to be done. Three common goals for our service system were set: (1) promoting economic self-sufficiency, (2) strengthening family functioning, and (3) building community capacity for prevention/ early intervention. Three major directions to work on together were identified: (1) monitoring client outcomes, (2) building community partnerships, and (3) creating responsive customer services. By working in a partnership approach, we were also able to improve our communication and develop better working relationships.

As an outcome of the strategic planning process, we created a human services advisory council to oversee the efforts to improve the system. It was comprised of staff from public and community-based organizations, former clients, political representatives, and a board member from a local foundation. This community group met monthly to oversee the implementation of our plan.

Discussion Questions

1. Why do you think the director proposed a strategic planning process to address the identified issues?

2. Can you think of alternative ways to reach the goal of systems change?

3. What benefits do you see in forming a human services advisory council?

Organizational Planning

Once the strategic goals and directions for the human services system had been set, we focused inside the agency to see what needed to change in order to achieve the strategic goals and directions. We went through an internal process of dialogue among the top managers to critically assess how we needed to structure ourselves and operate differently. It was not just a matter of having strategic planning goals. It was a matter of figuring out how the organization needed to change in order to implement those goals. A new mission, principles, and values were identified, written, and rolled out to staff for discussion and input. Getting staff buy in was a struggle. It does not happen overnight. It took about three years, with the assistance of some outside business consultants who were very interested in helping government improve the way it was serving the community. They donated their time to work with the executive and management teams, often challenging some of our thought processes. They brought their business expertise to our public sector organizational change effort. This was sometimes controversial because some staff had an anti-business bias and did not see how business approaches could improve our organization or customer service. We decided to approach our organizational change by first focusing on customer-service improvements.

Focusing on Customer Service

The organizational changes and innovations in HSA stem from the continual focus on improving the way we serve the customer. Our consultants helped us to think about the essence of good customer service and how to improve it. We conducted client satisfaction surveys to determine both satisfaction and dissatisfaction with all of our services. This enabled us to identify what we could improve and monitor over time. It was based on the continual messages "We are here to serve the community and to serve the customers more effectively." There was initially a lot of pushback and negativity from staff members who were more comfortable with the concept of client than the concept of customer. For example, staff claimed that clients do not have any choice to go anywhere else except our agency for the services they need, so they are not really customers. Continual dialogue with staff at all levels about our values, which included treating customers with dignity and respect and a commitment to excellence in delivering customer services, was necessary to get them focused on what they could do differently. Since the word "customer" seemed to be more an issue than the concept of improving service, we decided to use "customer" and "client" interchangeably. This concession reduced the resistance considerably. The shift to a customer-service approach to service delivery involved constantly pointing out where comments or actions diverged from the values identified in our strategic plan. We did lots of customer-service training. It didn't matter what program you were in, but rather how you could serve the customer more effectively. More intensive customer service training was offered for staff in areas where customer feedback was most negative. Customer satisfaction questionnaires are now a regular part of doing business, and results are now posted on the intranet quarterly, by office, trends identified, and customer service improvement actions undertaken.

Outcomes and Data-Informed Decision Making

One of the issues that emerged as we tried to focus on improving customer service was that staff members did not have information on how clients were doing. HSA had several large main-frame systems with "dumb terminals" that staff shared to enter data, but staff and management got only raw data printouts to work with and did not have information analyzed or presented in a way that was useful for decision making. The data focus was on tracking task completion and not on client outcomes. As a result, information on community needs and agency-based decisions on resource allocations were being made on anecdotal information. Community-based agencies that contracted with HSA had only individual client information available to them and had no automated, aggregate information on client outcomes. Managers were unable to hold contract providers accountable for performance.

Fostering a customer-service emphasis required focusing on identification of client and community outcomes agency-wide and for each program. It also required developing a special strategic plan for information systems that served the agency and its contract agencies. It included contracting with an outside vendor to analyze the current capabilities and gaps of the automation in place in HSA and our contract providers and developing a multi-year plan to implement a new information system. It required agency managers and staff to understand that resources would need to be committed to the development of this automated network, not just to hiring more staff. This was controversial, since previous management had taken the position that computers and automation were a waste of money.

I decided to provide concrete examples of how automation could help managers and staff do their jobs better by contracting with our county library system, which had created a database of human services available in the community. HSA had contracted with them for years to maintain and update that database. We decided to add resources and work with them to apply for a grant from our local community foundation to allow them to acquire staff and mapping software. We then contracted with them to map out all our client data from our multiple systems by city and zip code. These maps then became tools for structuring dialogue, both within HSA and with our community planning groups, regarding what services were needed in which areas of the county. This provided a model for data informed decision making, rather than the anecdotal approach of the past, and it was very enlightening for many participants.

The need to analyze data and look at trends has now become an accepted part of decision making at all levels of the agency. HSA spent several years developing a data warehouse that is capable of providing outcome reports to staff at all levels. Automation has been deployed to the desktops of all staff. Information on outcomes is regularly discussed for quality improvement purposes. It is an accepted practice to share information with community groups and partner agencies in an effort to have all parts of the system work more effectively together.

Discussion Questions

4. What do you see as the key success factors in this case thus far?

5. What was done that helped counteract staff resistance to change?

Service System Redesign

While customer service improved within our traditional service areas, the next step in creating a single point of entry for comprehensive services required different strategies. The emergence of welfare-reform waivers as a major policy tool for systems change in 1994 provided us with both an opportunity and a challenge. It was an opportunity to put our mission as a "catalyst for systems change" to work. Building on our successful community strategic planning process and with the strong support of another member of our elected board of supervisors, we decided to undertake a community-planning process to redesign the welfare system in San Mateo county. Through our ongoing efforts to work with the community, we learned that people disliked the welfare system because they saw it as promoting dependency and preventing people from getting out of poverty. The community-planning process included over 500 individuals from the community and HSA staff who were engaged in a series of focus groups and planning sessions. I challenged them, "Forget the system as it is now; forget the rules as they are now. If we are trying to help people become economically self-sufficient (one of the goals in our strategic plan) and get out of poverty, how would we design the system?" It was difficult for many participants to think that way. It took almost a year of continual meetings, focus groups, and draft proposals to reach consensus on a new service design and principles. The final plan—Shared Undertaking to Change the Community to Support Self-sufficiency (SUCCESS)—was presented to and approved by the board of supervisors, who charged me with working with the state's Department of Social Services to obtain approval to implement this pilot in our county. It took us almost two years to obtain approval for a waiver from state law and regulations to implement our program design. SUCCESS was implemented in four months, between the waiver approval in August 1996 and the actual roll-out on January 1, 1997. The HSA implementation planning incorporated a single point of contact for comprehensive family screening and assessment, the initial vision for human service delivery in the county when HSA was created. Continual focus on the goals, perseverance, and identifying opportunities had achieved results. SUCCESS sparked many service innovations.

Organizational Structure

Once the SUCCESS service model was created, the executive team searched for ways to support the integrated service model more effectively. Governmental structures tend to be top-down command and control organizations that mirror military structures. Hierarchical structures do not promote open, cross-program teamwork, which is crucial to making the SUCCESS model work. Therefore, with the help of our outside organizational consultants, we looked for organizational structures that the business world was using to change its culture and products. We developed a matrix organization adapted to meet the needs of the service model. In order to break down the program silos that operated in the agency, we began by looking at the outcomes we were trying to achieve. For example, if economic self-sufficiency is the outcome, how do we need to be structured so that we are bringing all of the resources to bear on promoting economic self-sufficiency? It was a different way of looking at service delivery.

We needed to create teams that focused on designing and building services so that everybody understood the whole system and how they contributed to improving client, program, and system outcomes. We took the matrix management concept (originally developed by NASA) and applied it to what we were doing. The organizational model that the executive team created recognizes the realities of our environment while still promoting community-focused, integrated services. We were mindful of the categorical nature of federal and state legislation, policy, and funding. We needed a way to relate our strategic-planning goals to our policy and funding streams and the matrix approach helped us link our integrated service system at the client level with strong integrated management focused on supporting integrated service delivery.

Instead of just having a director for welfare programs, employment programs, child-welfare programs and housing programs, we revamped these positions so that they had dual responsibility as lead for their program area and also served as directors of three geographic regions that covered the entire county. As regional directors, they are responsible for assessing client trends and needs in their region, promoting working relationships with community-based agencies, city governments, school districts, adult education programs, community colleges, and businesses in their region. Each of the three regional directors took the lead on one particular program area (e.g., child welfare, public assistance and welfare-to-work, integrated support services) by chairing a policy team with county-wide accountability for their specific program. For example, the Northern region director was most knowledgeable about children and family services, including child welfare, and provided leadership for the children and family services policy team. That policy team is comprised of children and family, staff from each of the other two regions, as well as the Northern Region. The policy team meets twice a month to assess all the policies, practices, funding, and outcomes related to that policy area. This enables HSA to continue its accountability to the state and federal government and to ensure consistent implementation of programs countywide (see Figure 8.3 for matrix model).

Another cross-program team structure was created at the service delivery level as part of the SUCCESS model. These teams were called Family Self-Sufficiency Teams. Three regional teams were instituted and comprised of line staff from welfare-to-work, child welfare, substance abuse, mental health, housing, probation, and our community-based core service agencies. The teams are convened by a supervisor in each region who serves as team leader and is responsible for coordinating, scheduling cases for presentation, and scheduling periodic case reviews. Clients are invited and encouraged to participate in their case planning in order to develop and agree to a case plan. One member of the team is assigned as primary case manager, depending on the primary needs of the family.

Figure 8.3

Human Services Agency
County of San Mateo

County of San Mateo
Human Services Agency
Director
Maureen Borland
Human Services Advisory Committee

Financial Operations

- Cost Accounting
- Revenue Enhancement
- General Accounting
- Claiming and Reporting
- Budget Monitoring and Audit Coordination
Development
  - Financial Policy Team
  - Financial Operations Team

Legislative/Public Information Officer

Planning and Development

- Special Investigations
- Clerical Support
- Staff Development
- Payroll/Personnel
- Planning
- Research and Evaluation
- Contract Management
- Facility Management
  - Human Resources Policy Team

Business Systems Group

- Automation
- Record Center
- Information Systems Policy

Direct Services
Support Services

Northern Region

Pacifica, Daly City, South San Francisco, Colma,
Brisbane, San Bruno

Countywide Services
- Juvenile Court Officers
- Children's Receiving Home
- CPS Emergency Response and Phone Intake
- Homefinding • Adoptions
- Community Liaison for Children and Families
- Therapeutic Foster Care
- Kinship Support Services Program

Regional Services
- Temp Assistance for individual and Families
  (CalWORKs, Food Stamps General Assistance)
- Work First Training Employment Services
- Health Insurance for (Medi-Cal) • ChildCare Assistance
- Rental Assistance • Children and Family Services
- Family Self Sufficiency Team • Screening Assessment
  • Children and Family Services Policy

Alcohol and Other Drug Services
- Prevention Services • Treatment and
- Tobacco Prevention Program Recovery Services
  • Alcohol and Other Drug Services/
  Tobacco Prevention Program Policy Team
  Drug and Alcohol Advisory Board

Office of Housing
- Property Management, FSS Coordination
- CDBG, HOME, Housing Rehabilitation, Homeownership
- Center on Homelessness, Continuum of Care Coordination
  • Rental Assistance Policy • Housing Policy
  Continuum of Care Collaborative

Central Region

San Mateo, Foster City, Belmont, San Carlos, Burlingame,
Hillsborough, Millbrae, El Granada,
Half Moon Bay, La Honda, Loma Mar, Montara
Moss Beach, Pescadero, San Gregorio

Countywide Services
- Rapid Response for Displaced Workers
- Workforce Investment Board
- workforce Investment Act
- Workcenter/Rehabilitation
- Economic Development
- Child Care

Regional Services
- Temp assistance for individual and Families
  (CalWORKs, Food Stamps General Assistance)
- Work First Training and Employment Services
- Health Insurance for (Medi-Cal) • ChildCare Assistance
- Rental Assistance • Children and Family Services
- Family Self-Sufficiency Team • Screening Assessment
  • Self-Sufficiency Policy Team
  • Medical and Nutrition Access Policy Team

Southern Region

Redwood City, East Palo Alto, Menlo Park,
No Fair Oaks, Woodside, Atherton, Portola Valley

- Adolescent Services

Regional Services
- Temp Assistance for individual and Families
  (CalWORKs, Food Stamps General Assistance)
- Work First Training and Employment Services
- Health Insurance for (Medi-Cal) • ChildCare Assistance
- Rental Assistance • Children and Family Services
- Family Self-Sufficiency Team • Screening Assessment
  • FSST Policy Team

g:\pubinfo\orchrt\hsa all no positions vsd 3\2002s

It was also critical that the agency administrative functions were realigned to support the integration in the SUCCESS model. A deputy director position was created to coordinate a number of the administrative support functions (e.g., facilities, human resources and staff development). Particular emphasis was placed on organizational development, job redesign and reclassification, re-training, and career development. The financial management, information systems, and research and planning functions were identified as critical to our new way of doing business. Therefore, a director of financial services and director of information systems positions were created from other positions within the agency and reported directly to the agency director. A research and planning unit (later planning and evaluation) that reported to the agency director was also created. This unit serves as the link between information systems and programs, provides data analysis for planning and management, and coordinates the knowledge management function and continual quality improvement functions of the agency. In 2005 (as part of the response to a child death crisis described later) some adjustments were made to this model. A separate policy director for children and family services was created to focus more attention on improving the cross-systems relationships in child welfare and on the implementation of the child welfare redesign in the county. At that time, due to a lack of available positions, a director for program support was added, which combined the administrative functions, including financial and information systems. The regional matrix model continues.

Discussion Questions

6. A matrix is the most complex and challenging organization design. Can you think of alternative designs that could have also had good results, perhaps with less effort?

7. What aspects of the new design were important in creating an integrated services system?

Organizational Development

The changes in the HSA organizational culture and the dual role assumed by each regional director represented a great deal of change. I knew that the directors, as well as their staff, would need some assistance in making this transition. The structural changes we were making required staff to operate in new relationships and structures, and they required a new level of mutual accountability. I researched the business literature for techniques that could be used to promote and implement these changes. Because the change was so large and complex, I decided that HSA needed to create a position for an internal organizational development (OD) specialist. The OD specialist worked with each one of the regional directors to build their policy teams. She also worked with each director (team leader) to help team members understand their roles in sharing information and leading action planning in their regions. Each team reviewed their composition to ensure appropriate representation and developed their mission, operating rules, schedule of team meetings, and other meeting management processes. Minutes were taken and disseminated so that everyone in the agency knew what was going on and the decisions being made by the team. The executive team (comprised of regional directors and other senior managers) serves as the coordinating body for all the policy teams.

The creation of policy teams also allowed us to open up the budgeting and financial management functions of the agency to comprehensive review and understanding. Each policy team reviews the allocations for their programs and works with their financial analyst (also a member of the policy team) to prepare the budget and make priority decisions about where those resources are most needed. These decisions are informed by data regarding client, program and system outcomes and linked to commitments to outcome improvement in our outcome-based management system. Annually, each team goes out into the community to get input on community needs, how services are working, and gaps in service. We have put together a community mapping process where we use zip-code data so that staff can actually see where there are clusters of problems and which neighborhoods and zip codes need attention. This information is shared with the communities in order to inform collaborative community action.

Each director also meets regularly with a regional management team and holds periodic regional staff meetings to share information and obtain input on issues and staff needs. This has helped to create a regional identity across programs and has resulted in better coordination and understanding between the program staff. The OD specialist also assisted the directors with building the operations of these regional teams.

Particular emphasis was placed on developing the Family Self-Sufficiency Teams (FSSTs). The internal OD specialist spent a good deal of time helping these multi-disciplinary teams understand their roles, how to function and make decisions as a team, how to schedule cases and hold productive case planning discussions as equals, and how to monitor and periodically review case progress. These teams became the core of our transformed service delivery system.

Discussion Questions

8. Could this change process have been successful without involving a consultant?

9. Without a consultant, what would the director have needed to do to move the change process?

Multi-Disciplinary Case Planning

The complex lives of our clients require multiple strategies. For example, poverty is very complicated, and it involves much more than economics. When we look at self-sufficiency in terms of family functioning and community involvement, there are different strategies needed to produce good client outcomes. These strategies vary depending on the family; where they live; and the resources, both family and community, that are available. We have tried to place special emphasis on working with those communities where poverty and social dysfunction are most prevalent. For example, we work with grassroots planning teams involving the police and a whole array of other organizations dealing with crime in high-crime communities. The problems of crime and poverty are so intertwined that we try to work together and develop multiple approaches, including job training; job placement, transportation supports, family resource centers, and schools. The Family Self-Sufficiency Teams, which include criminal justice and health representatives, are the mechanism for cross-system case planning when families are involved with multiple systems or have multiple needs. Nonprofit community agency partners, with whom we contract, are also involved in team meetings as necessary.

The FSSTs have become the mechanism for providing integrated services to multi-need families. The creation of those teams moved us toward the initial vision for the agency and the service system. It became clear to us that if we were trying to develop integrated service plans, all the relevant service providers needed to be at the table, with the client, to discuss and understand: (1) all the family issues, (2) the services they were receiving, (3) what they were trying to achieve, and (4) how they wanted to participate in the service plan.

When we initially put these teams together, the team membership was not so all-inclusive. It was a struggle to get staff, even from the smaller teams, to schedule cases for team discussion. Staff members were accustomed to doing individual case planning and did not regularly consult with multiple service providers. Staff needed to learn how to work in teams. Our OD specialist worked with the team leaders and the teams to clarify relationships, develop team rules, foster understanding of shared responsibilities, develop criteria for bringing cases to the team, discuss team meeting frequency, decide how cases would be followed up, and clarify the expectations for the outcome of the team work. We found that while effective team functioning is critical to providing integrated services, a managerial tracking and monitoring mechanism is needed to ensure that staff behavior shifts and that staff are bringing their cases to the team.

Today, staff members within both HSA and the community see the FSSTs as a critical resource in providing improved services to families. The teams have grown. Staff regularly take cases to the team for consultation and find them helpful. Inviting clients to participate in the team meetings has changed the culture of the way services plans are developed and implemented. Family responsibilities become a part of the discussion, as well. While there was initial concern about inviting families to participate in team meetings, approximately 75% of families are now coming to team meetings. The families are engaged in case planning, learning what to expect from the systems and programs, and agreeing to implement their case plan. Team meetings are now located in the neighborhoods where clients live.

Discussion Questions

10. What were the key factors in implementing the team structure?

11. What other tactics could have been used to enhance team functioning?

Creating a Culture of Innovation in a Learning Organization

I am a firm believer in identifying what needs to be done and trying to find the funding to do it. My experience has shown me that money often follows good ideas. Too often, public organizations limit their planning and thinking within their perceived fiscal constraints, rather than identifying community and client needs and encouraging new ways to meet them. Once you have a broad-based community strategic plan, it is possible to seek out ways to implement it. In San Mateo county, we worked closely with foundations to get one-time funding to initiate innovations in our community. Partnerships were developed with the Peninsula Community Foundation, the Center for Venture Philanthropy, and other regional foundations. Our partnerships focused on jointly meeting the needs of our community. Since the development of the San Mateo County Strategic Plan had involved community representatives (foundations, business, education, cities, community non-profits, health and criminal justice, and clients), it was owned by the whole community. We looked for opportunities to leverage public dollars with private matching funds.

The earliest innovative model piloted by HSA was the creation of the FUTURES family resource centers in 1992. The FUTURES project was a collaboration in Daly City (one of the cities in our county with the largest influx of new immigrant families with children) between the county and local school districts, community-based organizations, and county health and human services. It was the pilot for the concept of neighborhood-based, integrated, prevention/early intervention services for children and families. The involvement of HSA staff in this project informed the larger organization and created a concrete example of what neighborhood-based, integrated services could look like. The staff members that were part of the project became ambassadors for the new collaborative model of service and were given great exposure throughout the agency. While some staff members were jealous of the attention and resources committed to the pilot, the message was clear that those involved in implementing the strategic directions of the agency would be rewarded and seen as leaders.

When California's welfare reform program (CalWORKS) was implemented, we took the opportunity to use one-time federal incentive funds for the start-up of innovative programs to assist former welfare and low-income families in moving toward economic self-sufficiency. We also used those funds to create the one-stop service and employment centers in our low-income neighborhoods where we could co-locate multiple services. If you have a strategic plan, when the opportunities arise, you can target the funds to the priorities in your plan and interest your partners in doing the same.

Another major step in creating a learning organization resulted from the decisions we made in struggling with the change in job roles and the skills and abilities that staff would need as we implemented our service integration program (SUCCESS). Staff needed to become good assessors, interviewers, and case managers. We had staff with high school diplomas, some with AA degrees and some with BA degrees all working as eligibility workers in the old system. We realized we really needed to upgrade the level of skill and promote a culture that valued skill development and education as a part of career development. This message was consistent with the message we wanted staff to impart to welfare clients who were trying to move from welfare to work. Major alliances were formed with the community colleges that had previously worked as partners in welfare-to-work efforts for clients, to work with us to develop training for human services providers, including HSA staff. We also worked with the community colleges to offer an AA degree in Human Services and have been working with them over the past couple of years to co-locate a BA degree program in social work on a community college campus.

We also began to recognize the participation in educational and career development programs as a preference factor in promoting and selecting staff for special assignments and promotions. A major one-day HSA career conference was held annually to communicate our commitment to learning and education and encourage staff to take charge of their own career planning and development. These actually became models for county-wide human resources approaches.

It also became obvious to the executive team that our managers and supervisors needed training and assistance with the role changes we were defining for them. We brought in consultants to work with us on training topics that included facilitative leadership, managing with data, and project management. The executive team spent months identifying the core competencies that they needed in managers and supervisors and agreed that these would be rolled into the screening and interviewing processes for the selection of future supervisors and managers across programs. A comprehensive training program was developed for existing supervisors and managers to help them to develop these competencies. This training course is still in existence, and it is a valued program within the organization. The implicit goal of this training is to foster intellectual curiosity and critical thinking. The message conveyed is that although we may be doing good work, it can always be improved. This has led to an agency commitment to continual quality improvement.

My assumption in creating the original Research and Evaluation unit in 1996 was that by hiring a well-trained research person in HSA we would be more capable of evaluating our own efforts. This never really worked well, partly because the research staff struggled with organizational understanding and readiness for research and evaluation. It became obvious to us that training and a more collaborative working relationship between research and service programs would be required to build an organizational value for formal research and evaluation. It took time for managers to see how research information could help them improve their outcomes. Today, the Planning and Evaluation unit in HSA has taken the lead on coordinating the Continual Quality Improvement efforts of the agency. This unit is responsible for researching evidence-based and best practices and working with the service programs to review their outcomes and promote dialogue and decision making on what needs to be changed.

In San Mateo county, we have developed many of our own models and programs that we think make sense in meeting client and community needs. We are tracking outcomes and have created a culture committed to improvement. We have struggled with the fact that we have not had the resources to evaluate all these programs and their impact on client outcomes. Our planning and evaluation unit makes considerable use of administrative data and does the analysis for the programs to help them with their decision making. The limited availability of relevant research in the human services field has forced us to do the best we can through this unit and outside contracts with private research groups to evaluate our programs. It is hoped that the new emphasis on evidence-based practice and the improved linkages between program and researchers in the state will strengthen this effort.

Discussion Questions

12. What evidence do you see that a culture of innovation and learning was created?

13. What alternative or additional tactics might have helped to implement this change?

Advocating for Change

In addition to promoting change inside the agency, we have been actively involved in advocacy at the state level with our professional organizations and with the state's Departments of Social Services (DSS) and Health. As we began implementation planning for our SUCCESS redesign, it became clear that our thinking was ahead of the state's planning. We met with the DSS top management to present our community planning process and the plan we wished to implement, and they indicated that they were not interested in approving county pilot projects, no matter how innovative or community-supported. It took us almost two years to finally obtain approval for a waiver of state laws and regulations. We were told that a waiver could not be granted to do what we wanted to do because our design was too comprehensive and involved too many different components of the service system. By this time our board champion had been elected to the state assembly. I informed him of the DSS position, and we decided to have him sponsor legislation to allow us to pilot SUCCESS. It was only after legislation was introduced that the DSS Director decided that they did have the authority to grant a waiver.

This was both an education in the state political process for me and my executive team and a tremendous challenge to actually implement in four months. We were able to implement our own local version of welfare reform two years before the California CalWORKS program. We had an outside evaluator design a waiver evaluation and work with us as we tracked our welfare-to-work participants. We tracked exits from welfare, what kind of work clients entered, the average salary, and the availability of health benefits. We had the largest percentage of caseload reduction in the state, and it was because people went to work. The economy was strong at the time and 76% of our participants who had been on welfare went to work. That was a huge change. Subsequent studies have estimated that approximately 40% of the caseload reductions nationally during that time were due to the economy, but we worked with our community to take advantage of our good economy. Our SUCCESS program informed the thinking behind the design of the CalWORKS program for the state.

Two years into our three-year waiver, and after the CalWORKS legislation was passed, we were sued by a statewide advocacy group. Two of our rules in SUCCESS were more stringent than in Ca1WORKS. The advocacy organizations had fought the battle at the state level for less stringent rules and felt that allowing our project to continue the way it was would undermine that success. We lost in court and had to come into compliance with the CalWORKS process. The two major differences were: (1) in order to be approved for welfare and receive a check, clients had to participate in week-long employment services seminars, and if they did not cooperate, they did not get approved to receive a welfare check, and (2) while we had many more services in place than were in the state program (e.g., home visitors from community-based organizations), our clients who did not participate in welfare-to-work planning were given a full family sanction. We had the lowest sanction rate in the state (less than 3%), so this final sanction was used very sparingly. However, the advocates felt that they needed to make the point because other counties did not have a rich array of community services in place and might want to move to full family sanctions. We brought our SUCCESS program into compliance by modifying the entry and sanction policies and have been operating according to state rules ever since, while still maintaining the comprehensive screening and assessment and integrated case planning features.

While this was frustrating for us, we took the positive lessons from this experience and learned that it is important to advocate for the legislative and regulatory changes that you need to meet your community needs. We later had success in helping to design the Child Welfare Redesign approaches and the California Children and Families Accountability System. While it is a lot of extra work, volunteering to be part of the design and legislation development has great rewards. It often results in a more rational community service orientation in state and federal policy.

The Leadership Role

I have always envisioned myself as a team leader. I have worked hard to promote teamwork throughout our organization and in the community. Our organization has an executive team comprised of the regional directors and the directors of the key support services. It took several years to develop into a real team. We actually developed rules for how we operate. We agreed to bring major issues and policy team decisions to the team for discussion and input and to make decisions by consensus. I made the final decision if consensus could not be reached. That was not the environment that top managers had operated in previously. I obviously had a lot of influence in the team process, but if we did not all agree on something we took the time to work out our differences so that we could ultimately reach consensus.

Dialogue is critical to good decision making. The "command and control" approach to leadership does not promote common understanding and teamwork. Our organization has over 750 employees and an annual budget of about $185 million a year. Our community has over 700,000 residents. There is too much going on inside and outside the organization to think that you can control all of it. To me, leadership is promoting the vision, mission, values, and influencing the processes to move forward and achieve our goals. It takes constant effort to find ways to get feedback from people on what is working and what is not. I learned that sometimes I thought things were working a certain way, but they weren't. I sometimes think that leading teams by trusting others is my strength and biggest weakness. However, it is really effective in creating shared ownership. Nevertheless, you can get blindsided, which is why it is so important to continuously look for feedback.

One of the key roles I played as a team leader was to constantly look for opportunities to move our strategic plan forward and link external directions from the federal and state levels with the strategies our community had laid out. Some of the questions we would contemplate in our executive team meetings were: "How do the new laws or policy changes mesh with our strategic plan? How do we leverage or harness this new development as a catalyst for moving toward our vision and implementing our strategic directions more effectively?" Leadership is getting the team to think strategically within the framework of the overall vision and goals, rather than looking at each change as a mandated program to be implemented separately. Leadership is not waiting for others to do it to us, but figuring out what we think makes sense for our community and then formally putting in place a process to develop a plan that can inform federal or statewide thinking on implementation.

Another role of the leader is to model critical-thinking skills. This often takes the form of rigorous inquiry and may be viewed in a negative way by managers or staff members who do not think that top management should be probing or assessing ongoing operations. My experience has taught me that if you do not build a depth of understanding regarding how the organization operates, you cannot really change it. Discussions of processes and the need to redesign them were key in creating the organizational and service changes we made as well as promoting the culture of a learning organization.

Discussion Question

14. As a leader in this situation, what could you do to get feedback on your performance on a regular basis?

Managing Crises

Another key leadership role is to manage crises that affect the organization. One such crisis occurred in the process of creating organizational change. In late 1994, we were working with an external business consultant who was assisting us with the organizational change process. On his advice, I brought in an outside team to evaluate how things were going with the changes we were undertaking in the organizational culture. The team conducted focus groups and sent questionnaires to select staff and worked with an internal team to construct a report for management on how change was progressing, and where there were problems that needed intervention. The report was candid and laid out many areas that needed additional attention. This was to be expected, since it was early in the change process for such a large organization. The report was intended for executive team discussion and action planning. It was an internal progress report that we shared with staff.

I really trusted staff to use it in order to improve operations, but it became politicized. Although I had briefed the county manager on the report and our plan to address the staff concerns, the report was leaked to a board member with a cover note indicating that our agency was in a "mess." I had to manage the discussions with the board and county manager. The business consultant volunteered to join me in those discussions and lauded the openness and commitment to a process of continuous organizational improvement that the executive team and I had made. The board actually put the topic on a future meeting agenda, and the consultant did a presentation on the process we had used and praised the agency leadership. Ironically, the organizational self-assessment process was adopted by several other county department directors after they heard the consultant's presentation. Our staff learned a lot from the crisis and the way it was handled. It was a difficult process, personally, however, and I learned that I might be a bit too optimistic about openness and information sharing in a political environment.

The second major crisis of my tenure was a much more serious one. We had a child who was in foster care who went home on an unsupervised visit and became a victim of shaken-baby syndrome. The perpetrator was the father. It occurred over the Christmas holidays about three years ago. This was a very difficult situation, not only because of the emotions surrounding a child's death, but because there was a lot of controversy generated by the juvenile court judge. While the judge had actually approved unsupervised visits for this child, she criticized the agency for permitting it and proceeded with an open-court hearing to investigate the agency's behavior and decision-making process. It became a major focus of the local media, and she used that opportunity to criticize the worker, the agency, the director for child welfare, and me. Since she was part of the case decision making, I believe that she should have recused herself and had another judge oversee any investigation. The child's foster parent was very attached to the child, had wanted to adopt him, and was not pleased with the reunification process before the incident occurred. She became one of the harshest critics of the worker and the agency for allowing the child to go for this unsupervised visit. A detailed internal investigation, including county counsel, had found that there was no negligence on the part of the worker. There was, I believe, some miscommunication between the therapist and the worker. The therapist from the private contract agency was also very critical of the worker. However, there was no proof on either side of what was said back and forth to each other. It did point out some real gaps in the system in terms of the fact that we were not getting written reports and recommendations from our contractor provider agency. Most reports were oral, as had been agreed upon in the 1980s when the contract was first negotiated. I felt that it was my responsibility to support the worker, especially when there were many people calling for her termination. There was no reason to terminate her, and I felt that it was unfair for someone to lose his or her job because they made a judgment that did not work as planned. All indications in the reports had been that the child would be safe at home. In fact, an older sibling had already been reunified a month earlier and was doing fine.

I strongly supported both the worker and the child welfare director in my court testimony. The judge was not happy with me. It became a real political issue, since the judge is a good friend of the editor of the local newspaper, who continued to criticize me in print. I had no relationship with the editor and refused to get drawn into a public battle in the press. As a result, the county manager appointed a "Blue Ribbon panel" to look into the controversy. The agency was the only party not represented on the panel. The report issued was very critical of the agency and me. This continued to fuel the press coverage in the local paper. While some of my colleagues thought that I should have fought it out in the press and become as nasty as the judge, I refused to stoop to that level and would not do so today. I believe that leadership sometimes involves taking politically unpopular and principled positions, even at a risk to yourself, and even when the political establishment is searching for cover.

In response to these facts, I led the agency in conducting a comprehensive assessment of our policies and procedures and made improvements in several areas. The grand jury did an outside investigation and made some recommendations for policy, process, and service changes that we were already in the process of implementing. I think that our child-welfare system today is stronger than ever, including some new service providers and an improved documentation process.

In the spirit of using opportunities (even negative ones!) to promote strategic directions, I volunteered our agency to participate as one of the 11 counties piloting the new California Child Welfare Redesign as part of our child-welfare improvement strategy. California had developed a Child Welfare Redesign Plan that was issued in 2003. The plan involved developing a differential response system, in which community agencies provided services to families who had been referred for abuse and neglect, but who were determined not to need intervention from the child-welfare system. This system required the development of a community-service system to provide prevention and early intervention services to families. Since HSA had already developed a network of 14 family resource centers in high need areas of the county, an infrastructure already existed upon which the differential response services could be built. The second component of the Child Welfare Redesign was implementation of standardized safety and risk assessment at key points throughout the life of the case. Since this was one of the issues in our child-welfare death, our county participation in piloting new tools and retraining staff was part of our improvement plan. We utilized the state's mandate to develop a Systems Improvement Plan to convene a broad-based community and cross-systems advisory committee to review our child welfare outcomes (defined by the federal and state governments) and system. This committee reviewed all aspects of the system, including police and referral sources, court processes and legal representation, and community services and supports, including those from health, mental health and substance abuse systems. This committee was co-chaired by a member of the board of supervisors and the director of the Peninsula Community Foundation. The committee produced a systems-wide Child Welfare Systems Improvement Plan (SIP). The result has been a much better community understanding of the child-welfare system and the laws and processes surrounding it and a commitment of private foundation funds to help implement the systems improvements. Greater ownership of our strategic direction of building community capacity to support children and families has resulted, and services have been expanded in collaboration with schools, cities, and community-based organizations.

Discussion Questions

15.   As an agency leader, what would be your key priorities in handling unfavorable information about your agency?

16.   What would be your strategies and tactics in managing such crises?

Knowing When it Is Time to Leave

It is very difficult to know how long you should stay in the director position in the same organization. On the one hand, a long tenure can be a positive because you are in an organization long enough to really make deep changes in its culture. On the other hand, sometimes those changes are seen as only linked to you, instead of to the organization as a whole. Resistance to change can become personalized. This is very common in hierarchical organizations, where every success and failure is identified with the leader.

There were several points during my 13-year tenure when I thought about exiting, something everyone experiences at some time during a long period of employment. The work environment is very important to me, especially an organizational environment where I believe that I can move forward and make the changes to meet the strategic goals. If I do not think that I am going to be able to move anything forward, then it is time to leave. I think that sometimes you get to a point, emotionally and professionally, where you have taken on enough challenges and think that it may be time for the organization to have new leadership.

Quite honestly, I was ready to leave about two years before I retired. The child-death crisis is what convinced me to stay, because my work was not done. It was critical to guide the organization through this difficult time and enable it to make the improvements that needed to be made within the county systems and the community. It was important to re-establish the agency's credibility in our community and rebuild our partnership approach to service improvement.

Leaving an organization after investing so much of your life in it is very difficult. If you feel that you have hired the right people and that the team really owns the mission, values, and strategic directions, then the organization can carry on without you, and it makes leaving a little bit easier. That is why it is so critical to spend the time to identify the values, attitudes, and core competencies needed to lead the organization and to invest in training and developing managers. Succession planning is about the competencies, philosophies, and skills that you want to be a part of the organization, and how you make sure that you are developing a pool of people who could potentially become the director at some point and carry the vision forward.

Reflections and Implications

As I reflect back upon leaving the agency, it occurs to me that one of the most important legacies of my tenure is the fact that the mission, values, and strategic plan for human services have been implemented in HSA and in the county. The time that was spent working with senior staff paid off in terms of building a shared commitment to excellence, becoming big-picture thinkers, developing a sense of accountability for outcomes and performance, becoming team builders and collaborators, and developing flexibility and creativity in the way people worked together. These core competencies were much more important to me, and they have become much more important to the senior staff, than detailed program knowledge when selecting managers in the organization.

It has also become clearer to me how much organizational change is dependent on leadership setting the behavioral examples. For instance, the functioning of the executive team meetings as opportunities for team building and open dialogue on issues leading to consensus decisions set an example for how other teams in the agency could work. You can talk about the mission, values, and strategies all you want, but when managers and staff see it in practice repeatedly it becomes ingrained in the organizational functioning. Seeing things change for the better creates hope among staff and unleashes their ability to be creative, to think, and to develop the community relationships necessary to generate innovation.

My experiences in San Mateo have confirmed my commitment to proactive management. As difficult as some of the experiences were emotionally, I can see that perseverance can result in significant improvements in social service systems over time. Proactive management involves taking risks and challenging people or institutions. It can generate hostility. I have seen many managers who conceptually supported a direction, but were not willing to take the actions necessary to create real change in operations. The process of identifying, recruiting, and/or promoting proactive managers is complicated because reference-checking can be limited and superficial. It is only when you work with managers and see them in action that you can really assess their courage and willingness to work through conflict.

Reactive managers have a strong tendency to want to be liked. These are not the people who can promote organizational and systems change. However, they are often the managers who are most popular in public agencies. I believe that it is much easier to survive and thrive in public systems if you are a reactive manager and well liked, but this approach does not always serve the best interests of our clients, communities, or society. Reactive managers in your organization can undermine your best efforts.

Directors and top management can be easily diverted from the strategic vision by organizational crises. There is always something coming at you, and there is too much to be managed effectively. I can now see how important it is to continually bring the focus back to the mission and strategic plans. I think this requires the same set of skills that are needed to be an effective parent. Parenting is a balancing act between being permissive and being authoritative (not authoritarian—there is a real difference). Being authoritative (reminding staff of the mission; establishing realistic boundaries; using caring firmness to help everyone move in the same direction) is the most effective parenting skill and has similarities to effective proactive management. Even with these skills, however, it is clear that both children and staff can wait you out in order to find ways not to change. That is more difficult, however, if the proactive manager is persistent, consistent, and follows through.

My San Mateo experience also made me realize that while public sector leadership and management needs to improve, the vast majority of managers in human services systems work extremely hard and are emotionally committed to the work they do. While skill development and strategic approaches can help them to make these systems more responsive to the real needs of the poor in our society, the political realities with which they contend make this work extremely difficult and frustrating. It is important for everyone to be introspective enough to determine when they have done what they can in that environment and then find other ways to promote the cause of social change.

Discussion Questions

17. To what extent, and in what ways, do you think you need to be "liked" at work? How will you address the tension of wanting to be liked and also wanting change that may cause resentments?

18. What would you do as a leader when confronted with staff resistance or resentments regarding organizational changes that you believe are necessary?

19. Based on this case, what specific leadership skills would you like to develop to become an effective leader in a human service agency?

Suggested Debriefing Framework: 2.6 Policy Practice

❖ CHAPTER EXERCISES

Exercise #1

Using the Proehl (2001) dimensions of managing organizational change, this exercise provides students with an opportunity to work through a change management framework. Based on small group discussion to identify an agency structure or process that needs changing, students select the most interesting dilemma to analyze using the following eight steps:

1. Creating a sense of urgency: external forces, internal indicators, high performance standards, share data (e.g., management audit, employee survey)

2. Building the coalition for change: sponsor, champion, people with credibility, power, interest, informal leaders; formal group, e.g., steering committee, task forces; cross-functional representation from all levels ("diagonal slice"); communication systems

3. Clarifying the change imperative: problems, visions, resources needed, written contract including outcomes, legitimacy, communicating the vision

4. Assessing the present: strengths, obstacles, organizational readiness

5. Developing a plan for change: strategies, processes, activities, short-term successes, who will be involved

6. Dealing with the human factors: communication; resistance; involvement of staff; new skills, knowledge and attitudes; incentives

7. Acting quickly and revising frequently: quick results, timetables, involvement, monitoring, institutionalization

8. Evaluating and celebrating the change: assessing results, celebration, rewards

Exercise #2

One of the most challenging aspects of entering a managerial position in a human service organization is the capacity to quickly assess the structure, process, climate, and culture of the agency. Students could bring their responses to the following questions to use in a small-group discussions in which they indentify the area that they find most confusing in their fieldwork agency. In this way, the various areas could be identified and then shared with the entire class to note the similarities and differences and to explore possible explanations.

1. Agency Mission, Overview, and Environment:
   a. What is the mission of the agency?
   b. What is the governance structure (board of directors, elected officials)?
   c. What major programs are being operated?
   d. How many employees are there in the agency?
   e. What are the major environmental forces facing it? How does the organization adapt to environmental changes?
   f. What management theories do you see in use at the agency? How appropriate and effective do they seem to be?

2. Goals and Effectiveness:
   a. What are the organization's key goals and objectives?
   b. How is organizational performance defined and measured?
   c. How effective are the agency's programs?

3. Structure and Technology:
   a. How is the agency structured? (Attach an organizational chart.)
   b. What are the core inputs, service delivery technologies, and outputs/outcomes?
   c. Do the structure and technologies fit well with environmental demands and client needs and with each other? Are services based on evidence-based practice research?
   d. How are service and administrative processes coordinated?

4. Climate and Culture, Organizational Learning:
    a. How would you describe the organization's culture and subcultures, if any? What organizational values, beliefs, or norms are apparent in the organization?
    b. Are there rituals, ceremonies, traditions, symbols, or stories told about the agency or its leaders or founders that give clues as to how people are expected to behave?
    c. Does the organization use principles of organizational learning such as experimentation, learning from past experiences or from best practices, sharing knowledge, or creating a learning culture (see Austin & Hopkins, 2004)? Are there any other ways that the organization seems to learn from its experiences and change or adapt?

5. Quality of Working Life:
    a. How does the agency rate on dimensions of quality of working life such as adequate salaries, individual autonomy, enriching jobs, and a sense of community and support?
    b. How is morale? How much turnover is there?
    c. How much stress exists, and how is it dealt with?
    d. Is there evidence of staff burnout? If so, how is this addressed?
    e. How long do employees stay with the agency?
    f. Why do employees leave, and where do they typically go?

6. Life Cycles:
    a. At what stage is the organization in its life cycle?
    b. Is it managing its developmental needs for growth, maintenance, and survival?
    c. Are there any life-cycle issues the organization should be addressing? If so, what should it be doing?

7. Power, Politics, and Conflict:
    a. What are the major internal interest groups?
    b. Who are the most powerful actors?
    c. What power bases are used, and with what effect?
    d. What are the major areas of conflict?
    e. How does conflict get addressed? How effective are conflict management processes?

8. Leadership:
    a. What are the key behaviors of organizational leaders?
    b. What are some examples of effective and ineffective leadership?

9. Motivation:

   a. What are the motivational profiles of the main groups of employees?

   b. What seem to be the assumptions of managers regarding how employees are motivated?

   c. To what extent do job designs seem to motivate employees? How?

   d. What does the organization do or not do to respond to employee needs?

10. Diversity and Discrimination:

   a. How much diversity is there (race, ethnicity, gender, sexual orientation, disability, age, social class) in the agency?

   b. Describe key dynamics of communication processes with reference to diversity considerations. How effective is communication across groups?

   c. Is discrimination evident or a possibility (e.g., in promotions or work assignments, the ways clients are treated)?

11. Problems and Challenges:

   a. What are the major challenges facing the organization?

   b. How is the organization dealing with environmental changes and demands and internal problems or needs?

   c. What areas of the organization seem to be most in need of change?

References

Allison, M., & Kaye, J. (1997). *Strategic planning for non-profit organizations.* New York: John Wiley.

Argyris, C., & Schon, D. (1996). *Organizational learning II: Theory, method, and practice.* Reading, MA: Addison-Wesley.

Austin, M. J. (1988). Managing up: Relationship building between middle management and top management. *Administration in Social Work, 12*(4), 29–46.

Austin, M. J., & Hopkins, K. (Eds.). (2004). *Supervision as collaboration in the human services: Building a learning culture.* Thousand Oaks, CA: Sage.

Austin, M., & Kruzich, J. (2004). Assessing recent textbooks and casebooks in human service administration: Implications and future directions. *Administration in Social Work, 28*(1), 115–137.

Austin, M. J., & Packard, T. (in press). Case-based learning: Educating future human service managers. *Journal of Teaching in Social Work.*

Birren, J. E., & Fisher, L. M. (1990). The elements of wisdom: Overview and integration. In R. J. Sternberg (Ed.), *Wisdom: Its nature, origins, and development* (pp. 317–332). Cambridge, MA: Cambridge University Press.

Block, S. R. (2004). *Why nonprofits fail.* San Francisco: Jossey-Bass.

Bloom, G., Catagna, C., Moir, E., & Warren, B. (2005). *Blended coaching: Skills and strategies to support principal development.* Thousand Oaks, CA: Corwin Press.

Brock, J. (2004). *MORETOOLS: A framework for analyzing management dilemmas.* Seattle: Evans School of Public Affairs, University of Washington. Retrieved January 20, 2007, from evans.washington.edu/courses/2005–2006/autumn/syllabi/540-brock.pdf

Brody, R. (2005). *Effectively managing human service organizations* (3rd ed.). Thousand Oaks, CA: Sage.

Bryson, J. M. (1995). *Strategic planning for public and non-profit organizations.* San Francisco: Jossey-Bass.

Cossom, J. (1991). Teaching from cases: Education for critical thinking. *Journal of Teaching Social Work, 5*(1), 139–155.

Crow, R., & Odewahn, R. (1987). *Management for the human services.* Englewood Cliffs, NJ: Prentice-Hall.

Denhardt, R. B., Denhardt, J. V., & Aristigueta, M. P. (2002). *Managing human behavior in public and nonprofit organizations.* Thousand Oaks, CA: Sage.

Edwards, R., & Yankey, J. (Eds.). (2006). *Effectively managing nonprofit organizations.* Washington, DC: NASW Press.

Ezell, M., Menefee, D., & Patti, R. J. (1989). Managerial leadership and service quality: Toward a model of social work administration. *Administration in Social Work, 13*(3–4), 73–98.

Fauri, D., Wernet, S., & Netting, E. (2004). *Cases in macro social work practice* (2nd ed.). Boston: Allyn & Bacon.

Herman, R., & Renz, D. (1999). Theses on nonprofit organizational effectiveness. *Nonprofit and Voluntary Sector Quarterly, 28*(2), 107–126.

Hill, M., & Hupe, P. (2002). *Implementing public policy: Governance in theory and practice.* London: Sage Ltd.

Hopkins, K., & Austin, M. J. (2004). Coaching employees with performance problems. In M. J. Austin & K. Hopkins (Eds.), *Supervision as collaboration in the human services: Building a learning culture* (pp. 215–226). Thousand Oaks, CA: Sage.

Kadushin, A., & Harkness, D. (2002). *Supervision in social work* (4th ed.). New York: Columbia University Press.

Kahn, W. A. (2005). *Holding fast: The struggle to create resilient caregiving organizations.* New York: Brunner-Routledge.

Kearns, K. P. (2000). Private sector strategies for social sector success: The guide to strategy and planning for public and nonprofit organizations. San Francisco: Jossey-Bass.

Kelly, F., & Kelly, H. (1986). *What they really teach you at the Harvard Business School.* New York: Warner.

Kettner, P. (2002a). *Achieving excellence in the management of human service organizations.* Boston: Allyn & Bacon.

Kettner, P. (2002b). *Human service organizations.* Boston: Allyn & Bacon.

Kettner, P., Moroney, R., & Martin, L. (1999). *Designing and managing programs: An effectiveness-based approach* (2nd ed.). Thousand Oaks, CA: Sage.

Kettner, P., Moroney, R., & Martin, L. (2008). *Designing and managing programs: An effectiveness-based approach* (3rd ed.). Thousand Oaks, CA: Sage.

Kotter, J. (1990). *A force for change: How leadership differs from management.* New York: Free Press.

Lawrence. P., & Lorsch, J. (1967). *Organization and environment.* Cambridge, MA: Harvard University Press.

Lewis, J., Packard, T., & Lewis, M. (2007). *Management of human service programs* (4th ed.). Belmont, CA: Thomson/Brooks Cole.

Mayers, R., Souffle, F., & Schoech, D. (1994). *Dilemmas in human services management: Illustrative case studies.* New York: Springer.

Menefee, D. (1997). Strategic administration of nonprofit human service organizations: A model for executive success in turbulent times. *Administration in Social Work, 21*(2), 1–19.

Menefee, D. (2000). What managers do and why they do it. In R. Patti (Ed.), *The handbook of social welfare management* (pp. 247–266). Thousand Oaks, CA: Sage.

Menefee, D., & Thompson, J. (1994). Identifying and comparing competencies for social work management: A practice driven approach. *Administration in Social Work, 18*(3), 1–25.

Mintzberg, H. (2004). *Managers not MBAs: A hard look at the soft practice of managing and management development.* San Francisco: Berrett-Koehler.

Northouse, P. (2004). *Leadership: Theory and practice* (3rd ed.). Thousand Oaks, CA: Sage.

Packard, T., & Austin, M. J. (in press). Using a case-based comprehensive examination to evaluate and integrate student learning. *Journal of Teaching in Social Work.*

Proehl, R. (2001). *Organizational change in the human services.* Thousand Oaks, CA: Sage.

Quinn, R. E. (1988). *Beyond rational management: Mastering the paradoxes and competing demands of high performance.* San Francisco: Jossey-Bass.

Rapp, C., & Poertner, J. (2007). *Textbook of social administration: The consumer-centered approach.* New York: Haworth.

Roberts-DeGennaro, M., & Packard, T. (2002). A framework for developing a social administration concentration. *Journal of Teaching in Social Work, 22*(1/2), 61–77.

Thompson, J. (1967). *Organizations in action.* New York: McGraw Hill.

Webster, W. (1988). Student-developed case studies. *College Teaching, 36*(Winter), 25–27.

Index

About the Authors

Michael J. Austin, PhD, is the Milton and Florence Krenz Mack Professor of Nonprofit Management at the School of Social Welfare, University of California, Berkeley, as well as co-chair of Management and Planning Specialization. He teaches Management Practice, Assessing the Dynamics of Communities, Groups and Organizations, Working in Nonprofits, and Supervision. Over the past 38 years, he has authored 18 books, as well as numerous articles and research monographs. He currently serves as staff director of the Bay Area Social Services consortium, which operates an executive development program, research response team, and policy implementation and promising practices program. He also serves as Director of the Mack Center on Nonprofit Management in the Human Services, which promotes knowledge development in the areas of organizational histories, executive think tank, leadership development, and mapping the knowledge base of nonprofit management. He consults throughout the country in the areas of managerial team building, organizational restructuring, and strategic planning for nonprofit organizations (with a special focus on Jewish communal organizations). He received his PhD from the University of Pittsburgh in 1970 and his MSW from the University of California, Berkeley, in 1966.

Ralph Brody, PhD, was developing a casebook to accompany his best-selling textbook *Effectively Managing Human Service Organizations* when he passed away on February 8, 2006. As the book was in draft form, many cases were integrated into the current text with Michael J. Austin and Thomas Packard.

Prior to his death, Dr. Brody was on the faculty of Cleveland State University, where he taught social policy and social service administration. He also gave graduate courses on service delivery models at Case Western Reserve University. Previously, he served for 15 years as the executive director of the Federation for Community Planning, an organization that provides research, planning, and advocacy on health and human services. Dr. Brody authored books on case management, the state legislative process, fundraising events, community problem solving, service learning, and macro practice. He also produced documentaries on supervision and drug-free zones and chaired the Options Committee, which successfully planned and advocated for additional public funding for services for older persons in the greater Cleveland area. Dr. Brody's many years as a manager and teacher convinced him that the issues facing those in human service organizations were universal and applied to boards of directors as well as NGOs. He dedicated himself to developing tools to enhance the understanding and skills of those in leadership roles, from Cleveland to India, Spain, Ghana, Ethiopia, Egypt and Nigeria. His frequent workshops in Kenya led to the translation of his casebook into the Swahili language.

Dr. Brody's work touched millions, and his contributions will continue to educate, inform, and inspire future students and professionals in human services and human services administration.

Thomas Packard, DSW, is an associate professor in the School of Social Work at San Diego State University. His teaching specialties are administration and social policy. Since 2001, he has been a faculty consultant with the Academy for Professional Excellence in the School of Social Work at SDSU. Through the Academy, he works with the Southern Area Consortium of Human Services (SACHS), which consists of the directors of eight Southern California county human service organizations and two schools of social work. His SACHS activities have included a leadership development initiative for county human service managers and research projects on subjects including services integration and cutback management. His other Academy projects have included program evaluations and consultations with county child welfare organizations. Prior to his teaching career, he served as the director of two not-for-profit human services organizations. For more than 20 years, he has been an organization development consultant, specializing in government and not-for-profit organizations ranging in size from 10,000 to five employees. This experience includes six and a half years with the Organization Effectiveness Program of the City of San Diego. He earned his doctorate in social welfare at the University of California, Los Angeles, where he also studied at the Center for Quality of Working Life. His current research interests include organizational performance measurement and improvement, leadership, and organizational change. He is a member of the Editorial Board and Book Review editor for *Administration in Social Work*. He is a Certified Social Work Manager and an Advisory Committee member for the National Network for Social Work Managers.